HARD CHOICES

Russ Pannier

9-16-90

HARD CHOICES

Decision making under unresolved conflict

ISAAC LEVI
Columbia University

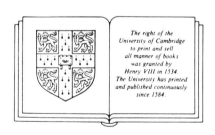

The right of the
University of Cambridge
to print and sell
all manner of books
was granted by
Henry VIII in 1534.
The University has printed
and published continuously
since 1584.

CAMBRIDGE UNIVERSITY PRESS
Cambridge
New York   Port Chester
Melbourne   Sydney

Published by the Press Syndicate of the University of Cambridge
The Pitt Building, Trumpington Street, Cambridge CB2 IRP
40 West 20th Street, New York, NY 10011, USA
10 Stamford Road, Oakleigh, Melbourne 3166, Australia

First published 1986
Reprinted 1987
First paperback edition 1990

Printed in the United States of America

Library of Congress Cataloging-in-Publication Data
Levi, Isaac, 1930 –
Hard choices.
Bibliography: p.
1. Decision-making (Ethics)   2. Values   3. Conflict
(Psychology)   4. Social conflict.   I. Title.
BJ1468.5L48   1986   170   864241

British Library Cataloguing in Publication Data
Levi, Isaac
Hard choices: decision making under unresolved conflict.
1. Knowledge, Theory of
I. Title.
121 BO161
ISBN 0-521-32527-7 hardback
ISBN 0-521-38630-6 paperback

TO MY MOTHER,
EVA LUNENFELD LEVI

IN MEMORY OF MY FATHER,
ELIEZER ASHER LEVI

Contents

Preface

For a long time, I have been interested in identifying the respects in which scientific inquiry is and is not value laden and have understood my ideas on this matter as a corrective to views advanced by Charles Peirce and John Dewey, in whose tradition I have located my own outlook. Dewey was also interested in the extent to which questions about values could be addressed in a manner exhibiting central features of scientific inquiry. In this volume, I have taken some first steps towards addressing this side of Dewey's concern.

I have had generous help and encouragement from many sources. Ruth Marcus read and commented copiously on an earlier version of what are now the first two chapters, inducing me to remove many errors. No doubt she will not be satisfied with the result, but I am very grateful for her help.

Norbert Hornstein read the entire manuscript and made several suggestions which, together with the comments of two referees for Cambridge University Press, led to a substantial reorganization of the contents of the book. I wish to thank him and the two referees (one of whom identified himself as Ned McClennen) for their kindness. Hornstein also suggested the title of the book. I am, of course, entirely to blame for accepting his suggestion.

Teddy Seidenfeld not only read a large portion of the manuscript, he participated in its construction through his encouragement and his positive contributions to the elaboration of the ideas contained therein.

I began work on this manuscript while on sabbatical leave at Cambridge University in 1980. I want to thank the members of the Faculty of Philosophy at Cambridge and the members of Darwin College for their kind hospitality. Special thanks are due to Hugh Mellor for his help and his attendance at the course of lectures I gave at Cambridge where I first elaborated the ideas which form the substance of this book.

I also thank those students who attended a recent seminar of mine at Columbia where I discussed the penultimate version of these ideas. Rebecca Berlow, Bruce Cooper, Yair Gutman, Melissa Mabon and Pinchas Ungvary were especially helpful.

Bruce Ackermann, Paul Lyon, Sidney Morgenbesser, Frederic Schick

---

and Amartya Sen have all read parts of this essay or discussed its ideas with me. My debt to Sen in chapters 8 to 11 and to Schick in chapter 4 will be apparent, but I have learned from all of them.

The work done at Cambridge in 1980 was partially supported by a fellowship from the NEH and a grant from the NSF.

My wife, Judith, has been a gold mine of moral support. Without her encouragement, I would not have managed to see this or any other large project I have undertaken to a conclusion.

This book is dedicated to the memory of my father, Eliezer Asher Levi, whose passionate commitment to his values bred a model of integrity for me to emulate, and to my mother, Eva Lunenfeld Levi, whose love and support enabled me to stand on my own two feet.

New York City
June 1985

1

Moral struggle

1.1 Two kinds of struggle

Adam lost his innocence and acquired a taste both for good and for evil. Yet he ate the forbidden fruit and after, it was clear what was good and what ought to be done.

According to this vision of our moral predicament, there are no gaps in our moral knowledge requiring completion through inquiry as there are gaps in our scientific knowledge. We may be ignorant of the consequences of our choices; but given any conjectured consequence, there is no doubt about its value. The remedy for our ignorance of consequences is, indeed, to be found either in scientific inquiry or in better decision theory. Aside from these aids to conduct, however, the best that can be done for Fallen Man is to institute a regimen of character building designed to strengthen his will. Moral problems are problems of moral training and therapy. There is no need for moral inquiry because there is no dearth of knowledge of good and evil.

To claim that we know everything there is to know about nature is quixotic arrogance. The results of science offer knowledge of some things but insist on our ignorance about others. In my view, the same holds for knowledge of good and evil. Our knowledge is fragmentary and incomplete. As in science, it is open to revision and improvement, and no amount of therapy will indicate how we should proceed. No doubt we have a taste for good and for evil. But our wickedness is often the product of our ignorance and not our perversity. Therapy should be supplemented by inquiry.

Dewey and Tufts point in a congenial direction when they distinguish between two kinds of moral struggle:

One kind, and that the most emphasized in moral writings and lectures, is the conflict which takes place when an individual is tempted to do something which he is convinced is wrong. Such instances are important practically in the life of an individual but they are not the occasion of moral theory. The employee of a bank who is tempted to embezzle funds may indeed try to argue himself into finding reasons why it would not be wrong for him to do it. But in such a case, he is not really thinking but merely permitting his desire to govern his beliefs. There is no sincere doubt in his mind as to what he should do when he seeks to find some justification for what he has made up his mind to do.

Take, on the other hand, the case of a citizen of a nation which has just declared war on another country. He is deeply attached to his own State. He has formed habits of loyalty and of abiding by its laws, and now one of its decrees is that he shall support war. He feels in addition gratitude and affection for the country which has sheltered and nurtured him. But he believes that this war is unjust, or perhaps he has a conviction that all war is a form of murder and, hence, wrong. One side of his nature, one set of convictions and habits, leads him to acquiesce in war; another deep part of his being protests. He is torn between two duties; he experiences a conflict between the incompatible values presented to him by his habits of citizenship and by his religious beliefs respectively. Up to this time, he has never experienced a struggle between the two; they have coincided and reënforced one another. Now he has to make a choice between competing moral loyalties and convictions. The struggle is not between a good which is clear to him and something else which attracts him but which he knows to be wrong. It is between values each of which is an undoubted good in its place but which now get in each other's way. He is forced to reflect in order to come to a decision. Moral theory is a generalized extension of the kind of thinking in which he now engages. (Dewey and Tufts, 1932: 174–175)

A moral struggle of the first kind is a struggle against temptation. The challenge to the agent is to do what he recognizes he ought to do, all things considered when desire, habit, fear and the like incline him in some other direction. Moral reflection and inquiry directed at finding out what one ought to do are unnecessary. There is no doubt as to what ought to be done. Strength of character aided and abetted by psychomoral therapy or exhortation must be summoned to ensure that what ought to be done will be done.

In contrast, strength of will is of little help when an agent is undecided as to what he ought to do. Inquiry, not therapy, is required to address the issue at hand. Of course, if such inquiry is brought to a successful conclusion so that it becomes clear that some given option ought, all things considered, to be performed, moral struggle of the second kind should cease to be followed, perhaps, by moral struggle of the first. But struggle against temptation presupposes that the task of moral inquiry has been completed or was unnecessary in the first place.

Anyone wishing (as I do) to follow Dewey and Tufts in emphasizing the importance of moral inquiry will resist the suppression of moral struggle of the second kind in favor of moral struggle of the first. The need for such resistance demands as much advertising today as it did, according to Dewey and Tufts, when they wrote.

A subtle and interesting suppression of moral inquiry is found in D. Davidson's discussion of weakness of the will. According to Davidson (1980: 33–34), all occasions where strength of will is demanded arise when there is moral conflict in a "minimal sense", which exists "whenever the agent is aware of considerations that, taken alone, would lead to mutually incompatible actions." Davidson cites as illustrations of moral conflict in this minimal sense predicaments which exemplify situations Dewey and Tufts would take to be illustrative of moral struggle of the second kind, such as the conflict between patriotism and pacificism. Two or more principles apply to a specific case and do so in a manner which yields prescriptions which cannot, in that case, be implemented jointly.

Davidson (1980: 34) asserts that very little attention has been paid to this problem, and even then it has been focused on one of two unsatisfactory solutions. One of these approaches insists that there be only one ultimate moral principle – an outlook Davidson rejects.[1] An alternative suggestion denies that the allegedly conflicting principles prescribe actions which are not jointly feasible. According to this view, the principles prescribe no choice at all. In the case of the agent torn between pacificism and patriotism, pacifism supports a *prima facie* case for conscientious objection. Considerations of patriotism afford a *prima facie* warrant for signing up. Neither pacificism nor patriotism taken alone makes categorical recommendations as to what ought to be done.

Davidson appears to think that when the two values are taken into account together, they will "add up" to a verdict concerning the relative merits of conscientious objection and joining the army.[2] But this verdict is also a *prima facie* verdict. What remains to be addressed is how the agent is to determine what ought categorically to be done. Davidson's recommendation is that the agent determine which of the options is *prima facie* best, "all things considered" – i.e., relative to all the known relevant reasons. He should then identify the categorical appraisal of his options which is to guide his conduct with the *prima facie* appraisal all things considered. To determine categorical valuations in this way is to follow a "principle of continence" analogous to Carnap's requirement of total evidence for inductive reasoning. It is well known that statistics can be made to lie by a partial and selective use of the available evidence. The statistician who lies in this way parallels the incontinent agent who loses the struggle against temptation by recognizing as better an option which is *prima facie* better relative to some partial set of the relevant reasons rather than all things considered (Davidson, 1980: 41–42).

According to this account, an akratic agent may be said to have acted for a reason even though he recognizes his action to be *prima facie* wrong, all things considered. We may seek explanations as to why he fails to live up to the practical analogue of the total evidence requirement and, perhaps, find them by examining such factors as "self-deception, overpowering desires, lack of imagination and the rest".

Davidson concedes that the akratic agent's actions are not fully rational. They do not cohere well with his values, desires and beliefs. This failure of rationality parallels the failures exhibited by the agent who does not obey the total evidence requirement and whose failures may sometimes be subject to some kind of explanation appealing to psychological disturbances rather than to an account which provides a full and cogent rationalization.

Strength of will requires character through training, therapy, exhortation and the like in Davidson's view, just as it does in Dewey's. To this extent, there seems to be little difference between moral struggle of the first kind as depicted by Dewey and Tufts and Davidson's *akrasia*.[3]

The interesting and important differences between the views of Dewey and Davidson concern the analysis of conflict. Nowhere in his discussion does Davidson acknowledge the possibility that when all the relevant considerations are taken into account there is no uniquely permissible value ranking of the feasible options. The agent divided between patriotism and pacifism might think that, all things considered, enlisting is neither better than, worse than or equal in value to conscientious objection. If he does, Davidson's principle of continence should recommend that the agent refuse to make a categorical appraisal of the first option as better, worse or equal to the other. As Dewey and Tufts maintain, the agent should recognize that he does not know what ought to be done and acknowledge that his predicament is an appropriate occasion for moral reflection and inquiry. No amount of willpower will be of use to the agent (except the strength of character needed to carry on the inquiry) until such inquiry is brought to a successful conclusion. Davidson's account of weakness of the will is consistent with recognizing this possibility, but he nowhere acknowledges the possibility or its importance. To the contrary, he seems to think that contexts of moral dilemma are precisely the occasions where challenges to willpower arise.

This is simply false. When moral conflicts arise because the relevant moral considerations yield conflicting *prima facie* recommendations, it will usually be the case that there is no clear *prima facie* recommendation if these moral considerations are taken together. Further inquiry will be needed. To suppose otherwise is to assume that before the conflict a definite all-things-considered *prima facie* verdict was provided by the available arsenal of moral principles, that direct inspection of the specific situation provides the required *prima facie* verdict or that this verdict is rendered arbitrarily. In my judgement, it is better to admit that one does not know what is for the best, all things considered, than to invoke the shaky authority of intuition or arbitrary fiat. And although it may be true sometimes that we have ready-made recipes for resolving conflicts, the supposition that we always have such recipes at our disposal is just not credible. When we do not, weakness of will – at least in the sense envisaged by Davidson – is not an issue.

Davidson should have said that when moral inquiry is over and a settled verdict as to what ought to be done, all things considered, has been reached, the agent must then gird his loins and implement what he recognizes he ought to do. When moral conflict is over, the testing of the will begins. When it is clear what ought to be done, all things considered, the agent may be tempted to follow a course of action which can be rationalized by taking into account only some of the relevant considerations while neglecting others. Succumbing to this kind of temptation is, indeed, incontinence just as Davidson says, but it is not an example of moral dilemma or conflict.

Genuine dilemma or conflict presupposes that what ought to be done, all things considered, is as yet unsettled. The only weakness the will can exhibit in such a context is coming to a conclusion as to what ought categorically to be done when, all things considered, no verdict is warranted. In emphasizing the importance for moral reflection of moral struggle of the second kind, Dewey and Tufts were warning against this very special form of *akrasia*.

1.2 Withholding judgement

A moral struggle of the second kind arises when the following four conditions are satisfied:

1. The agent endorses one or more value commitments $P_1, P_2, \ldots, P_n$.

2. Value commitment P_i stipulates that in contexts of deliberation of type T_i, the evaluation of the feasible options should satisfy constraints C_i.

3. The specific decision problem being addressed is recognized to be of each of the types $T_1, T_2, \ldots, T_n$ so that all of the constraints $C_1, C_2, \ldots, C_n$ are supposed to apply.

4. The decision problem currently faced is one where the constraints $C_1, C_2, \ldots, C_n$ cannot all be jointly satisfied.[4]

Sometimes value commitments are represented in the guise of moral principles (e.g., the prohibition against breaking promises), but they need not appear that way. They may be represented as expressions of life goals, personal desires, tastes or professional commitments. Nor need moral struggles of the second kind be restricted to conflicts involving one or more value commitments of an allegedly distinctive moral type. Choosing one of several careers often entails a moral struggle and is widely recognized to do so by agents who face such choices. This is so even though no issue raised by the Decalogue or other systems of categorical imperatives appear to be at stake.

Given a specific context of choice with a specific set of feasible options as described according to the information available to the agent, a constraint C_i is intended to impose requirements on the permissible ways of evaluating feasible options. An account of ways of evaluating feasible options will be developed in chapter 5. For the present, it suffices to think of a way of evaluating feasible options as a comparison of the feasible options as better or worse. A way of evaluating feasible options is permissible according to the agent if the agent has not ruled it out for the purpose of determining which feasible options are admissible – i.e., not prohibited from being chosen. A constraint C_i imposes conditions which every permissible way of evaluating the options must satisfy.

If several constraints are imposed on a given set of options, more and more ways of evaluation will tend to be ruled out. The agent's "value structure" or evaluation of the feasible options is given by the ways of evaluation which meet the requirements imposed by all the constraints imposed by the agent's value commitments.

The constraints are not satisfiable for a given set of feasible options if there is no way of evaluating all the feasible options which satisfies all of them. Thus, if constraint C_1 requires that option x be ranked better than option y and constraint C_2 demands that y be ranked as better than x, the constraints are not jointly satisfiable over the pair $\langle x, y \rangle$.

A constraint imposes restrictions on the ways a given set of feasible options is to be evaluated by specifying how options of different types are to be compared with one another. Hence, whether a constraint or set of constraints is satisfiable in a given option set depends on how the members of the set are described. Whether condition 4 is met, therefore, depends on the information available to the agent about the feasible options.

The circumstance that constraints $C_1, C_2, \ldots, C_n$ are not jointly satisfiable in some context of choice does not entail inconsistency in the system of constraints themselves. Constraints $C_1, C_2, \ldots, C_n$ are consistent (consistently applicable) if they are jointly satisfiable in some context of choice regardless of whether they are satisfiable in others.

Value commitments $P_1, P_2, \ldots, P_n$ (in contrast to the constraints they impose) are logically consistent if and only if it is logically possible to satisfy the constraints $C_{i1}, C_{i2}, \ldots, C_{ik}$ in all contexts of choice simultaneously of types $T_{i1}, T_{i2}, \ldots, T_{ik}$ (for any subset of the scope restrictions $T_1, T_2, \ldots, T_n$).

The n value commitments are universally applicable if and only if, for every subset T_{i1}, T_{i2}, . . . , T_{ik} of the n scope restrictions and every context of choice satisfying all of the k scope restrictions, the constraints C_{i1}, C_{i2}, . . . , C_{ik} are jointly satisfiable.

The strong generalization condition (SGC) requires that when an agent endorses value commitments P_1, P_2, . . . , P_n, he assume the universal applicability of the n value commitments as part of his body of knowledge. If one accepts SGC (as I shall), the agent's endorsement of the n value commitments will contradict what he knows given that he knows there is at least one context of types T_1, T_2, . . . , T_n where the constraints are not jointly satisfiable. Thus, when conditions 1–4 obtain, the decision maker embraces value commitments making presuppositions inconsistent with what the agent knows. This epistemological inconsistency in the value commitments should not be confused with logical inconsistency. The n value commitments may be logically consistent and recognized to be so by the agent even though their universal applicability contradicts what he knows.[5]

Thus, there is nothing logically inconsistent in the hero of the Dewey–Tufts example embracing the "habits" of loyalty and patriotism simultaneously with his opposition to war. According to SGC, endorsement of both value commitments implies that in all decision contexts within the scopes of both principles, both constraints are satisfied by ways of evaluating feasible options. As long as there is no logical inconsistency in supposing that they are satisfied in all such decision contexts which have obtained or will arise, the joint endorsement is also logically consistent.

Nonetheless, specific occasions can arise in which the expectations of the hero in a Dewey–Tufts scenario are frustrated. A decision problem may be presented to him in which the requirements of patriotism and pacifism are to apply but in which the joint satisfiability of the constraints is inconsistent with what the agent knows. Given what he knows, he cannot consistently impose constraints required by both commitments in all decision contexts within the scopes of the two principles.

In some respects, recognition of this inconsistency is analogous to recognition that two or more mutually consistent hypotheses entail a result confounded by experiment. The set of hypotheses may be mutually consistent, but this set and the report of the experimental results are inconsistent.

Sometimes questioning the experimental results may be appropriate. Often, however, it is preferable to question the hypotheses. To question the hypotheses, however, is to move to a position of suspense between them. This involves a change in the agent's body of knowledge or settled assumptions. It has been modified so that it is no longer inconsistent. Once this is done, inquiry aimed at settling the emerging controversy among the several hypotheses may be undertaken without begging the question as to which (if any) of the hypotheses jointly inconsistent with the data ought to be reinstated in the evolving doctrine (Levi, 1980a: ch. 3). Thus, the inconsistency between the several hypotheses and the data must be distinguished from the conflict generated by the recognition of this inconsistency. The conflict or dilemma arises when the investigator shifts to a position of suspense among the hypotheses. Since the posture of suspense does not entail inconsistency, being in a state of conflict is not to be confused with being in the state of inconsistent belief which provoked it.

Moral struggles of the second kind are provoked by inconsistencies between value commitments and information concerning the kinds of decision problems which arise. One might remove such inconsistencies by questioning some of the assumptions concerning the types of decision problems which obtain. Although it is far from obvious that this response is always unattractive, it often is. Typically, the joint endorsement of the value commitments is questioned. A shift is made to a state of suspense concerning the evaluation of options in contexts of choice like the problematic one being confronted. At a minimum, the scopes of the original value commitments, if not the constraints, have thereby been modified so that the constraints no longer apply to the problematic cases. A conflict in value emerges. But this conflict is not a case of inconsistency. The conflict or "dilemma" involves suspension of judgement among competing value commitments. When removal of the conflict is sufficiently urgent, inquiry is undertaken and may be undertaken without begging any questions concerning which of the constraints being considered ought to be satisfied in the predicament presenting the dilemma and others like it.[6]

Thus, the agent's habits of loyalty should be modified to the extent that the scope of his patriotism is restricted to situations where his country has not declared war. Likewise, the scope of his pacifist principles should be reduced so that they no longer require opposition to war declared by his native land. Pending further inquiry, neither patriotism nor pacifism can be ruled out as applying to the kind of situation where the native land has declared war. But neither can be taken to be mandatory for that kind of situation. Although no single evaluation of the options can consistently meet both the requirements of patriotism and pacifism, the agent must consider evaluations to be permissible which meet one or the other system of constraints.

Suspending judgement in scientific inquiry removes inconsistency, but only at the cost of a loss of information. Had the investigator removed inconsistency by deleting one of the conflicting theories while retaining the other, he would have minimized the loss of information while still avoiding contradiction. Doing so, however, would beg the question in favor of the hypothesis which is retained. The additional loss of information incurred by removing both of the conflicting theories from the body of settled assumptions is justified by the desirability of adopting a viewpoint with respect to which both alternatives can be given a hearing without prejudice.

Nonetheless, shifting to a position of suspense is only the beginning of inquiry. The main task remains – to wit, undertaking investigations in order to choose one of the rival hypotheses or some new proposal which, perhaps, was not envisaged when the inquiry began.

Much the same procedure should be followed when inconsistency in the application of two or more value commitments to a given situation arises. The scopes of the value commitments are modified so that neither constraint applies to the given context. In such contexts, judgement is suspended as to which, if any, of the erstwhile conflicting constraints is to apply. This is generally preferable to retaining the applicability of one commitment at the expense of the other without giving a nonprejudicial hearing to the rival commitments.

Moving to a position of suspense, however, does not eliminate moral struggle of the second kind. It is merely the first step in that direction. When an investigator is in suspense between rival hypotheses, he is in doubt as to the truth values of these hypotheses. The truth (and falsity) of each rival is a serious possibility as far as he is concerned.

Suspension of judgement should be understood differently in the evaluation of feasible options as better or worse. Each way of evaluating feasible options as better or worse is intended to furnish the decision maker with a criterion for determining which of his options are optimal. The agent's doubt as to the ranking of the feasible options is not reducible to suspension of judgement between rival truth value bearing hypotheses even though questions of fact and scientific theory may have an important bearing on the weights to be accorded different rankings. When the hero of the Dewey–Tufts scenario is in suspense between a pacifist and patriotic evaluation of his options, the question before him is not which of the rankings or evaluations is true. That question does not even arise.

Thus, when the agent's value commitments generate no conflict but constrain the agent to evaluate his feasible options in an unequivocal manner, the agent is obligated by those commitments to restrict his choice to one of the feasible options which is optimal according to the mandated ranking. It is not a question of the ranking being true or being believed true by the agent. Rather it is that the ranking is the only one the agent is permitted to use (according to his commitments) in determining which options are admissible for him.

If, however, the agent starts off committed to two or more value commitments which on the specific occasion mandate different rankings of the feasible options, he should avoid contradiction by moving to a position of suspense which avoids prejudicing the resolution of the conflict among the rival value commitments.[7] In contrast to the scientific case, the agent does not hold that one of the rankings is true while professing ignorance as to which it is. Rather he regards all of the rankings as permissible for the purpose of assessing optimality. The upshot is that any option which comes out optimal relative to some permissible way of evaluating options has not been prohibited by the agent's value commitments from being chosen by the agent. The options which have survived criticism in this manner are called *V-admissible* − i.e., admissible relative to the agent's valuations of the feasible options as better or worse, all things considered. There is no implication in all of this that one of the V-admissible options is the best, all things considered, but the agent does not know which it is. In contrast to suspension of judgement among rival scientific hypotheses, the agent does not presuppose that there is a "truth of the matter" unknown to him and that the rival ways of evaluation are possibly true hypotheses as to what that truth is. They are permissible to use in evaluating options and not possibly true conjectures.

An important ramification of the difference between possibility as applying to truth-value-bearing hypotheses and permissibility as applying to ways of evaluating feasible options concerns the concept of compromise or potential resolution. When in suspense as to the truth of some hypothesis *h*, the agent refuses to rule out the assignment "true" or the truth value "false" as possible truth value assignments for *h*. However, there is no third possibility between these possibilities which represents a "compromise" between them. To be sure, probabilities may be assigned to *h* and its negation, but we should no more confuse probability assignments with intermediate truth values than we should confuse certainty with truth.

The situation is different in the case of suspense among different rankings of feasible options as better or worse. Not only should the agent regard each of the different rankings as permissible; but other rankings different from those originally in conflict may be recognized as representing potential resolutions or compromises and as such should also be regarded as permissible.

The technical presentation of the notion of a potential resolution will be given in section 5.4. For the present, its ramifications will be explained through illustration.

Suppose Jones, the manager of an office, is looking for a new typist-stenographer. He requires all applicants to take standardized typing and stenography tests. Three persons apply: Jane, Dolly and Lilly. Their typing scores are 100, 99 and 90 respectively, and their stenography scores are 90, 99 and 100 respectively. Jones is committed by his responsibilities as office manager to two constraints on how candidates should be evaluated as better or worse. One requires that the candidates be rated according to their performance on the typing test. The other requires rating according to the stenography test. Suppose that in the past, the scores on both tests have coincided to a sufficient degree that Jones has had no trouble living up to both commitments. I have suggested that he should move to a position where neither value commitment is regarded as applicable but the verdicts of both tests are permissible evaluations of the feasible options.

According to one permissible evaluation, hiring Jane is optimal. According to another, hiring Lilly is optimal. Hence, all things considered, both of these options are V-admissible. What about hiring Dolly?

There are ways to weight the two scores and to compile average scores which yield a ranking according to which Dolly comes out best on average. After all, she is nearly as good a typist as Jane and nearly as good a stenographer as Lilly. Of course, if Jones considered typing much more important than stenography for the job, he might use a method of weighting which placed Jane first. Or if he thought the need for a stenographer much more urgent, he might hire Lilly. I do not mean to suggest that there is an *a priori* appropriate way in which Jones should weight the scores so as to come out with an evaluation of the job applicants. To the contrary, I mean to suggest that when Jones is in suspense between evaluating the candidates according to typing and according to stenography, he should regard all possible ways of weighting the importance of the two desiderata as determining permissible ways of evaluation as well. Each weighting yields an evaluation of the feasible options which represents a potential resolution of the conflict between the two desiderata. In a state of suspense, no potential resolution should be eliminated as impermissible.

Of course, when in doubt, Jones faces a moral struggle of the second kind (even though the value commitments generating conflict are professional, not moral). Even so, he might come up with some way of resolving the unresolved conflict through reflection, inquiry or consultation with his superiors. Such a conclusion would mark the termination of moral struggle of the second kind and adoption of a new value commitment covering the erstwhile problematic case.

The verdict might favor hiring Dolly. Yet Jones might have a hankering after excellence in typing and be tempted by the incontinent act of hiring Jane. The resolution of the conflict still carries a trace of the original conflict in that it prescribes a way of evaluating feasible options which is a function of the ways of evaluating the feasible options recognized by the value commitments which came into conflict originally. The commitments to stenography and to typing are compromised but not forgotten.

It may be objected that this story relies excessively on averaging and cannot account for cases where the ways of evaluating feasible options involved in conflict are not susceptible to numerical representation in any useful sense. In chapter 5 and those which follow, I hope to show that the framework I am hinting at here is an extremely flexible one and does not presuppose that value structures need be characterizable by numerical functions.

For the present, however, I may, perhaps, allay some anxiety by showing that weighted averaging of scores captures an important feature of our presystematic judgement. Moreover, I shall argue that this feature can arise not only in the case of professional conflicts of the sort facing Jones but in the moral dilemmas described by Dewey and Tufts.

Suppose that instead of scoring 99 Dolly had scored 91 on both tests while the scores of Jane and Lilly remained as before. In the previous case, I argued that hiring Dolly should be V-admissible as long as conflict goes unresolved because rankings where hiring Dolly is optimal are potential resolutions of the conflict and, hence, ought to be permissible. In the present case, however, no matter how the scores are averaged, Dolly cannot come out with a best average score. This is because she is almost as bad as the worst according to both the desideratum of typing and the requirements of stenography. No permissible ranking rates hiring Dolly optimal. That option is not V-admissible.

I think the difference between the two scenarios conforms with presystematic precedent. In the second scenario, conventional wisdom tells us that hiring Dolly is a nonstarter. That is not so in the first case. The difference is brought out nicely by the contrast between second best and second worst and the appeal to averaging in determining aggregate scores.

Jones' predicament is not made of the stuff which furnishes the text for moral sermons. Consider, however, the hero of the Dewey—Tufts story. He is given the option of becoming a combat medic rather than bearing arms or refusing to serve altogether. The option of becoming a combat medic might appear second best according to both the agent's pacifist and his patriotic value commitments even though his two commitments identify the best and worst options differently. Surely the opportunity of becoming a combat medic expresses a potential resolution of the agent's conflict in the sense that there is a way of evaluating his options which (a) ranks that option best and (b) is a weighted average (in some suitably specified sense) of his conflicting desiderata.

Contrast this situation with one where the conflicted agent is offered the opportunity to work in a recruiting office but not the opportunity be a combat medic. This option is second worst according to the agent's pacifist sentiments and quite possibly according to his patriotic commitments as well. If so, it seems quite plausible that the agent should rule that option out. It cannot express a potential resolution of the conflict.

Whichever variation of the scenarios envisaged here obtains, suspension of judgement, though different from suspension of judgement between rival truth-value-bearing hypotheses, shares with such agnosticism the weakness of the conclusions warranted. In the first version of Jones' predicament, all three options are V-admissible. In the second, hiring Jane and hiring Lilly are V-admissible, although neither option is categorically optimal. The weakness of this conclusion is itself impetus for undertaking efforts to resolve the conflict among the rival ways of evaluating options which are held in suspense so that more definite conclusions may be reached in this or in future predicaments of a similar kind.

Thus, as already indicated, removal of the inconsistency among value commitments which occasions moral inquiry is but the first step. Inconsistency is removed, but conflict in the sense of suspense among alternative valuations remains pending the identification of a satisfactory resolution.

This kind of conflict, to reiterate, requires inquiry, not therapy. To be sure, one must guard against the temptation to fix on a solution arbitrarily so as to avoid the need for inquiry. And the better the agent's computational capacity and memory and the more stable his emotional constitution, the more effective is his capacity to carry out inquiries. The proper conduct of inquiry demands strength of character and acuteness of mind, just as does any other challenge to the will. This should not blind us, however, to the important difference between the kind of conflict which occasions inquiry and the kind which tests our character.

1.3 For the best, all things considered

The dichotomy between types of moral struggle identified by Dewey and Tufts combined with the emphasis they place on the importance of considering moral struggle of the second kind will seem untenable to anyone who doubts the feasibility or, perhaps, the intelligibility of remaining in suspense among rival value commitments and rival ways of evaluating feasible options licensed by such commitments.

Dewey's vision of deliberate inquiry as exemplified by scientific investigations insists that a solution to the problem under investigation not be presupposed in advance; and it is an important feature of Dewey's philosophy that reflection about values be patterned after scientific inquiry:

. . .improved valuation must grow out of existing valuations, subjected to critical methods of investigation that bring them into systematic relations with one another. . . .
This method, in fact, simply carries over to human or social phenomena the methods that have proved successful in dealing with the subject matter of physics and chemistry. (Dewey, 1939: 60)

The implication is clear. It must be possible for the hero of the Dewey–Tufts scenario to remain in suspense because his evidence fails to warrant favoring either patriotism or pacifism or, perhaps, some third alternative. Just as the state of investigation may not warrant adopting a definite solution in a scientific inquiry, so too it may be appropriate to suspend judgement in moral inquiry as well.

But practice is more peremptory than theory. Our conflicted hero will have to decide whether to join the war effort or resist doing so regardless of whether he has or lacks warrant for favoring one system of constraints or another. The beleaguered office manager, Jones, will have to reach a decision if he is to keep his own job. The luxury of reflection and inquiry is not available. At the moment of choice, there can be no more suspense. Moral struggle of the second kind becomes impossible – or so we are told.

Those who take this position do not necessarily say that at the moment of choice the agent must have some warrant for resolving his conflicts one way or another. T. Nagel (1979: 135) suggests that "judgement" or "practical wisdom" can in many cases "be relied on to take up the slack that remains beyond the limits of explicit rational argument". As is well known, J. P. Sartre denied that there is or can be any sort of warrant for conflict resolution. Nor can we trust our "instincts". Yet we should regard the decision we make as the best thing to do in the situation and, moreover, it should be generalizable into a value commitment applicable to every agent in a relevantly similar situation:

To choose between this or that is at the same time to affirm the value of that which is chosen; for we are unable ever to choose the worse. What we choose is always for the better; and nothing can be better for us unless it is better for all. (Sartre, 1956: 291–292)

Of course, those suspicious of allusions to "judgement" and hostile to irrationalism have sought to devise some all-purpose constraint on modes of evaluation which can be used to resolve conflcits between other value commitments when they arise. Thus, J. S. Mill wrote as follows:

There is, then a *philosophia prima* peculiar to art as there is one which belongs in science. There are not only first principles of knowledge, but first principles of conduct. There must be some standard by which to determine the goodness or badness, absolute and comparative, of ends or objects of desire. And whatever that standard is, there can be but one; for if there were several ultimate principles of conduct, the same conduct might be approved by one of these principles and condemned by another, and there would be needed some more general principle as umpire between them (Mill, 1949: 620–621).

Of course, Mill (1949: 621) goes on to declare "that the promotion of happiness is the ultimate principle of teleology".

Kant too is clear that "a conflict of duties is inconceivable":

It may, however, very well happen, that in the same subject and the rule which he prescribes to himself there are conjoined two grounds of obligation, of which, however, one or the other is inadequate to oblige, and then one of them is not a duty. When two such grounds are in conflict, practical philosophy does not say that the stronger obligation prevails, but the stronger ground of obligation prevails. (Kant, 1909: 280)

Whether one insists on the existence of some all-purpose constraint on valuations potent enough to eliminate conflicts, relies on instinct or judgement or declares that the very act of choosing coincides with the resolution of the conflict, it is being assumed that at or by the moment of choice the rational agent must be in a position to choose for the best, all things considered. He must have resolved his conflicts sufficiently so that he can recognize some of his options to be at least as good as all others according to all ways of evaluating his options he considers permissible.

I reject this assumption. The agent torn between patriotism and pacifism may have to decide whether to join the army or become a conscientious objector. Whatever his choice might be (suppose he joins the army), he need not maintain that the option he chooses is better than or even at least as good as the other. Instead, he might admit that what he did was for the worst according to one of his value commitments (pacifism) while insisting that it was for the best according to another (patriotism). He might deny that he has, therefore, come down on the side of patriotism. He can insist and quite reasonably so that he cannot settle the conflict between patriotism and pacifism by the deadline for choice. Precisely because he is compelled to choose, he does choose; but he refuses to consider the conflict in value commitments to be settled. As far as he is concerned, the issue remains open to further moral inquiry and reflection.[8]

If this is right, two tasks become urgent:

1. Efforts should be made to give an account of the conduct of inquiries aimed at alleviating moral struggles of the second kind. This, as I understand it, is the topic Dewey invited us to consider.

2. We need an account of decision making under unresolved conflict. When decisions must be made before reflection and inquiry can warrant an acceptable resolution of conflict, it remains entertainable that the decision problem is subject to some sort of critical control. In any case, one need not assume in advance what the extent of such critical control might be in order to recognize that the determination of this extent is a question worth pursuing.

To my knowledge, Dewey did not address the question of decision making under unresolved conflict. Yet he should have done so. The alternative is to suppose that there is no question to raise because rational agents invariably choose for the best, all things considered. To suppose, however, that inquiry could always lead to warranted resolution of conflicts in value by the time a choice is required is to indulge in fantasy.

The main topic of this volume is rational decision making under unresolved conflict in values. The value commitments which come into conflict need not be moral commitments in any distinctive sense of "moral". They may be cognitive, aesthetic, professional, economic or political. And, as we shall see, conflict in values is often generated by uncertainty concerning the consequences of the feasible options. Our topic is relevant to moral deliberation, to scientific inquiry insofar as it is controlled by cognitive values, to approaches to decision making under uncertainty and to social choice theory in general and questions about the fair distribution of benefits in particular.

In addressing the question of decision making under unresolved conflict, I do not mean to downgrade the importance of reflection on the conduct of inquiry aimed at resolving such conflicts. To the contrary, Dewey's question remains as important as it is difficult. The topic of this essay, though of some interest in its own right, is significant because by addressing it we might clear away some of the difficulties facing anyone who hopes to come to an adequate understanding of moral inquiry. If we are successful, we shall be in a position to claim that the peremptoriness of choice does not compel us to reach conclusions when, all things considered, there is no warrant for doing so.

1.4 The plan of this book

Chapter 2 compares the outlooks towards moral conflict represented in recent discussions by R. Marcus, B. van Fraassen and B. Williams with the view I favor. These writers maintain that in moral conflict or dilemma, conflicting moral obligations remain in force even when they are not jointly implementable. I argue, to the contrary, that in such contexts a form of suspense between the rival obligations is appropriate pending resolution. This means that neither obligation is in force.

Chapter 3 points out that value conflict can arise in scientific inquiry. There can be conflict between cognitive values, on the one hand, and between cognitive values and moral, aesthetic, political, economic and other practical values, on the other. It is argued that the autonomy of scientific inquiry boils down to the irreducibility of cognitive values to other practical values. Advocates of such autonomy (like myself) are thereby committed to forms of value pluralism. It is within the matrix of such value pluralism that the importance and rationality of decision making under unresolved conflict arise.

Before elaborating the technical aspects of the proposed account of decision making under unresolved conflict in chapters 5 and 6, it seems desirable to make explicit the assumptions which an ideally rational decision maker ought to make about the feasibility and effectiveness of his options, his evaluations of them and the rationality of his choices. In chapter 4, I argue that no matter what principles are endorsed as regulating rational choice, the deliberating agent should not presuppose that he, she or it will follow such principles. To do so, I shall claim, frustrates deliberation.

Chapter 5 provides the general characterization of the conditions for decision making under unresolved conflict and the principles of choice which ought to prevail under those conditions.

Chapter 6 discusses certain ambiguities which emerge in the notion of preference or valuation and the related notion of "optimality" when unresolved conflict is taken seriously. In particular, it argues that the presence of unresolved conflict can lead to violations of principles of so-called choice consistency widely advocated by students of individual and social decision making and accounts of revealed preference. Rather than regarding these violations as signs of the irrationality of recommendations supported by the theory I am advocating, I regard them as marks of good sense on those occasions where value conflicts ought to go unresolved. Those who insist on preserving such "choice consistency" conditions as generally applicable are seen to be antagonistic to the idea that decision making under unresolved conflict may sometimes be reasonable.

Chapter 7 explores the application of the account of decision making under unresolved conflict abstractly presented in chapters 5 and 6 in the context of decision making under uncertainty. After summarizing ideas already elaborated (Levi, 1980a), I focus on the ramifications of the views being advocated for phenomena of so-called preference reversal – including much discussed responses to decision problems introduced by M. Allais and D. Ellsberg. I argue that both apologists for Bayesian decision theory and their critics respond to these and kindred puzzles in ways which deny decision making under unresolved conflict. Although several proposals have been made concerning phenomena of preference reversal which deny unresolved conflict, none have succeeded in systematizing all the phenomena involved in a useful manner. All of them entail awkward consequences concerning the avoidance of dominated options. Once one is willing to allow for unresolved conflict, a systematic approach to these phenomena can be constructed. Moreover, one can guarantee obedience to so-called sure-thing and independence principles as well as avoidance of embarrassing recommendations of options dominated by other options.

Chapters 8 and 9 consider some possibilities of applying the approach to rational choice developed earlier to questions concerning social choice. Chapter 8 argues that institutions, like persons, may be coherently regarded as agents and subjected to critical appraisal with respect to the rationality of their propositional attitudes. It argues further that the question of decision making under unresolved conflict arises with force in the context of both social choice and individual decision making.

Chapter 9 discusses a family of value commitments marked by a concern to promote benefits of some kind for each member of a group of clients, patients or citizens in a way which removes conflicts among the competing interest of the clients in conformity with the requirements of chapter 5. Various forms of utilitarianism are members of this family of value commitments. I shall argue that such criteria for resolving conflicts among the demands to promote the benefits of different clients or citizens cannot succeed at this task and also be sensitive to the demands of fair distribution. Counter to widely held views, invoking some form of average benefit principle, as utilitarians do, can be made sensitive to questions of fair distribution. However, this can be done only if one abandons the aim of resolving conflicts among commitments to promoting the interests of each citizen.

Chapter 10 builds on the framework and results of chapter 9. It examines the extent to which utilitarianism in particular can be held to provide a basis for avoiding decision making under unresolved conflict. Chapter 11 discusses the relations between the ideas developed in chapters 9 and 10 and social choice theory in the tradition of Arrow as developed by Sen. Chapter 12 is a brief summary of the main theme of the book.

The aim of these discussions is to establish the coherence of the approach to decision making under unresolved conflict advocated in this volume and demonstrate its applicability in diverse contexts. The richness and generality of the proposal preclude doing more than exploring its most obvious ramifications. I hope, however, to persuade others that accepting the coherence and reasonableness of decision making under unresolved conflict need not lead to the sort of intellectual chaos or anarchy which apparently offends or frightens many philosophers, decision theorists and social scientists. To the contrary, recognition of the reasonableness of decision making under unresolved conflict on occasions where responsible inquiry has failed to yield a resolution ought to remove an important obstacle to taking seriously the Deweyite project of clarifying the structure of inquiries aimed at resolving conflicts in value.

2

Dilemmas

2.1 Conflict and deontic logic

B. van Fraassen (1973: 6) has argued that the presence of unresolved conflict in a decision problem confounds the "axiological thesis" that "what ought to be is exactly what is better on the whole". As the preceding discussion indicates, I agree with van Fraassen on this score. Moreover, I agree that rational agents often find themselves in conditions of unresolved conflict.

Van Fraassen also holds that a certain "classical" principle of deontic logic precludes the existence of unresolved conflict. According to that principle, when A and B are not jointly feasible, it cannot be obligatory that A and obligatory that B. Van Fraassen (1973: 12) comments, "I can only conjecture that the original devisors of deontic axioms had a certain ethical bias; perhaps they were utilitarians, or accepted some other axiological creed".

In my view, there is not the slightest reason to understand the offending principle as precluding the existence of unresolved conflict. My motive for insisting on this is not to save the "classical" principle. That principle is too trivial to be either in need of or worth rescuing. It seems to me, however, that there is an important misunderstanding about unresolved conflict lurking behind van Fraassen's view (a view he shares with many others) which ought to be clarified.

I shall suppose that an agent's decision problem is representable by a set of feasible options from which, as far as the agent knows, he must choose exactly one. In 4.2 (particularly, note 6) some questions pertaining to the representation and individuation of options will be discussed. For the present, it will suffice as a first approximation to think of a decision problem as being represented by a set of sentences or propositions such that the agent is able to make one and only one of these sentences true and is constrained to make at least one of them true. In the context, these sentences can be viewed as giving relevantly complete descriptions of possible or, perhaps more accurately, feasible worlds relative to what the agent knows. Consider those sentences which are equivalent, given what the agent knows, to Boolean combinations of these complete descriptions. I shall say that any such sentence is feasibly true if and only if it is true in some feasible world.

Suppose, as before, that Jones, the office manager, is able to hire Jane, Lilly or Dolly but not more than one of them. Moreover, he is constrained to hire one of them. For the purposes of the deliberation, the feasible worlds are representable by "Jones hires Jane", "Jones hires Dolly" and "Jones hires Lilly". In this framework, we may also consider claims like "Jones does not hire Jane", which is equivalent given the available knowledge, to "Jones hires Dolly or Lilly" and so on.

A feasible world is admissible if and only if it represents an admissible option – i.e., a feasible option which is not prohibited by the agent's values and beliefs and the principles of rational choice. I shall say that sentence h ought to be true if and only if h is true in every admissible world – i.e., if and only if the performance of any admissible option entails, given what the agent knows, the truth of h.

An extended discussion of admissibility will be postponed until later chapters. However, the notion of V-admissibility has been introduced. For present purposes, this special conception of admissibility will suffice.

When there is no conflict in value, the agent's value commitments identify a uniquely permissible way of evaluating feasible options. Under such conditions, the "axiological thesis" applies and the optimal worlds are those van Fraassen (1972: 419) calls "ideal". If the number of feasible worlds to be considered is finite (and to avoid niggling complications I shall focus on such cases now), there will be at least one ideal world according to the "standard of value" (van Fraassen's term) or "way of evaluation" (my term) used to rank the feasible worlds. The set of such ideal worlds coincides, in this case, with the set of V-admissible worlds so that one can substitute "ideal" for "V-admissible" in the specification of the conditions under which h ought to be true. The result is the definition of "ought" van Fraassen uses to secure the "classical" principle of deontic logic he questions.

Observe, however, that V-admissibility is well defined even when there is value conflict. An option or feasible world is V-admissible if it is optimal according to some permissible "standard of value" or way of evaluation. This is so even if there are two or more such permissible ways of evaluation, as there will be in cases of unresolved conflict.

Furthermore, when "V-admissible" is substituted for "ideal" in specifying the feasible worlds forming the basis of the interpretation of the obligation operator, the resulting notion of obligation satisfies van Fraassen's "classical" principle, which precludes the obligatoriness of A and the obligatoriness of B when A & B is not true in any feasible world. This interpretation of the obligation operator makes perfectly good sense even though it does not presuppose the axiological thesis he means to criticize.

Van Fraassen holds that conflicts in values are expressible by asserting that h ought to be true and ~h ought to be true. He and others who take this view think that such conflict arises when the relevant principles of the type I have called "value commitments" applicable in a given context of choice impose constraints on the permissible ways of evaluating the feasible options or "worlds" as better or worse which cannot, in that context, be jointly satisfied. One constraint (pacifism) when taken alone might generate one set of optimal or ideal feasible worlds for that context. Another (patriotism) might generate another nonoverlapping set. Sentence h might be true in the first set and ~h in the second. Hence, it appears appropriate to assert that h ought to be true and also ought to be false.

In contrast, there is no value commitment identifying a permissible way of evaluating the given feasible options according to which h & ~h is true in all ideal worlds. Even though h ought to be true and ~h ought to be true, it is not the case that h & ~h ought to be true. The latter asserts a straightforward deontic contradiction and not merely a conflict in values.

Thus, if one wants to insist, as van Fraassen clearly wants to do, that one may consistently recognize conflicts in values representable in the manner he claims such conflicts should be represented, the following two assertions cannot be regarded as equivalent as they are often assumed to be.

1. ~(h ought to be true & ~h ought to be true).
2. ~(h & ~h ought to be true).

Van Fraassen thus agrees with Williams (1973: 166–186) and Marcus (1980: 121–136) that the equivalence of 1 and 2 ought to be rejected on the grounds that rational and moral agents might and do find themselves in value conflicts or moral dilemmas. This conclusion requires understanding the deontic operator "ought" differently than I have suggested – at least in contexts of value conflict.

Given the characterization of the conditions under which h ought to be the case relative to a conflict-free evaluation of the feasible worlds (a characterization I share with van Fraassen), van Fraassen's interpretation amounts to requiring that h ought to be the case categorically (or all things considered) if and only if it ought to be the case relative to ways of evaluating feasible options permitted by at least one of the value commitments in competition.[1]

Van Fraassen and I agree that value conflict is absent when there is a single permissible way of valuation in the context of a given decision problem. Conflict arises when two or more ways of evaluating options are permissible or "in force".

Van Fraassen says that for each way of evaluation in force, the agent ought to perform an option optimal relative to that standard. Thus, if there are n standards in force, there can be n options, each of which ought to be performed even though they cannot be performed together. In contrast, I say that the agent ought to perform some option which is optimal relative to some permissible way of evaluation or standard of value in force. However, the agent is not obliged to implement an optimal option relative to each standard.

Is there some substantial point at issue, or is the difference just sketched merely verbal? Van Fraassen and I appear to agree on the properties of the structures in terms of which a semantics for deontic primitives is to be fashioned. Hence, the distinctions one of us makes could be made by the other. Insofar as the debate focuses on supplying a "semantics" for deontic primitives, the dispute appears to be over the way to use "ought" in making distinctions.

If there is some substantial difference between van Fraassen's approach and my own, it should be sought in differences in the way van Fraassen and I intend our deontic formalisms to be applied in the context of decision making. Let us return then to the case of the Dewey –Tufts hero, who must choose between being a conscientious objector and joining the war effort. Van Fraassen and I agree that he is in conflict because he takes two ways of evaluating these options into account which rank the options differently.

In my account, both options are V-admissible and, hence, are not prohibited as far as the considerations grounded on patriotism and pacificism are concerned. Van Fraassen would say that the agent's values imply that he ought to go to war and also that he ought to refuse to go to war.

What help does all this give to the agent in deciding what to do? In my approach, it is frankly admitted that the agent's values fail to render a verdict between conscientious objection and joining the war effort. Van Fraassen appears to be making a different recommendation. But what is it? Van Fraassen cannot be telling the hero to go to war and also telling him not to. Such advice is inconsistent with the assumption that the agent cannot perform the actions required to comply. So what does the van Fraassen formula provide in the way of counsel? Does it instruct the agent to join the war effort? Does it tell him to refuse? Does it declare both options to be admissible? Or does it fail to give any advice whatsoever?

Both Marcus (1980: 135–136) and Williams (1973: 184–186) explicitly address this question and concede that the formula which they, like van Fraassen, use to represent moral conflict gives no advice concerning what to do. What they concede explicitly, van Fraassen (1973: 8–11) acknowledges indirectly. The concession is important, for it acknowledges that the revisions of deontic logic they entertain are not focused on the use of ought statements in giving advice to decision makers facing value conflict.

In contrast, the interpretation I have suggested according to which h ought to be true if and only if it is true in all V-admissible worlds (or more generally all admissible worlds) construes ought statements in a manner relevant to their role in making recommendations as to what is to be done. In this respect, the interpretation of "ought" I have suggested has something in its favor which the conceptions considered by Marcus, van Fraassen and Williams do not.

One by-product of this usage is that the deontic principles van Fraassen calls "classical" need not be abandoned in order to acknowledge the existence of moral conflict. Nor do advocates of these principles need to be saddled with a commitment to utilitarianism or any other axiological creed. In saying this, I do not deny the important insight shared by Marcus, van Fraassen and Williams that moral conflict is not a form of incoherence. To the contrary, the account I favor makes it plain that moral conflict is conflict akin to that of an investigator when he is in doubt as to which of two rival hypotheses is true. Once this is clear, it should be obvious that moral conflict may be perfectly coherent and appropriate.[2]

2.2 Guilt

I have argued that the senses of "ought" used by Marcus, van Fraassen and Williams offer no advice to agents experiencing value conflict as to what to do. I have also denied the need to represent the condition of unresolved conflict with the aid of this notion of obligation. Is there any other consideration which might warrant our taking seriously a sense of "ought" which flouts condition 1 and the equivalence between 1 and 2 mentioned in 2.1?

Williams invokes the consideration of moral "regret". Marcus and van Fraassen speak of "guilt". Van Fraassen alludes to a sense of regret according to which Buridan's ass, had he finally picked one of the bales, might still regret having foregone the opportunity of eating the other. This is not the sense of regret discussed by Williams or of guilt considered by Marcus and van Fraassen. All three authors agree that the agent facing an unresolved conflict in values feels guilt (or regret) appropriately; for no matter how he chooses, he will violate a moral obligation. For the present purpose, no distinction need be drawn between Williams' regret and the guilt of Marcus and van Fraassen.

My account suggests that in a context of unresolved conflict, the evaluations of the options mandated by the moral principles in conflict are permissible but not mandatory and that the options recommended to the agent are recommended as admissible, not obligatory.

This may be relevant to giving advice concerning what the agent ought to do, but it fails to render either guilt or regret appropriate (except, perhaps, in the sense in which regret is appropriate for the hay-eating ass).

Thus, it may be argued that the conception of obligation suggested by my interpetation of deontic operators fails to capture an important dimension of moral experience which the conceptions canvassed by Marcus, van Fraassen and Williams do.

I disagree. Suppose a person commited to the injunction against breaking promises confronts a decision which does not involve conflict between that value commitment and others he endorses, "all things considered". It is noncontroversial that he ought to keep his promise. Suppose, however, that due to weakness of will the agent fails to live up to his commitments and breaks the promise.[3] We have a clear case where the agent is guilty. Perhaps he ought to feel guilty; but setting aside his feelings of guilt, it is clear that he should make amends in some appropriate manner if that is feasible.

To say this is to endorse a widely held value commitment. In enjoining against the breaking of promises, not only are promise-breaking options not to be ranked optimal according to permissible ways of evaluating feasible options but breaking promises and making amends is to be ranked over breaking promises and not making amends according to all permissible ways of evaluation. Thus, the propriety of guilt in this case of weakness of will is built into the value commitments which constrain the ways of evaluation used to rank options as better or worse.

Consider now an agent committed to promise keeping and the clause concerning making amends. Suppose, as Marcus rightly envisages as a possibility, he makes two promises he cannot jointly keep. Keeping one promise is breaking the other. In such a case, the agent recognizes that he needs to modify his value commitment (counter to Marcus' view) by restricting the scope of applicability of the promise-keeping obligation so that it no longer covers this case. However, the agent does not turn his back on his earlier value commitment altogether. The obligation to keep promises retains its applicability over a wide range of cases, and in the particular case under consideration it may still be regarded as obligatory to keep one of the promises without it being mandated that some particular one of them be kept.

The authors we are discussing seem to think that the guilt or regret generated by breaking a promise in this dilemma must be the same as in the case of breaking a promise due to weakness of will, for in both cases the agent has disobeyed a moral injunction which is in force. Williams does, to be sure, acknowledge that confrontation with moral conflict sometimes induces an agent to realize some moral commitment to which he was wedded to be "too naive or simpliste". But precisely in such cases, according to Williams, the agent is relieved of guilt. When guilt is unavoidable, as in moral dilemmas, it must be because conflicting obligations are in force. The agent can try to avoid such predicaments in the future without necessarily being able to do so (Williams 1973: 176–177). Marcus (1980: 135) is even more extreme. She urges the avoidance of morally hard cases as a regulative second-order principle of morality.

Thus, for these authors, the notion I have been floating that value commitments are revised in order to remove the contradiction and that the surviving value conflict is a form of suspense seems untenable, for they do not see how this view can support an account of guilt as anything other than a form of neurosis. But we have already noticed that even in cases of promise breaking due to incontinence, it is not the breaking of the promise which is the critical condition generating guilt. Rather it is the circumstance that built into the agent's value commitment regarding promising is the constraint that breaking promises and making amends is to be ranked over breaking promises and not making amends. If that constraint were not present, then even though the agent's value commitment enjoined against ranking promise breaking as optimal, the agent's choosing to break a promise due to weakness of will would not render it appropriate according to the agent's values (or those of the community upholding the value commitment) that he make amends rather than not.

In contrast, some people might endorse the desirability of making amends for broken promises even though they did not think that keeping promises was obligatory, just as many resisters to the Vietnam War did not deem it obligatory to observe the law (indeed, thought they ought to violate it) but did think they ought to be willing to "pay the price" and serve prison terms.

Thus, I think we must grant Williams that acting while in doubt as to what is right is not in itself a sufficient basis for moral regret or guilt. But acting in violation of what is right while in no doubt as to what is right is also not in itself a sufficient basis for moral regret or guilt. More to the point, even when the obligation to make amends for some act is acknowledged, this does not imply that the performance of the act violated some obligation.

Let us return then to the case of the agent who has made two promises he cannot jointly keep. Suppose he has four options: Keep promise A and make amends for breaking promise B. Keep promise A and make no amends for breaking B. Keep B and make amends for breaking A. Keep B and make no amends for breaking A. In my view, he must deny that he is obliged to keep both promises, all things considered. There is no way in which he can restrict ways of evaluation

counted as permissible to those which avoid ranking promise breaking optimal. Consistency requires that he abandon this constraint for
decision problems of this kind. The agent, however, is not compelled
by the dilemma to abandon the constraint *to which he was antecedently
committed* that keeping A and making amends for breaking B is to be
ranked over keeping A and not making amends for breaking B and
likewise for keeping B in the two ways. And this constraint effectively
precludes any permissible way of valuation from ranking the keeping
of A (B) and failing to make amends for breaking B (A) as optimal.
The only options which could be V-admissible would be keeping A
and making amends for breaking B and keeping B and making amends
for breaking A. If the conflict is unresolved, presumably both would
be V-admissible.

Clearly it is obligatory for the agent to make amends for the broken
promise. Yet in the situation, the agent was not obliged to keep the
promise he did break. The obligation to make amends does not require that the obligation violated remain in force.

It may be asked why, given that the injunction to avoid breaking
promises is not consistently applicable in the dilemma-like situation
according to the account I give, the requirement to make amends
should not be abandoned for those situations as well. I contend that
when the need to revise value commitments arises because of the lack
of feasibility, we should, indeed, modify the network of value commitments to avoid inconsistency, but we should modify it as little as is
necessary. In our example, it is not necessary to abandon the requirement to make amends even though it is necessary to relax the injunction against breaking promises.

This argument parallels a principle I have advocated as operative
in revising knowledge when one must abandon erstwhile secure assumptions because of the need to remove inconsistency. Not only is it
desirable to suspend judgement among rival hypotheses brought into
conflict, it is also desirable to make no more additional modifications
than necessary which call settled assumptions into question. One should
minimize the loss of information consistent with the need to open up
one's mind in order to remove contradiction (Levi, 1980a: 59–62).

I do not mean to suggest that in all cases of dilemma it will be appropriate to retain an obligation to make amends or to give expression to guilt. Sometimes there may be additional considerations which
warrant deeper revisions of value commitments including such demands. My point is that often an obligation to make amends may remain as a trace of an obligation no longer in force, and for perfectly
sensible reasons.

This view of the matter retains the idea that "ought" statements represent advice as to what is to be done rather than fragments of moral

epiphenomenology, and it does so without obliging us to follow Marcus' advocacy of the desirability of avoiding conflict in values.

I do not mean to deny that her advice makes good sense on some occasions. When conflict can be easily avoided or when at least the chances of such conflicts can be reduced with relatively little effort while the difficulty involved in resolving such conflicts is considerable, Marcus gives us excellent advice. It may often be easier to avoid making more promises than one can keep than to resolve the dilemmas thereby engendered.

However, the occasion of conflict may be one which threatens to recur in the future as a result of changes in social policy, technology, political structure or the allocation of wealth. Following Marcus' policy will not be feasible and, even if it is, it may be morally dubious. Rather than becoming moral Luddites, it will be preferable to follow Dewey's advice and engage in inquiries aimed at transforming our moral commitments so as to relieve our moral doubts.

2.3 Choosing without resolving conflict

Marcus, van Fraassen and Williams all use "ought" so that in a situation of unresolved moral conflict an agent ought to do A and ought also to do B when it is not feasible to do both A and B. I have already complained that this way of employing "ought" is useless in providing guidance to the agent. Williams explicitly concedes that his characterization of "ought" does not address the "deliberative question 'what ought I to do?' " (Williams, 1973: 185; see also Williams, 1981: 114–123). He contrasts the notion of a "deliberative ought" with moral oughts and also with desires and other ways of evaluation determined by value commitments which he considers nonmoral.

In the course of his discussion of deliberative oughts, Williams observes that moral commitments can come into conflict with value commitments other than moral value commitments. Moral commitments represent but one kind of value commitment an agent may have. There are many other kinds as well. Thus, Jones, the office manager, has value commitments requiring him to seek a secretary who is a good typist and a good stenographer. These commitments would not usually be called "moral" by those who are fond of talking of moral principles. Perhaps that might be due to the fact that we are not as prone to speak of "regret" or "guilt" when considering that Jones may have to violate his commitment to hire the best typist he can or his commitment to hire the best stenographer he can. Nonetheless, Jones faces a value conflict just as certainly as does the hero of the Dewey–Tufts scenario. We are focusing here on the identification of the general principles (if there are any) which regulate rational choice in the face of unresolved conflict. The principles under investigation are to be applicable regardless of whether the value commitments in conflict are labeled moral, are all nonmoral, or involve conflict between moral and nonmoral commitments or whether the conflict is between any of these and unreflective desires. In all such cases, the conflict is due to the fact that the agent has endorsed principles or has "habits" which induce him in the particular situation to evaluate the same set of feasible options in different ways as better or worse and, hence, to modify these commitments so as to allow him to be in suspense among them.

Although there can be no serious objection to identifying certain kinds of value commitments as moral in contrast to others, it can be misleading if it suggests that the principles of rational choice – including choice under unresolved conflict – are somehow different when the conflict involves moral principles. To be sure, some writers (Marcus, unlike Williams, appears to be one of them) tend to take the position that when there is a conflict between moral and nonmoral commitments, the conflict should usually be resolved in favor of the moral commitments. Like Dewey, I doubt that we can find any value commitments which can claim such a systematic privilege. But I am not concerned to argue the point here. If we are interested in exploring the problem of value conflict without adopting relatively specific views concerning the values we ought to uphold (and that seems to be van Fraassen's aim at any rate), we should entertain the possibility that conflict among moral and political, aesthetic, cognitive, professional and other value commitments can go unresolved at the moment of choice. This alone implies that precedence need not always be ceded to moral commitments. And if we acknowledge the entertainability of such a view, we should also concede the relevance of studying decision making under unresolved conflict in contexts of conflict not only among moral commitments but between moral and nonmoral commitments and among different nonmoral commitments. I maintain that there are principles of rational choice covering all these cases.

Not only is Williams prepared to admit that there can be conflicts between moral and nonmoral commitments; he is even prepared to concede that sometimes there might be a resolution of the conflicts in favor of the nonmoral commitments (Williams, 1973: 185). Even so, Williams appears to think that at the end of deliberation and before making a choice, the agent will have reached a conclusion as to what he deliberatively ought to do and that this will be acting for the best. Indeed, he boasts that the distinction between deliberative oughts and other oughts such as moral ones can clarify how a man in moral conflict can claim to have "acted for the best" in, say, joining the war effort while insisting that he ought to have refused and thereby registering his regret (Williams, 1973: 185). He acted for the best in the sense that he did what he ought to have done in the deliberative sense of "ought". Yet, he transgressed a moral ought.

The agent who has managed these maneuvers has apparently resolved his value conflicts after all and has succeeded in identifying enough of a ranking of his options as mandatory on him to determine a set of categorically optimal options. Otherwise it is difficult to understand how Williams can say that the agent has "acted for the best".

In this reading of Williams' view, the only sense in which moral conflicts go unresolved at the moment of choice is that the resolution is not achieved by invoking some second-order principle. It is done through "deliberation", which may involve invoking nonmoral considerations or other values in a manner Williams does not explain. Be that as it may, what is crucial is that appearances to the contrary notwithstanding, Williams does not allow for decision making under unresolved conflict when the agent does not know what is for the best.

There are grounds for suspecting that van Fraassen is also hostile to the notion of decision making under unresolved conflict. To be sure, he does insist that there can be unresolved conflict between moral values, and in such cases we cannot speak of what is morally best. Still, the conflict can be resolved: "If two duties, equally sacred, conflict, an exercise of the will can settle the conflict, but not a calculation of values" (van Fraassen, 1973: 9). Unlike Williams, van Fraassen does not claim that value conflicts are settled by some process of deliberation involving, perhaps, the citation of reasons, but they are, nonetheless, settled – not by an act of deliberation but by an act of will.

Marcus comes closer than either van Fraassen or Williams to a genuine recognition of decision making under unresolved conflict. Like van Fraassen and Williams, Marcus insists that in a genuine "moral dilemma" the agent is under moral obligation to choose option *A* and also to choose option *B* when his performing these two options jointly is not feasible. Nonetheless, the agent must finally choose:

> But, it may be argued, when confronted with what are apparently symmetrical choices undecidable on moral grounds, agents do finally choose. That is sometimes understood in a way in which, given good will, an agent makes explicit the rules under which he acts. It is the way an agent discovers a priority principle under which he orders his actions. I should like to question this claim. (Marcus, 1980: 135)

Thus, Marcus explicitly denies that an agent resolves his conflicts through his choice. She thereby seems to reject both the notion that moral conflicts are always solvable through deliberation as Williams suggests and the view that they can be solved by an exercise of the will as van Fraassen says.

Referring to a remark by E. M. Forster from *Two Cheers for Democracy*, Marcus contrasts Forster's hope that he would betray his country rather than his friend when faced with the cruel choice with the prayer of a hypothetical Worster that he would betray his friend rather than his country. Marcus (1980: 135) contends that neither of them need pretend that his choice is a morally obligatory one – i.e., there need be "no moral reason for generalizing his own choice to all". By putting matters in this way, Marcus has conceded (rightly I believe) that when it comes to determining what Forster ought to do in such a predicament (in the sense of the ought of deliberation), moral considerations offer no recommendation.

Like van Fraassen and Williams, Marcus claims that when moral considerations fail to resolve conflict, we can invoke other factors to help us decide. There appears, however, to be an important difference between Marcus and the others. Williams seems to think that the other considerations, whatever they may be, determine what is "for the best" in the situation. Van Fraassen is less explicit but appears to take a similar position.

In discussing the Forster–Worster case, Marcus asserts that Forster and Worster do not disagree over moral principles but "about the kind of persons they wished to be and the kind of lives they wished to lead". She does not seem to think that value commitments pertaining to personal ideals are moral commitments. Such personal ideals are, in her view, normally ruled out of consideration whenever they come into conflict with moral principles on the grounds that moral commitments take precedence over nonmoral ones. I have already dissented from this aspect of her view.

Nonetheless, there is an important aspect of her discussion of decision making when conflicts among moral principles are unresolved which deserves serious consideration. Even if Forster invokes his personal ideals to determine what to do when he cannot decide on the basis of his moral principles, Marcus does not maintain that Forster has resolved the conflict. The conflict remains as it was.

The appeal to personal ideals provides guidance concerning what to do when the "moral principles" are impotent to legislate by furnishing a criterion for discriminating among those options which the moral principles in conflict allow to be V-admissible. Such a criterion does not determine what is "for the best". There is no categorically "best" option. Forster cannot choose for the best as long as the conflict goes unresolved, for there is no best to choose. But among the V-admissible options – i.e., the options which have not been eliminated by those value commitments with respect to which Forster is in suspense – he can distinguish between those which are better or worse with respect to a yardstick of value which he has ignored in determining V-admissibility but which he is prepared to consider precisely in situations like this one.

Let us return to the second version of the problem facing Jones, the office manager – i.e., where Dolly scored 91 on both the typing and the stenography test and, hence, was "second worse" according to both desiderata. Observe that Jones' conflict is not between moral principles. Yet the structure of his dilemma parallels that of Forster. By focusing on it first, we can remove the red herring of special moral principles and eliminate irrelevancies from our discussion.

In this decision problem, hiring Jane is V-admissible. So is hiring Lilly. But hiring Dolly is not V-admissible because there is no way to weight the desiderata which yields a ranking according to which hiring Dolly is optimal. Suppose that Jones decides in this situation to hire the prettiest of the two candidates. He judges Jane prettier than Lilly and so regards the hiring of Jane as uniquely admissible.

The yardstick of feminine pulchritude figures in this calculation in much the same manner as personal ideals appear in the calculations of Worster and Forster. Consideration of feminine pulchritude is not one of the value commitments in conflict with Jones' commitments to hiring a good typist and to hiring a good stenographer. Even if Jones judges Dolly prettier than Jane and, hence, prettier than Lilly, he is committed to grounding his decision as to whom to hire, in the first instance, in professional desiderata (typing and stenographic skills). Hence, hiring Dolly is not a V-admissible option because the ranking with respect to feminine pulchritude is not a permissible way of evaluation. Only when professional considerations fail to render a verdict is Jones free with good professional conscience to bring in other considerations.

Of course, there can be disputes and doubts about secondary desiderata and value commitments as there can about the primary ones which determine V-admissibility. Some may complain that male chauvinism has no place in the office even as a secondary criterion, perhaps because it gives an advantage to those who need none. It may be argued that in hiring people for jobs, when professional considerations can no longer render a verdict, one should favor disadvantaged ethnic and racial minorities. There are many who object to stronger forms of "reverse discrimination" but who are sympathetic to this type of policy.

Suppose that the ranking with regard to disadvantage is the same as with regard to feminine pulchritude: Dolly is first, Jane is second and Lilly third. As before, Dolly is ruled out because hiring her is not V-admissible on professional grounds. The secondary criterion rules in favor of hiring Jane.

2.3 CHOOSING WITHOUT RESOLVING CONFLICT

Jones cannot claim that by choosing Jane he has chosen the best option, all things considered. To be sure, he has chosen the best typist, but not because she is the best typist. He has not chosen the best stenographer. (He has chosen the worst.) He has not chosen the prettiest applicant or the one belonging to the least advantaged of the minorities represented. There is no best option according to his primary (in this case professional) value commitments. There are V-admissible options. Hiring Jane is hiring the best candidate with respect to the secondary criterion (pulchritude or disadvantage as the case may be) among those allowed by V-admissibility. But this is a far cry from the claim that hiring Jane is for the best, all things considered.

A critic may insist that this is nothing more than a verbal trick. By choosing to hire Jane, Jones has revealed that he prefers hiring Jane, all things considered, to the other options. The widespread dogma that an agent's choice reveals his preferences to the extent of indicating that he values the option chosen at least as much as any other feasible option differs from the view I am advocating in a way which involves more than terminology. An extensive discussion of the issue will be undertaken in chapter 6. But a further elaboration of Jones' decision problem may serve to illustrate a pivotal consideration in the argument of that chapter.

Suppose that Jones has invoked the appeal to favoring handicapped minorities to render a verdict when professional considerations fail. He decides to hire Jane. Before informing Jane that she is hired, he is told that Lilly has found another job and taken it so that only two candidates are left, Jane and Dolly. Dolly is the better of the two in stenography and worse in typing. Hiring Dolly has suddenly become V-admissible. Hiring Jane remains V-admissible. But Dolly belongs to a more disadvantaged minority than Jane. Hence, Jones should conclude that he should hire Dolly.

Thus, in a pairwise choice between Dolly and Jane, Jones should choose Dolly; but in a three way choice between Jane, Dolly and Lilly, Jones should choose Jane. He should proceed in this way even though he does not change his values or resolve his value conflict.

The practice just portrayed would be regarded as irrational by nearly every decision theorist in the book. The objection is to a transgression not against morals but against reason. The alleged principle of reason violated has sometimes been called "independence of irrelevant alternatives" (Luce and Raiffa, 1957: 288). However, this label generates some confusion with K. Arrow's principle of the same name, so it is better to call it something less colorful. I adopt A. K. Sen's (1970a: 17) suggestion and call it "property α".

Luce and Raiffa (1957: 288–289) cite the following "incongruous exchange" as an illustration of the violation of property α:

Doctor: Well Nurse, that's the evidence. Since I must decide whether
    or not he is tubercular, I'll diagnose tubercular.
Nurse: But, Doctor, you do not have to decide one way or the other,
    you can say you are undecided.
Doctor: That's true, isn't it? In that case, mark him not tubercular.
Nurse: Please repeat that!

The nurse's bewilderment is justified because he assumes that the
doctor's first judgement is grounded on an assessment of the evidence
as furnishing stronger support for a diagnosis of tuberculosis rather
than none whereas the doctor's second judgement suggests that she
thinks the evidence for the diagnosis of no tuberculosis has greater
warrant than either the diagnosis of tuberculosis or suspension of
judgement.

Unless the physician has changed her assessment of the evidence or
the evidence does not, in fact, provide an ordering of her options with
respect to evidential warrant, her two responses are out and out inconsistent.

Not every violation of property α, however, exhibits inconsistency.
When Jones chooses Dolly, this does not reveal that he thinks Dolly is
at least as good as Jane for the job. Jones is in conflict as to who is
better, all things considered. He chooses Dolly because in the face of
such conflict among the values to which he is committed, he invokes
considerations which otherwise would not have counted for him. When
he contemplates the three-way choice, hiring Dolly is ruled out because of his values. This does not mean that his values have changed
or that he has inconsistent values. Hiring Dolly is neither better nor
worse than hiring Jane in the two-way choice. The same remains true
in the three-way choice.

This example illustrates an important difference between resolving
a conflict so that one can choose for the best and failing to resolve a
conflict. In the latter case, some consideration which otherwise would
not be taken into account is used to provide counsel as to what to do
when one cannot choose for the best, all things considered.

None of the three authors I have been discussing makes this sort of
distinction so it is difficult to assess their intentions when addressing
what an agent ought to do in the face of unresolved conflict. The
rhetoric of van Fraassen and Williams suggests that in the final analysis they suppose that by the moment of choice all rational agents resolve value conflicts. Marcus, in contrast, appears to take the other
view allowing for unresolved conflict and the use of secondary and
possibly tertiary, etc., principles to guide action when values at the
primary level are so conflicted as to preclude choosing for the best.

Whatever the actual intentions of these authors, my own approach
to this issue is close to that of Marcus as I understand her.

2.4 Unresolved conflict generalized

Marcus, van Fraassen and Williams focus attention on conflicts among value commitments of a distinctively moral kind. Dewey's view of moral struggle is broader than that. It includes conflicts among value commitments of any kind, whether they are economic, legal, political, aesthetic, generated by self-interest or desires or are identified as moral. Even so, Dewey's discussion of moral struggle of the second kind is focused primarily on the question of individual decision making. I suggest that the question of decision making under unresolved conflict arises in the context of the decision making of insitutions as well as the deliberations of individuals. Furthermore, it applies to cognitive decision making in which the aims are of a special epistemic variety and it arises in a special form in the context of decision making under uncertainty.

In this volume, I wish to explore a certain structure which seems to be shared by all contexts of decision making under unresolved conflict. My aim is not to reduce all forms of such decision making to a common denominator but to supply a framework of invariant features within which similarities and differences can be explored in an orderly fashion.

In the next chapter, a first step towards establishing the ubiquity of conflict in values and the presence of unresolved conflict will be taken. The role of values in scientific inquiry will be explored with an eye to ascertaining whether there are autonomous and distinctive cognitive values involved and the extent to which they come into conflict with one another and with other, noncognitive values.

3

Values in scientific inquiry

3.1 Cognitive values

In *The Will to Believe,* William James wrote:

There are two ways of looking at our duty in the matter of opinion – ways entirely different, and yet ways about whose difference the theory of knowledge seems hitherto to have shown very little concern. *We must know the truth;* and *we must avoid error* – these are our first and great commandments as would-be knowers; but they are not two ways of stating an identical commandment, they are two separable laws. . . .

Believe truth! Shun error! – these, we see, are two materially different laws; and by choosing between them we may end by coloring differently our whole intellectual life. We may regard the chase for truth as paramount, and the avoidance of error as secondary; or we may, on the other hand, treat the avoidance of error as more imperative, and let truth take its chance. (James, 1956: 17–18)

Here James discusses value commitments concerned with the promotion of cognitive values. His rhetoric is infused with moral language, but the duties to which he alludes are "in the matter of opinion" and are not customarily counted as moral. Moreover, James suggests that there are at least two different kinds of cognitive values and that these can come into conflict with one another. On both scores, I think James is right.

To agree with James about these matters is not to endorse the main drift of the argument of *The Will to Believe.* James sought to defend his and everyone else's cognitive right to embrace religious beliefs. There is much to complain about in James' superficially clear but genuinely obscure argument.

Thus, James' identification of truth and avoidance of error as two kinds of cognitive value which conflict is terminologically misleading at the very least. James (1956: 19–20) allows that an agent has the option of suspension of judgement which, if exercised, enables him to avoid error at the cost of throwing away the chance of gaining truth. But if the agent cared only for truth – i.e., whether his beliefs were true or false – giving up that opportunity would be no loss. All the beliefs he had would be true – i.e., free of error – and that is all that would matter.

What the agent gives up by suspending judgement is the opportunity of ruling out possibilities that had heretofore been left open or unsettled, of relieving agnosticism or of obtaining something of informational value.[1] Once this is appreciated, it should also be recognized that what is prized here is independent of truth value. It is relieving agnosticism, eliminating doubt, ruling out possibilities or obtaining something of informational value regardless of its truth value that is of interest. Thus, if the agent did not care at all about avoiding error, it would not matter one bit whether or not the new "truth" or information were true.

A second serious difficulty with James' view is found in his tendency to think of these two desiderata as "materially different laws" between which we must choose when determining how to fix our beliefs. Thus, James seems to think that in certain scientific contexts we choose against informational value (i.e., "truth") and in favor of avoidance of error so as to follow the policy advocated by W. K. Clifford (as misconstrued by James) of suspending judgement (James, 1956: 19–22). For those who find some religious hypothesis to be a "live option", however, the concern to avoid error is discounted in favor of the interest in believing an important truth (James, 1956: 25–29).

Thus, James fails to countenance the possibility that an investigator might resolve the conflict between the competing desiderata by finding a distinct mode of evaluating his cognitive options which trades off avoidance of error against informational value in some definite manner. According to proposals I have made elsewhere, such trade-offs determine how improbable a hypothesis should be before information gained by rejecting it is worth the risk of error incurred thereby.[2] If this is so, it is entertainable that an agent ought to take avoidance of error as well as informational value into account both in scientific investigation and in theological reflection – at least if he is to live up to scientific ideals of probity.

In addition, James fails to identify those contexts and that sense in which opinions are to be adopted. C. S. Peirce had recognized at least two distinct tasks in inquiry in which the question could be raised: in abduction and in induction. In abduction, hypotheses are appraised with respect to their value as potential answers to the question under consideration. They are judged testworthy if they gratify the demands for information sufficiently well and are not ruled out in advance as impossible relative to the available background knowledge. Once a system of alternative hypotheses is identified through such abductive efforts, the consequences of the hypotheses are elaborated (at the "deductive" stage in inquiry) and they are prepared for experimental test. At the inductive stage, one evaluates the rival hypotheses in order to identify which of them are to be rejected on the basis of the evidence so that the disjunction of the survivors can be added to the background knowledge.

At the abductive phase of inquiry, adding new hypotheses to the settled assumptions in the background knowledge is not at issue. Hence, concern about importing error does not arise. All that matters is whether the hypothesis proposed via abduction is sufficiently informative to merit serious attention.

At the inductive phase of inquiry, items may be added to the background knowledge. Risk of error is incurred. In such contexts, it makes sense to consider both avoidance of error and informational value whereas at the abductive phase only informational value can matter.

I suspect that James intended his plea for a right to believe theological hypotheses to be a plea for the right to entertain such hypotheses for further investigation. Since the testing of such hypotheses, in his view, involves living as if they were true, he might be construed as invoking only the informational values here on the grounds that only such considerations matter at the abductive phase. Unfortunately, this interpretation of James' intent is underdetermined by the text. James appears to have understood the fixing of opinion in some uncritical manner as if it were crystal clear what one were doing when one was determining what to believe. In any case, there is no indication of sensitivity to the Peircean distinction between abduction and induction.[3]

If we factor these errors, obscurities and confusions out of James' discussion, an important residue of truth remains. In efforts to expand a body of knowledge via induction, investigators ought to be concerned to obtain new error-free information – i.e., ought to evaluate their "cognitive options" in a manner which represents a trade-off between the desideratum of avoiding error and the desideratum of obtaining new information.

This observation characterizes a value commitment in the sense of chapters 1 and 2 – i.e., a general principle imposing constraints on the way options should be evaluated in a certain type of situation. As such, it does not specify fully the way such options are to be evaluated. Thus, except for requiring that no error be valued more than any potential correct answer, no restriction is imposed on the trade-off between avoidance of error and obtaining new information (Levi, 1967a: 76–77, 107).

I do not and never have claimed that conformity to such a value commitment could be justified by some form of *a priori* reasoning. Nor do I claim that I could show that scientific investigators actually conform to the requirements of this kind of value commitment. I am inclined to think, however, that a value commitment of this kind ought to be applied in evaluating strategies for adding new information via induction – as is done when a case is being made for favoring the adoption of one theory rather than another, for adopting some estimate of the value of a parameter or for deciding whether to accept some putative law. Such a value commitment may be vindicated by appealing to ramifications of its use for scientific practice.

The value commitment I characterize as seeking new error-free information does not uniquely determine the way in which cognitive options are to be evaluated in a given context of inductive inference. Other value commitments may be invoked to make a more definite determination.

One problem is to determine the degree of caution. Sometimes scientists may be able to identify an appropriate trade-off between the demands for information and the desirability of avoiding error, but conflict regarding such trade-offs cannot always be resolved. Nonetheless, it may be possible to give sensible recommendations even in the presence of such unresolved conflict (Levi, 1979: 415–419; 1980a: 35–137).

Setting aside the question of determining degrees of caution, there is still another important source of conflict among cognitive values. The general constraints imposed on quests for new error-free information do not determine uniquely how informational value is to be assessed. Competing cognitive value commitments (representing rival research programs) may impose different demands for information. These different demands can generate conflict in the way rival strategies for adding items to a body of knowledge are to be evaluated. Even when it is agreed that hypotheses which are of great explanatory power and simplicity satisfy demands for information better than complex and explanatorily weak hypotheses, controversies may arise as to what is to count as simple or as explanatorily powerful, and this can generate conflict in the way rival hypotheses are appraised with respect to informational value.[4]

Sometimes such conflicts in informational value do not matter much because the risks of error (as assessed relative to the available background knowledge) argue in favor of one conclusion over alternatives according to all permissible ways of evaluating informational value and trading it off against risk of error. However, assessments of risk may not be sufficiently robust to settle controversy in this way. If the differences in the evaluations of informational value are not removed, several different conclusions may turn out to be V-admissible. The decision theory I have proposed for handling such predicaments when conflict in assessment of informational value goes unresolved recommends suspending judgement pending further inquiry. Doing so permits the acquisition of new evidence, which leads to new assessments of risk of error, justifying more definitive conclusions.[5]

Thus, conflicting visions of explanatory adequacy underlay disputes between Newton, on the one hand, and Hooke and Huyghens, on the other, concerning the relative merits of corpuscular and wave theories of light. These disagreements expressed differences in the cognitive value commitments characterizing different programs of research. Yet if the compelling discussion of H. Stein is to be credited (in an unpublished talk delivered at Yale in 1976), Newton did not think that inquiry need or should be impeded pending resolution of the conflicts in informational value lurking behind the dispute. Nor did he suggest that the question be begged in favor of his assessment. Newton recommended remaining in suspense between the rival theories. He hoped that through further inquiry, one could obtain information which would be robust enough to settle controversies concerning which of the competing theories was true without having to settle in advance the dispute as to which way of evaluating explanatory adequacy should be adopted.

According to T. Kuhn (1970), avoidance of error cannot be a desideratum when one faces a choice among incommensurable theories. There is no way to specify truth conditions for the rival theories or to assess risk of error from a vantage point relative to which judgement is suspended among the rival theories. Truth conditions for T' can be specified relative to T in a way which entails the falsity of T' and the truth of T, but such an assessment begs the issue in favor of T and against T' (Levi, 1980a: 65–70). When one is choosing among incommensurable theories, begging the question in this way is unavoidable.

This does not mean that Kuhn denies the importance of epistemic values to theory choice. However, the only values he considers correspond to what I call informational values.

Kuhn concedes that there is broad agreement concerning what these values are: accuracy (in predicting observable phenomena), simplicity, fruitfulness and the like. He insists, however, that serious investigators can differ concerning the ways these values trade off against one another. Furthermore, there can be genuine differences regarding the values represented by any one of them. There is a consensus that simplicity is a value but very little agreement as to what simplicity is. In other words, Kuhn acknowledges, as I do, that there can be conflict among different informational values (Kuhn, 1970: 199–200).

According to Kuhn, however, there is no hope of deciding among rival theories without settling such disputes concerning informational value. Every dispute among incommensurable theories depends upon the presence of an unsettled dispute among rival informational values. It is not possible for the dispute concerning rival theories to be resolved by inquiry, leading to an assessment of risk of error favoring one side or the other. The only way to settle the controversy is to settle the conflict among informational values.

Kuhn rightly observes that there is no fixed algorithm for resolving conflicts between ways of evaluating feasible options in general and cognitive options in particular. It does not follow, however, that such conflicts cannot be resolved through inquiry. Kuhn nonetheless appears to think that inquiry is powerless to settle them.

If Kuhn is right in maintaining that avoidance of error is not a desideratum when one is choosing among incommensurable theories, the only way to settle such disputes is to settle disputes concerning informational value. Kuhn seems to take for granted that the only way to settle disputes concerning value commitments is through persuasion or coercion. The attitude which Stein admiringly attributes to Newton is taken to be fruitless, if not incoherent.

I reject both assumptions leading to this conclusion. Avoidance of error ought to be a critical desideratum in all inquiry. I have argued for this view in many other places and shall not belabor it here except to say that Kuhn has not marshaled a single shred of evidence for the view that theory choices are sometimes incommensurable in the sense that one cannot move to a "neutral" position relative to which we may avoid begging the question as to which of two or more rival theories is true. Hence, there is no obstacle to taking the desirability of avoiding error seriously due to incommensurability.

Although Kuhn and I agree that scientific inquiry is value laden and, moreover, laden with cognitive or epistemic values (in contrast to moral, political, economic or aesthetic values), Kuhn denies the feasibility of undertaking a moral struggle of the second kind to settle conflicts among cognitive values. Instead of the sort of inquiries envisaged by Dewey as appropriate to such struggles, Kuhn recognizes only processes of persuasion.

If, however, one may hope on some occasions to settle conflicts among cognitive values through inquiry, then pending such resolution it makes sense to favor suspension of judgement. This means that questions about decision making under unresolved conflict are relevant to disputes concerning cognitive values as well as disputes among moral, political, economic or aesthetic values.

In this sense, scientific inquiry can be the scene of moral struggle of the second kind. This remark may seem exaggerated to those who take a narrow view of moral struggle and value conflict. My aim, however, is to urge on us a broader conception of conflict in values – a conception which is sensitive to the similarities between decision making under unresolved conflict in scientific inquiry and in practical deliberation.

3.2 Cognitive and practical values

I have suggested that when scientific investigators are adding new information to their body of knowledge, they should be committed to evaluating their cognitive options with respect to two desiderata: how well these options promote the acquisition of new information and whether they avoid error. But the decision to add new information to the body of evidence and background knowledge can have signifigant practical ramifications impinging on agents' moral, political, economic and personal concerns as well as on their commitment to acquiring new error-free information.

Whether the new information added to the resources for subsequent inquiry and deliberation consists of a more or less precise estimate of the value of some parameter (e.g., the size and frequency of dosage at which treatment of experimental mice produces approximately one cancer in a thousand), the adoption of some theoretical hypothesis (e.g., concerning the mechanisms explaining the genesis of some genetically determined disease) or a prediction about the future (e.g., as the approximate levels of interest rates in the next quarter), the acceptance of some conclusion of these kinds as evidence in subsequent deliberation and inquiry may have a bearing on how the investigators or those who accept their authority on the issues under consideration will conduct themselves on questions having economic, political, moral or aesthetic import.

On this basis, James Leach has argued that these economic, political, moral, aesthetic or, more generally, noncognitive values should be taken into account in deciding whether to add some specific conclusion to the resources of inquiry.[6]

In a sense, Leach's thesis is unexceptionable. Consider the predicament of Jones, the office manager, hiring a secretary. The decision he makes will have consequences for the typing and stenographic competence of the office staff. It will also have a bearing on the ethnic composition of the staff. Whether Jones commits himself to ignoring the latter consideration or not in deciding among the candidates (except, perhaps, when all other considerations fail to provide a verdict) or insists on taking it into account, Jones has, in a sense, made an evaluation of ethnic composition. Nonetheless, if he takes the strictly professional attitude, we can still say that *qua* office manager he is neutral on the question of ethnic composition, focusing exclusively on the issues of competence in typing and stenography in deciding whom to hire. To adopt a neutral stance is to place a value on pulchritude of a very special kind. We can acknowledge with Leach that such a value judgement is made and still insist on the strictly professional character of Jones' commitments.

Similar remarks apply *mutatis mutandis* to Leach's effort to rescue R. Rudner's (1953: 1–6) arguments against the value neutrality of scientists *qua* scientists.

Scientific investigators are in a position akin to Jones' predicament. They have value commitments to which they have declared loyalty insofar as they have taken up a specific kind of profession. The values they are enjoined to take into account in deciding what to add to the assumptions to be used as resources in subsequent inquiry ignore moral, economic, political and aesthetic considerations of many diverse kinds even though the conclusions they reach may be consequential for moral, economic, political and aesthetic interests. In suppressing these interests, such investigators are taking a definite valuative stance, just as Jones does when he ignores ethnic composition while deciding which candidate to hire.

In this sense, it is absurd to deny that scientists must make value judgements.[7] But when Rudner insisted that scientists *qua* scientists must make value judgements in a typically ethical sense and Leach sought to support him in this, they intended to sustain a stronger thesis. They insisted that scientists *qua* scientists must assign positive weight to moral, economic, political, aesthetic or other practical values when deciding what to accept into the body of scientific knowledge. The addition of the new items to the body of knowledge is thereby construed as an act undertaken to promote these practical objectives. This thesis is no better supported by Leach's argument than it was by Rudner's original discussion.

Had Leach been successful, he would have reduced the importance of one of the most interesting features of Rudner's original discussion – to wit, his appeal to the relevance of the seriousness of mistakes in deciding what to add to a body of knowledge via induction.

Even if, counter to fact, I were initially certain that what was to be added were true, taking it for granted and acting as if it were true might have morally, politically or economically offensive consequences. Practically speaking, it might be preferable not to take the hypothesis to be true than to do so. By focusing on the practical considerations exclusively, I would ignore the seriousness of errors entirely. According to Leach, one should attach some positive weight to the practical considerations. The more weight given to them, the less there will be given to the seriousness of mistakes.

It may be maintained in reply that Jones is a man of flesh and blood subject to temptation like anyone else. He may be engaged in moral struggle of the first kind in order to avoid succumbing to the temptation of ignoring his professional obligations and gratifying his sense of justice by hiring the candidate who best promotes a well-balanced ethnic composition regardless of professional skills. More to the point, Jones may be in genuine unresolved conflict as to whether to live up to his professional obligations or satisfy his sense of justice. In this case, Jones confronts a moral struggle of the second kind.

What is true in Jones' case is applicable to scientists as well. Scientists are, after all, human beings who endorse moral value commitments, belong to political parties and have economic interests. Just as these diverse practical values can come into conflict, the professional commitments of scientists entailing the promotion of cognitive values may come into conflict with these practical values.

Had Leach intended to emphasize this important possibility, there would have been no dispute; but the importance of the possibility of such conflict resides in the fact that it is a conflict between cognitive interests and other "practical" interests. That is to say, such conflict implies the correctness of the thesis which advocates of value neutrality are most anxious to defend – to wit, the autonomy of the cognitive interests of science. Unless cognitive commitments are recognized as distinct from moral, political, economic, aesthetic or other practical interests, no conflict can arise.[8]

Leach (1968: 102–106) and several others have complained that the way in which a trade-off is determined between avoidance of error and informational value (i.e., the way a degree of caution is determined) is either arbitrary or determined by practical considerations. Hence, appeal to practical values is inescapable in any event.

Objections of this sort confuse two distinct factors involved in efforts to resolve conflicts in values: (a) the potential resolutions of the conflict under consideration and (b) the reasons for favoring one potential resolution over others.

To understand the difference, let us return once more to the predicament of Jones, the office manager. He could achieve a potential resolution of the conflict by taking some weighted average of the typing and stenography scores of the candidates and ranking the options accordingly. But which of the infinitely many schemes for weighting the two scores should be adopted?

The values (performance on the typing and stenography tests respectively) involved in the conflict are to be distinguished from the potential resolutions, which evaluate the options in still different ways. Nonetheless, we may say that the potential resolutions are resolutions of the conflicts in these values (proficiency in typing and stenography).

Different considerations may be invoked in deciding which of the potential resolutions to eliminate and which to retain as permissible pending further inquiry. For example, Jones might consider how much time the new secretary will spend typing as opposed to taking dictation. He might use this information to fix on a method of weighting the rival desiderata. In such a case, he will have evaluated the potential weightings of the competing desiderata according to a distinct standard of value and chosen a potential resolution.

The way of evaluating options ultimately chosen by Jones differs from the appraisals of the rival desiderata for which it is a potential resolution and which form the basis on which Jones chose that particular resolution.

Similar remarks apply *mutatis mutandis* to contexts of scientific inquiry. Scientists *qua* scientists should seek error-free information when engaged in efforts to enlarge their body of knowledge. This value commitment imposes restrictions on the way they should evaluate the cognitive options. Nonetheless, many degrees of freedom remain for determining how cognitive options are to be assessed. In particular, the value commitment just mentioned fails to specify how risk of error is to be traded off against informational value – i.e., how a degree of caution is to be chosen.

Sometimes there is no problem. The degree of caution may have already been standardized for investigations of a certain type. But it may also be the case that an investigator chooses a particular degree of caution to exercise because he or she suspects that doing so will somehow flatter the ego of the director of a major grant-giving agency. This self-serving motivation does not detract from the fact that the value commitment determined by the choice of a degree of caution qualifies as a cognitive value commitment.

I do not mean to suggest that such an investigator's reasons for making a choice of a degree of caution in this way are beyond criticism. My point is rather that someone could object to the reason without objecting to the degree of caution chosen or to the conclusions reached using the value commitment thereby determined.

Similar remarks apply when the question concerns the topics to be investigated. Investigators sometimes select topics they expect will promote their careers. And choosing such topics will, of course, impose constraints on how cognitive options are to be identified and evaluated. Nonetheless, as long as the values built into the demand that error-free information be sought are observed in the evaluation of cognitive options, the autonomy of scientific interests will have been respected.

Of course, as stated previously, one may pursue inquiry without resolving conflicts in cognitive values regarding degrees of caution or demands for information. On some occasions, such conflicts may be settled by an appeal to other cognitive interests rather than to practical ones. Even so, scientific inquiry is carried on in the same world as is the commerce, politics and amusements which preoccupy scientists and laity alike. To advocate a notion of value neutrality which insists that scientific inquiry be hermetically sealed off from these other activities would be pernicious and quixotic.

Nonetheless, it would be equally unfortunate for us all if the recognition of the distinct aims of scientific inquiry were lost or assimilated into other moral, political or economic values. Nor is such a position congenial with the value pluralism associated with the pragmatist Dewey.

Dewey complained that utilitarians applied an all-purpose system of principles immune to revision or criticism to the reduction of all value commitments to a single system. Unfortunately, Dewey himself failed to do justice to the cognitive interests of science in his pluralist axiology. We should respect truth as much as we respect goodness and beauty. Not only is such respect compatible with the pluralism Dewey advocated. Insisting on the respect should deepen and fructify the pluralism.[9]

3.3 Pluralism and conflict

In this chapter and in chapter 2 attention was focused primarily on conflicts in value generated by commitments customarily understood to be moral. However, the notion of value conflict with which I am concerned has a far greater applicability than the domain of moral dilemmas. In this chapter, the point was illustrated by an examination of cognitive values and the sorts of conflicts which may arise among cognitive values and which are generated when cognitive values clash with moral, political, economic and other practical considerations.

There is no point in providing more examples of the diversity of value commitments which reasonable agents may endorse. And advocates of value pluralism often acknowledge the inevitability of conflict. My purpose in discussing epistemic values is twofold. (a) Even those philosophers, like Dewey, who acknowledge the diversity of value have failed to be sufficiently generous in this recognition. There is a tendency among some pragmatists to reduce epistemic values to moral or other practical values. Value pluralists ought to resist this tendency. (b) To the extent that there is diversity of values, there is the opportunity for conflict in value and, more to the point, there is the occasion for decision making under unresolved conflict. The discussion of epistemic values illustrates this point.

It is now time to develop an account of decision making under unresolved conflict in a systematic and general way.

4

Choice and foreknowledge

4.1 Ability and possibility

According to the proposal informally sketched in 1.2 and to be elaborated in chapter 5, value commitments impose constraints on the ways in which feasible options are evaluated. The totality of value commitments endorsed by an agent delimit a set of permissible ways of evaluation of the feasible options available to the agent. (This set of ways of evaluation will be called a *value structure* in the more technical discussion.) The set of feasible options which rank best according to some permissible way of evaluation in the value structure comprises the *V-admissible* options. Given his value commitments and his knowledge of the feasible options, a rational agent ought to restrict his choice to the set of V-admissible options.

Chapter 5 will elaborate and slightly modify this formula. However, the criterion of admissibility just sketched is intended to apply to the options open to the decision maker or, more accurately, to the options open to the decision maker insofar as the decision maker recognizes them to be available to him. In this chapter, some remarks will be made about the kind of assumptions the decision maker must make about feasibility if he is to apply criteria for admissibility of the sort I am proposing (and, indeed, criteria proposed by a broad range of alternative decision theories) in his deliberate decision making. These remarks address questions about feasibility whose answers do not depend on the presence or absence of unresolved value conflict in the decision problem being faced. Yet the issues raised are relevant to the concerns of this essay precisely because they are relevant to any theory of rational choice.

Having a choice presupposes having options. Having the option to perform some action entails having the ability to perform the action upon choosing it. Hence, having a choice presupposes having abilities to perform various actions upon choosing them.

Abilities may be attributed to objects and systems when no question of choice arises. Iron bars are capable of being magnetized. Coins are able to land heads up on being tossed onto a smooth surface. Before we discuss choice, a brief examination of abilities in general should be useful.

Coin *a* is able to land heads up on a toss. We may also say that it is possible for coin *a* to land heads up on a toss. The existence of actual or possible tosses of coin *a* is not implied by such claims. A property of the coin is being predicated, a property it has regardless of whether the experiment (tossing the coin) is ever conducted. Furthermore, whether the coin has or lacks the property is independent of the attitudes of those who make the attribution. In this sense, abilities or possibilities are real. There are, however, no unactualized but possible entities or worlds. I offer no analysis of the ability of coin *a* to land heads up on a toss yielding nontrivial necessary and sufficient satisfaction conditions for the predication of the ability. Attribution of the ability is equivalent to the assertion that object *a* is not constrained to fail to land heads up on a toss or, alternatively stated, that *a* has the "sure fire" disposition to fail to land heads up on a toss. Thus, we could take sure-fire disposition predicates to be primitive rather than ability predicates. One way or the other, however, we end up with a primitive as far as armchair semantics is concerned.

But all is not lost. By taking one of these notions to be primitive, we may still identify principles linking that type of predicate with regularities pertaining to test behavior. This practice imitates Carnap's practice when he introduced disposition predicates through reduction sentences. Those who are discontented with such an approach are urged to relieve their malaise through scientific inquiry, which, on some occasions, yields the integration of ability and disposition predicates within some theoretical framework (Levi, 1980a: ch. 11).

Ability so understood plays an important role in characterizing stochastic processes. When considering stochastic processes, we direct our attention to a "sample space" of possible outcomes of a trial or experiment of some kind. For example, on a tossing of coin *a* 100 times, there are 2^{100} possible sequences in which coin *a* can land heads and tails. These are representable as "points" in the sample space relative to that kind of experiment on coin *a*.

Associating a sample space with a kind of trial on a setup is predicating an objective property of it. That property is characterizable as a congeries of abilities and constraints (or sure-fire dispositions). The coin is able to land in any one of the 2^{100} sequences of heads and tails in a single series of 100 tosses. It is incapable of landing in more than one of these ways in such a trial, but it is constrained to land in at least one of the 2^{100} ways in a 100-fold tossing.

The relativity of the sample space to the kind of trial should be emphasized. The sample space of 2^{100} different sequences of heads and tails is relative to 100-fold series of tosses of the coin. Relative to those kinds of trials characterizable as 100-fold series of tosses of the coin in which the coin lands heads on the first toss, the sample space consists of 2^{99} different sequences of heads and tails. Relative to the type of trial described by specifying for each toss in a 100-fold series that it is in an initial mechanical state which, for the sake of brevity and out of ignorance, I call a "heads-inducing state", there will be exactly one point in the sample space. Coin a might have all three properties at the same time. It can have all of them even if none of the trials is instantiated at the time the coin has these three properties.

Suppose a trial event does occur. It could be of all three kinds of trial just mentioned, the first two or the first alone. No matter which it is, a can still have all three congeries of abilities and dispositions.

It is objectively possible for coin a to land heads on a toss and also to land tails on a toss. Hence, one cannot causally explain why the coin landed heads at time t by asserting that it was tossed. In this sense, the landing heads up was not causally determined by the tossing. However, the tossing might be redescribed in terms of a specification of the mechanical state of the coin at the inception of the toss (together with the prevailing boundary conditions), and the landing heads up might also be redescribed in terms of the corresponding mechanical state of the coin. Hence, by suitable redescription of the tossing and the landing heads up, one might furnish a causal explanation where initially there was none.

E. Nagel observed a long time ago:

. . . in discussing the causal or noncausal character of a given theory, two factors must be examined: the *state* (or system of properties) in terms of which the physical system under discussion is described and the *laws* (or systems of equations) which connect the states at different times and places. (Nagel, 1939: 25–26)

Nagel goes on to point out that when the specification of states and laws is taken into account, it becomes apparent that depicting some process in terms of objective probabilities does not preclude offering a deterministic characterization as well. Nagel's point does not depend upon the adoption of a frequency interpretation of objective or statistical probability of the sort J. Venn invoked in defending a similar conclusion. The point may be appreciated if one recognizes that it applies *mutatis mutandis* to claims about objective possibility or ability when the question of a frequency interpretation does not arise.

Thus, if the sample space for a coin relative to trials which are tossings contains the two points "landing heads" and "landing tails", that suffices to prevent a deterministic, nomological or causal explanation of why the coin landed heads (under that description) by stating that it was tossed. But this need not preclude redescriptions of the tossing and the landing heads by reference to mechanical states so that a deterministic explanation is available. Just as the recognition of such objective possibility is compatible with determinism at some other level of description, the same applies to recognition of objective probability.[1]

Ability or objective possibility should be distinguished from epistemic or serious possibility. In deliberation, an agent must distinguish between truth value-bearing hypotheses whose logical possibility of truth should be taken seriously and those hypotheses whose logical possibility should be ruled out of consideration. If the agent takes for granted that coin a has the ability to land heads up on a toss but is incapable of landing heads up on a tails-inducing toss in a situation where he also knows that the coin has been tossed in a tails-inducing way, he should rule out the hypothesis that the coin landed heads on that occasion as a serious possibility. This is so even though the agent knows that the coin at that time had the objective ability to land heads up on a toss. It was possible *for* the coin to land heads up on a toss at time t, but it was not seriously possible (according to the agent X) *that* the coin landed heads up at t. If, however, the agent knew only that the coin was tossed at t but not that it was a tails-inducing toss (even though it was, in fact, tails-inducing), it would be a serious possibility according to X that the coin landed heads up at t. Serious possibility is epistemic. It is relative to what the agent knows or assumes. And it applies to truth-value-bearing propositions. Ability or objective possibility is not epistemic. It is not *de dicto*. It is the possibility for an object or system to respond in a manner of some kind in a certain type of trial.

The temptation to confuse the possibility for coin a to land heads up with the possibility that coin a lands heads up seems extremely potent – especially in cases where coin a is known to have been tossed. Thus, S. Kripke considers a pair of dice, A and B, which are tossed once. He notes that there are 36 possible "states" of the dice when states are described in terms of the pair of sides which show up. This type of observation, Kripke points out, is familiar from high school exercises in calculating probabilities. He claims that these exercises in probability thereby introduce us "at a tender age" to a set of miniature possible worlds (Kripke, 1982: 16–18).

It is, indeed, true that if one knows that the pair of dice has been tossed at time t and nothing else about the tosses or the dice except the ability to land in the 36 different ways on a toss, it is consistent with what one knows that both A and B land with one-spots up, a one-spot up on A and a two-spot on B, etc. Given one's knowledge, 36 hypotheses qualify as serious possibilities. However, suppose one also knew that the pair of dice was tossed in some special way which prevented either A or B from landing with a one-spot up. Relative to such a toss, the sample space is reduced from 36 cases to 25 – so the agent knows. Hence, only 25 of the original 36 hypotheses remain serious possibilities.

As I understand him, Kripke would not think the space of possible worlds he has in mind is so readily altered by a change of knowledge. The system of mini possible worlds associated with the possible outcomes of tossing the dice is generated by the tossing of the dice regardless of what is known about the dice. But what is this objectively given space of possible worlds? Is it the space of 36 cases "every schoolboy knows" relative to the tossing? Is it the 25 relative to the type of trial precluding the showing of one-spots? Or consider that the tossing of the dice positioned them in some initial location in phase space from which their trajectories and the eventual outcome could be determined by the laws of Newtonian mechanics. If the dice were tossed in a manner of this sort (whether we knew it or not) and Newtonian mechanics were applicable to the process, there would be only one possible world – neither 36 nor 25.

Perhaps Kripke denies that Newtonian mechanics applies and insists that the system is indeterministic. The elementary schoolboy exercise in probability to which Kripke refers then depends for its interpretation on whether the process is taken to be governed by Newtonian mechanics or by some non-Newtonian indeterministic system of laws. The exercise is not so elementary after all!

But even if the process is indeterministic, the tossing of the dice might be characterizable in stronger terms relevant to the outcome and in a manner reducing the space of 36 possibilities to 25. Hence, the space of 36 possible outcomes may be recognized relative to the characterization of the trial as a tossing of the dice but not as a tossing of the dice in the special way. Which of the different spaces correctly ascribing the abilities of the dice to respond to trials generates the space of possible worlds? Kripke seems to think it is the space of 36 possibilities every schoolboy knows. Does every schoolboy really know *that?*

These difficulties would disappear if a space of possible worlds were relativized to the kind of trial which generated the sample space. In that case, on any occasion when some event occurred which was correctly describable as an instance of several different kinds of experiment, there would be many different spaces of possible worlds corresponding to the diverse kinds of experiments instantiated on that occasion.

It is not clear (to me at any rate) why anyone should be interested in possible worlds so construed. To be sure, there is some importance to be attached to ascertaining the abilities systems have and the constraints to which they are subject. But we do not need to appeal to *de dicto* modal representations to characterize such a possibility. *De dicto* modality becomes important in deliberation when one seeks to discriminate between hypotheses which are serious possibilities and hypotheses which are not. What must be answered is whether the sort of possibility assignable to hypotheses which Kripke seeks to characterize by reference to the analogy with the tossing of dice helps us to understand ability or to understand serious possibility. I do not see that it contributes to the clarification of either concept. Even when relativized to kinds of trials along lines I have suggested, possible worlds seem like gratuitous or *verdoppelte* metaphysics of the sort Neurath sneered at when discussing correspondence theories of truth.

In any case, when discussing deliberation I shall follow the practice of distinguishing *de dicto* serious possibility and abilities which are real, nonepistemic possibilities relativized to kinds of trials. We shall have no need for possible worlds or *de dicto* nonepistemic possibilities.

Still, there remains an important issue deserving some brief consideration. We have seen that sample spaces representing networks of abilities and dispositions relative to different kinds of trials may be true of the same setup at the same time. Furthermore, the same trial event may be of all the different kinds. The pair of dice was known to be tossed, to be tossed in a way preventing a one-spot from showing up and tossed in a way which positioned the dice in a "double-sixes"-inducing mechanical state. Relative to the description as a tossing, the sample space contains 36 points, relative to the description as a one-spot-preventing tossing, there are 25 points; and relative to the description as a double-sixes-inducing tossing, there is 1 point. The problem is to determine how the agent who knows all this should make judgements of serious possibility concerning the outcome of the specific toss under scrutiny.

The answer here appears to be that the agent should invoke the strongest description available to him concerning the kind of experiment which has taken place to identify a sample space of objectively possible outcomes. He should then regard each hypothesis, asserting that a specific one of these possible outcomes occurs as a serious or epistemic possibility. If the agent knows only that the pair of dice is tossed without knowing whether the toss is one-spot-preventing or double-sixes-inducing, he should judge each of 36 hypotheses about the outcome as a serious possibility. If he knows in addition that it is a one-spot-preventing toss, he should judge 25 hypotheses to be serious possibilities. If he knows that the toss is double-sixes-inducing, only 1 of these hypothesis is a serious possibility.

The principle of reasoning linking knowledge of objective abilities and judgements of serious or subjective possibility in this way is analogous to principles of direct inference linking knowledge of objective probability or chance with judgements of subjective probability (Levi, 1980a: 254–256).

4.2 Choice

Choice and chance have more than assonance in common. Coin a is constrained to land heads or tails upon being tossed. Jones is constrained to choose to hire Jane, to choose to hire Dolly or to choose to hire Lilly in a search for a new secretary. Just as the coin has the ability to land heads up on a toss, so too Jones has the ability to choose Jane in the search for a new secretary. Both the chance setup and the agent have congeries of abilities and dispositions representable by sample spaces relative to given kinds of trials.

The kind of "experiment" or "trial" relative to which the "sample space" appropriate to deliberation is specified is a process of deliberation (such as Jones' searching for a new secretary). The "possible outcomes" of the experiment are the various feasible options. In spite of the artificiality, I have represented these outcomes as "choosing sentences true." The reasons for this will emerge subsequently.

Suppose Jones concludes on Tuesday that he will not hire Dolly on Wednesday, leaving open whether he will hire Jane or Lilly. He remains able to hire Dolly in one sense; for he can renege on his conclusion on Tuesday. That is to say, he has the ability to choose to hire Dolly in a search where he concludes that he will not hire her on Tuesday but reneges before Wednesday ends. And the conclusion he reaches on Tuesday does not deprive him of the objective ability to hire Dolly in his search for a secretary (where the description of the search leaves entirely open what conclusions he reaches on Tuesday or anytime before the choice point on Wednesday).

Thus, Jones might very well know that he is able to choose to hire Dolly in his search for a new secretary where he has concluded that he will not hire Dolly on Wednesday and will not renege subsequently and also where he has concluded that he will not hire Dolly on Wednesday but does not know whether he will or will not renege subsequently. He might also know that he is not able to hire Dolly in a search where he has concluded on Wednesday that he will not hire Dolly and will not subsequently renege on that conclusion.

There is no inconsistency in supposing that Jones has the objective ability to hire Dolly relative to some descriptions of the "experiment" (the search for a secretary) but not according to others. Nonetheless, the question arises as to how Jones is to identify the set of feasible options to which he is to apply his value commitments and canons of rational decision making in deliberation. The problem appears to resemble the analogue of the problem of direct inference to which I alluded at the end of the previous section. The option of choosing to hire Dolly is subjectively feasible for Jones relative to what he knows if and only if Jones is objectively able to hire Dolly in a search having all the features he knows apply to the search he is undertaking. Jones' judgement of subjective feasibility should be derivable from his information about objective feasibility and the circumstances of his deliberation.

A possible outcome of a process of deliberation (i.e., a feasible option relative to a process of deliberation of a given kind) can be described as a choosing true that something be the case. Jones might terminate deliberation with the decision that he will hire Jane. In this case, the proposition chosen true specifies that Jones himself perform some action. In another context, the agent might choose true that somebody else perform an action. Thus, Laban decided that Jacob marry Leah. In other cases, the proposition chosen true need not specify that an action be performed by any specific agent. Thus, someone might decide to have the walls of his or her room painted pale blue.

According to G. L. S. Shackle, a decision is a

transition between a psychic state in which the individual is holding in contemplation a number of distinct action-schemes each of which is open to him, to a psychic state in which he has mentally committed himself to one of these schemes. (Shackle, 1958: 20–21)

In chapter 8, I shall argue that institutions ought sometimes to be counted as agents. Shackle's formulation leaves institutional agents out of account, but his thesis could be modified so as to apply to such agents as well. Setting this point to one side, Shackle appears to take the following view of choice. Before reaching a decision, agent X knows he is compelled to choose exactly one of the options $A_1, A_2, \ldots, A_n$ through his deliberation, but he is able to choose any one of them. However, X does not know which of the options X will choose. If X had such knowledge, the issue would be settled for him. In Shackle's view, X has chosen. Deliberation would be over. This is so whether X is a person or an institution.

Shackle is, indeed, correct in saying that agent X will terminate his reflection on what he should choose once he has concluded that he will choose some particular option; and if X concludes that he will not choose some one of a particular subset of his feasible options without venturing a view on how he will choose from the remaining options, he may carry on his deliberations as if the remaining options were the sole feasible ones. Still, I think it useful to distinguish X's conclusion as to what he will choose from his choosing. The "transition" from one psychic state to another to which Shackle refers seems to me to characterize concluding rather than choosing.

Consider the case where Jones concludes on Tuesday that he ought to hire Jane but fails to implement this conclusion until Wednesday. Ordinarily we might say that Jones decided to hire Jane one day before he implemented his decision. Observe, however, that Jones is able to renege on the "decision" he made on Tuesday up until the moment he implements that "decision". Until the fateful moment on Wednesday, Jones is able to hire Dolly and to hire Jane on a reconsideration of the conclusion reached on Tuesday and in that sense has retained all the hiring options he had on Tuesday.

I propose restricting the notion of choosing so that Jones does not choose that he will hire Jane until he has lost the ability to choose true other alternatives on a reconsideration of his concluding that he will hire Jane. And that ability is lost only when Jones has implemented what he has concluded. To be sure, the actions which implement a choice could, in general, have been performed without having been done out of choice. Jones could have been compelled to hire Jane because of a court injunction or the orders of a superior officer of the firm. Still, choosing that Jones hire Jane presupposes that Jones hires Jane and, therefore, that the opportunities to choose that Jones hire Lilly and to choose that Jones hire Dolly on a reconsideration of the conclusion that Jones will hire Jane are lost. Choosing true is a concluding true accompanied by an act which implements what is concluded.

From the point of view of someone interested in the explanation of an agent's actions,[2] distinguishing between choosing true that h and successfully implementing the choice may seem worthwhile. But the explanation of action is not the topic of this discussion. The focus is on criteria for choice given the agent's background knowledge and value commitments, especially in contexts where value conflicts are unresolved at the moment of choice. Such criteria are to be applied to the assessment of the admissibility of members of the set of feasible options when feasibility is assessed relative to the agent's background knowledge. We are interested in the presuppositions embraced by the decision maker when he recognizes a feasible option. If an agent takes for granted that choosing true that h is an option for him, he takes for granted that exercising that option will be efficacious. That is to say, if the agent chooses true that h, then h is true. From the deliberating agent's point of view, choice not merely is the mental commitment to one option rather than others but entails successful implementation.

Given the concerns of this volume, there is no need to settle controversies as to whether the predicate "chooses h true" describes some event or process distinct from the the action implementing the choosing or is the same event described differently. As the considerations introduced in 4.3 will indicate, it would be a mistake to maintain that describing an action as done by choice entails that it be explained in some special way – e.g., in terms of the reasons for the action. At least, this would be a mistake from the point of view of the deliberating agent. As I shall argue in 4.3, the deliberating agent should not assume that the policy followed will be explainable by reference to the agent's reasons in conformity with some principles of choice. From his point of view, describing an option as a choosing true makes no presupposition as to how the choice is to be explained.

How in the final analysis does Shackle's view of choice bear on this? Shackle and I agree on focusing attention on choice from the agent's point of view. I differ from him in insisting that choice, from that point of view, entails implementation as well as psychic commitment. Concluding that h, as I have understood it, resembles Shackle's psychic commitment. But concluding that h without implementation does not preclude the opportunity to renege upon reconsideration. Concluding is not choosing.

Even so, Shackle's position contains an important kernel of truth. Should Jones conclude on Tuesday that he will hire Jane but delay implementation until Wednesday, the choice (so I propose saying) is made on Wednesday. On Tuesday, Jones did not choose but concluded. Even from Jones' point of view, there is a difference. To be sure, Jones retains the ability to renege upon reconsideration of his conclusion, but in concluding on Tuesday that he will hire Jane he will become certain that he will not reconsider.

On Tuesday Jones has no intention of reneging on Wednesday and comes to be certain that he will not renege. He takes for granted that the hiring of Jane will be implemented on Wednesday. His certainty of this is consistent with his conviction that he remains able until Wednesday to choose to hire Dolly and to choose to hire Lilly upon a reconsideration of his conclusion. There is a sense in which these options remain open to him; but relative to what Jones knows, his implementing them (and, hence, his choosing them) are not serious possibilities.

Hence, from Jones' point of view on Tuesday, there is no further point in deliberating. The hiring is as good as done. Jones has not lost the objective ability to renege on what he has concluded through reconsideration. But he is certain that he will not do this. To this extent, he has renounced these objectively feasible options on Tuesday. The matter is settled. Although the options are objectively feasible in the sense explained until the moment of implementation on Wednesday,

from the point of view of the deliberating agent the only feasible option he has after the conclusion reached on Tuesday is the hiring of
Jane. That is to say, that is the only feasible option in the sense relevant to the application of value commitments and principles of choice.

The conclusion reached on Tuesday is, I suggest, a "psychic shift"
in Shackle's sense. It is a shift from a state where hypotheses predicting the implementation of several different options are countenanced
as serious possibilities to a state where only one such hypothesis is
recognized as seriously possible. I have argued that this psychic shift
may not be an appropriate characterization of choosing even from
Jones' point of view if we want to take into account the ability to renege. But if we are focusing on a characterization of the domain of
options to count as feasible for the purpose of assessing admissibility,
the psychic shift becomes critical. Through the psychic shift the set of
feasible options for the purpose of assessing admissibility is reduced
– at least from the decision maker's point of view. This is the important kernel of truth in Shackle's characterization of choice.

The import of such renunciation of "objectively" feasible options
through concluding before implementation can be further illustrated
by a case where Jones concludes on Tuesday that he will not hire
Dolly without making up his mind about Jane or Lilly. Since his only
three options initially were hiring Jane, hiring Dolly and hiring Lilly,
it is quite obvious that when implementation takes place on Wednesday in accordance with his conclusion on Wednesday, we do not want
to say that the choice was to hire Jane or Lilly. To be sure, Jones does
choose true on Wednesday that Jane is hired or that Lilly is hired. But
"Jane or Lilly is hired" is not the strongest statement relative to what
he knows that he chooses true. It does not provide a univocal characterization of the option chosen on Wednesday.[3]

Notice, however, that although Jones merely concluded true on
Tuesday that he will hire Jane or Lilly and this proposition is the
strongest he concludes true at that time, the concluding at that time
reduces the three serious possibilities to two. This is not merely a shift
in psychic state whereby Jones comes to be certain that he will not hire
Dolly. From that moment on, pending further revisions in his body
of knowledge, criteria of admissibility are to be applied to two options
and not three.

Much contemporary decision theory is concerned with choosing
among long range strategies or plans when questions of reneging at a
later date may arise. Such plans are not implemented until they are
carried through without reneging. And yet we often say that the plan
is chosen before the onset of implementation. I have suggested instead that we say that the agent concludes that the plan will be chosen
and, hence, implemented. Or one might say that alternative strategies

have been renounced so that their implementation is no longer a serious possibility. Often enough, making the distinction between concluding and choosing will appear to be excessive pedantry in a discussion of planning. Unless the distinction is critical to the discussion here, I shall ignore it.

Let us rehearse the chief reason for emphasizing the distinction between choosing and concluding. We are concerned with criteria for the admissibility of options feasible for the agent from his point of view. I have been arguing that the domain of feasible options involved here consists of options which he knows he is able to choose in a deliberation and the choosing of which is a serious possibility according to what he knows. Shackle's insight is that renouncing a feasible option is a coming to know that it will not be chosen. When all but one feasible option has been renounced in this sense, the agent comes to know that he will choose the sole survivor. Although, strictly speaking, it is not chosen until implemented, from the point of view of the deliberating agent it is as good as chosen.

In this sense of choosing (i.e., concluding), choosing or concluding true that h entails coming to know that h is true. Through choosing we may add information to our knowledge. This way is an alternative to observation and inquiry as a road to knowledge.

Of course, expanding our knowledge through choice is not something we claim a right to do under any circumstances. We are entitled to do so when we can assume that we have the ability to choose in various ways through deliberation. We are not always entitled to make such an assumption. I would choose true that I receive $10 million tax free if I could and so enlarge my knowledge by coming to know that I have received $10 million tax free. Unfortunately for me, I cannot choose in that way and, hence, lack a warrant for expanding my knowledge so profitably. Still, choosing does involve a revision of doctrine which is describable as a ruling out of possibilities of a special kind – rather as Shackle suggested.[4]

4.3 Foreknowledge and freedom

Shackle's view implies that when an agent has foreknowledge that he will not choose a certain option in a given deliberation, that option should not count among the options feasible for him to choose when assessing admissibility. The agent is not, in that sense, free to choose the given option. This is so even if the agent continues to know (as may be appropriate on some occasions) that he is able to choose the option upon a reconsideration of the deliberation.

Recognition of this point is widespread among action theorists. Thus, A. Goldman concedes:

The agent who knows, as a result of reading his book of life, that he is going to commit suicide, cannot *deliberate* about whether or not to commit suicide. For deliberation implies some doubt as to whether the act will be done. (Goldman, 1970: 194)

Goldman's remark is in agreement with Shackle's much earlier observation that if an agent could predict the option he will choose, his decision problem would be "empty" (Shackle, 1958: 21).

The notion of freedom just depicted is not relevant to questions of moral or legal responsibility, but it is of central importance when attention is focused on identifying the options feasible for the agent to which he is to apply his value commitments and criteria of choice in the context of deliberation. An agent must be free to choose in this sense in order for deliberation to have any point.

We must, therefore, attribute to the deliberating agent a system of assumptions about the feasibility of his options which do not commit him to a definite view as to how he will choose. Shackle as well as R. C. Jeffrey (1977: 135–141) and F. Schick (1979: 235–252) appreciate the ramifications of this demand. Shackle formulates the issue as follows:

If a man believes himself to have in his mind a complete range of the distinct results, each fully stated in so far as he is interested in it, any one of which he can bring about by some action of his own, and if he likewise has in mind a range of distinct actions open to him, and if between the actions and the results he sees a one–one correspondence whose correctness he takes for granted, and if lastly he can order the whole class of results, each embracing *every* consequence that concerns him, according to his own desires, then his decision upon one action rather than another will be as it were *empty*, the mere registering of a formal solution to a purely formal problem. (Shackle, 1958: 21)

Criteria for rational choice are intended to determine a set of admissible options relative to information concerning (i) the options identified as feasible relative to what the agent knows, (ii) the agent's beliefs concerning the consequences of his actions and how likely they are to ensue and (iii) the agent's assessments of the values of the options and their possible consequences.

Discussion of the items mentioned under (ii) and (iii) will be postponed until chapter 7. Nonetheless, we may suppose with Shackle that the problem of determining the set of admissible options given (i), (ii) and (iii) is a problem of calculation and that the deliberating agent should be expected to carry out the calculations insofar as limitations of memory, computational capacity and emotional (or sociological in the case of institutional agents) stability do not prevent him from doing so. We should also expect the deliberating agent to be in touch with his own views concerning items (i), (ii) and (iii) insofar as failures of memory, calculation or emotional (sociological) stability do not prevent him from doing so. I gloss over but do not disparage the difficulties sometimes involved in securing such stability. Subject to the same qualifications, therefore, the deliberating agent should know what the admissible options for him are in the situation according to his values and beliefs. Finally, insofar as the agent takes for granted that he will live up to his commitments to choose in conformity with principles of rational choice relative to his values and beliefs, he knows that he will restrict his choice to the options in the admissible set.

In the special case where the admissible set contains exactly one option, the agent knows that he will choose that option. Deliberation must indeed be empty in Shackle's sense. That option and that option alone will be feasible for him to choose in the sense of "feasibility" according to which the domain of feasible options is the set of options to which the principles of choice are to be applied. But, by hypothesis, the domain of options to which the agent applied the criteria of choice was not a unit set. It turns out that either that hypothesis is false or one of the assumptions made about the information available to the decision maker must be given up. To put the point in a slightly different way, if the decision maker has the information specified above and if the set of admissible options is a singleton, the set of feasible options to which the criteria of admissibility are applied must be that same singleton.

This result generalizes obviously enough to the case where several options are admissible. There too, the set of feasible options to which the criteria of admissibility are applied must coincide with the set of admissible options.

As a general rule, principles of rational choice are expected to apply to a set of feasible options with the expectation that the set of admissible options will be a proper subset of the set of feasible options. There will be exceptions to this. Feasibility and admissibility will sometimes coincide, but they should not coincide in every case. Any theory of rational choice which entails that they always do is, indeed, empty and should be abandoned or modified. The difficulty we now face, however, applies to a wide variety of decision theories. If the decision maker has the information ascribed to him above, his decision theory is reduced to impotence no matter what it is.

Suppose that Jones, conflicted between the values of hiring a good stenographer and hiring a good typist, recognizes that hiring Jane and hiring Lilly are admissible but that hiring Dolly is not. If he also knows that he will decide in conformity with his current values and beliefs relative to principles of rational choice which yield this assessment of admissibility, he knows that he will not choose to hire Dolly. Hence, from his point of view, hiring Dolly is not feasible in the subjective sense relevant to the applications of principles of choice. Yet Jones' assessment of admissibility was grounded in the assumption that hiring Dolly is feasible in just that sense.

Suppose that Jones alters the desiderata he uses in deciding whom to hire. This need not change the set of objectively feasible options from which Jones is able to choose. More crucially, it should not alter the set of subjectively feasible options to which Jones applies criteria of admissibility in deciding how to choose. But if the change in desiderata leads to different assessments of admissibility and admissibility coincides with feasibility, what ought to be feasible no longer is.

Goldman seems content with the observation that the agent who knows he will commit suicide because he has read his book of life cannot deliberate over whether to kill himself. This contentment is unwarranted. Suppose the agent knows he will commit suicide because his value commitments and principles of choice single out that option as uniquely admissible. In this case, the agent has read his book of life through his deliberation.

If we are to avoid these embarrassing results, we must question some of the assumptions made above as to what the agent is committed to taking for granted in applying his value commitments and principles of choice to his decision problem, but we must do so in a manner which allows the decision maker to have sufficient information so that the criteria for choice can, indeed, be applied in a nontrivial manner.

R. C. Jeffrey endorses the strict Bayesian view that a rational agent should identify as admissible all and only those feasible options which maximize conditional expected utility. Jeffrey (1965: 74–75) derives a variation of the foreknowledge problem tailored to this approach to rational choice. His first suggestion for solving the problem favored weakening the assumption that the agent's choices are efficacious. The agent may suppose that he can try to make h true (perform some action), but he should not assume that if he chooses h true, h is true. In Jeffrey's view, trying to make h true may enhance its probability to nearly unity, but the agent should not assign probability 1 to h conditional on his choosing h true.

This proposal does not appear to be of much help. Jeffrey is denying that choosings are feasible options. Only tryings are. But surely the agent is able to choose to try to make h true, and when he presupposes this to be so, he does presuppose his choice to be efficacious. That is to say, he assumes that if he chooses to try to make h true he will succeed in trying to make h true even if he fails to make h true. This circumstance is enough to restore the result that admissibility must coincide with feasibility.

Jeffrey (1977: 136–137) subsequently abandoned this suggestion in favor of another approach. According to this second proposal, the agent lacks some of the information presumed to be available to the agent in the argument leading to the equation of feasibility and admissibility. Either the agent has failed to identify his ranking of feasible options (in this context Jeffrey assumes that there is a uniquely permissible ranking), has failed to identify his feasible options or, granted that he has done these things, is not certain that he will choose an option which is admissible (because optimal) relative to the current list of feasible options and the current preference ranking.

It remains the case, however, that when an agent becomes clear about all these matters, admissibility and feasibility collapse into one another. Jeffrey seems to think of choosing as coming to know oneself fully in the relevant respects in the state one was in immediately before choice.

F. Schick (1979: 237–244) has offered us the best discussion of the foreknowledge puzzle. He sums up the issue by concluding that during the process of deliberation up to the moment of choice "logic alone rules out our knowing the whole truth about ourselves" (Schick, 1979: 243). Schick does not maintain that the agent who assumes that A_1, $A_2, \ldots, A_n$ are admissible options relative to information of types (i)–(iii) about his predicament and also assumes that he will restrict his choice to the admissible options is logically inconsistent. (One of the admirable features of Schick's exposition is that, unlike Jeffrey, he avoids presupposing a Bayesian approach to admissibility and thereby reveals the full generality of the problem.) He does claim that such self-knowledge is indefensible in a sense that slightly extends J. Hintikka's (1962) conception of doxastic indefensibility.

Schick's argument, however, fails to sustain this conclusion. The type of doxastic indefensibility Schick is talking about obtains only if the set of admissible options A_1, $A_2, \ldots, A_n$ is a proper subset of the set of feasible options listed in the information provided by (i). Schick explicitly takes for granted that this will be the case. (In his discussion, as in Jeffrey's, the admissible set is a unit set, but this is not essential.) There is no inconsistency – not even extended doxastic indefensibility – in insisting that the feasible and admissible sets coincide.[5] And whether the two sets coincide or not is not a restriction on the self-knowledge of the agent. The limitation on self-knowledge to which Schick correctly directs our attention is based on "logic" (or extended doxastic indefensibility) together with the assumption that, before choice, admissibility should not in general coincide with feasibility.

Having formulated the issue, Schick asks how disturbing this result is:

. . . Not very, I think. No one has a commitment to full self-knowledge. We want to know ourselves better. Some of us want (for protection) to know ourselves better than others do. This is not ruled out. All that must go is expendable. (Schick, 1979: 243)

Schick's equanimity is not entirely in order. He is right that "no one has a commitment to full self-knowledge" if that means that full self-knowledge is not required in order to apply criteria of choice before the moment of choice to identify admissible options as a proper subset of the set of feasible options. However, we should require that, ideally at least, an agent should have sufficient self-knowledge before choice to be in a position to apply criteria of rational choice to his feasible options to determine which of these options are admissible for him. If we were not concerned before choice to determine admissibility, a crucial feature of principles of choice understood as normative principles to be used in evaluating feasible options in the context of deliberation would be lost.

When the matter is put in this way, it becomes apparent why the approaches of both Jeffrey and Schick are, in the last analysis, unsatisfactory. Both authors recognize that the agent cannot be required to have the full self-knowledge which leads to the emptiness of principles of rational choice embodied in the equation of feasibility with admissibility. Both seem to think that there is no difficulty in giving up this requirement. I agree, but a question remains. Some of the items are needed in order to apply the principles of choice, and the ideally situated agent ought to have this information. Otherwise he cannot apply the criteria for admissibility. The question arises: Which items are needed to apply the criteria for admissibility? Neither Schick nor Jeffrey addresses this question. They do not seem to think it matters.

The sort of self-knowledge presupposed in knowing items (i)–(iii) is presupposed in determining admissibility. However, the assumption that the agent will choose an admissible option relative to the information supplied by (i)–(iii) is not required to determine the set of admissible options before choice and, hence, is not presupposed in the application of criteria for rational choice.

As I understand Jeffrey's approach, before choice the agent may fail to have the self-knowledge involved in items (i)–(iii), just as he may not know whether he will choose an admissible option. That is no doubt true. Both human agents and institutional ones may fail to identify the set of admissible options to which they are committed because of failures of memory, inadequate computational ability, self-deceit or other emotional or social difficulties. Agents often do lack the self-knowledge required for applying principles of rational choice.

But full self-knowledge of the information required to determine admissibility is a regulative ideal for deliberation before the moment of choice. Both individuals and corporations sometimes take great pains in order to live up to it. Much (though by no means all) of the activity in deliberation involves calculation so as to identify the assumptions to which the deliberating agent is tacitly or implicitly committed. Observe, however, that if living up to the regulative ideal would entail a collapse of feasibility into admissibility, that would be a serious blow to our decision theory. Insofar as I understand Jeffrey's second resolution of our problem, in the course of deliberation before choice we must perforce be unclear about our preferences and our beliefs. That lack of clarity precludes our applying our principles of choice. The moment we have enough clarity to apply the principles, admissibility and feasibility must coincide. I am not sure that Jeffrey intends this, but that seems to be suggested by his discussion. Nor do Schick's remarks prevent this reading. These views trivialize principles of choice by denying the existence of knowledge situations relative to which the agent can deliberately invoke his value commitments and principles of choice to identify a set of admissible options which is a proper subset of the set of feasible options.

The proposal I am making specifies that all we need give up until the moment of choice is the assumption that the agent will choose an admissible option. This assumption is not needed by the agent or anyone to identify the admissible options, and without it admissible options can be a proper subset of the feasible options.

The proposal I am suggesting resembles in some respects the approach of Shackle, who also recommends allowing the agent to have the information contained in (i)–(iii), to know that he has it and to recognize the logical consequences of this and any other information he has insofar as it is relevant. His view, like mine, allows the agent to determine a nontrivial reduction of the set of options recognized as feasible to a proper subset which serves as the admissible options relative to (i)–(iii). To do this consistently, Shackle's proposal, like mine, insists that the agent not assume that he will choose an option which is admissible relative to that determination.

Shackle holds that until the moment of choice the agent has the ability to revise his knowledge and his values and, in particular, to do so by identifying new hitherto unrecognized policies as feasible. The agent's creative capacity is a wild card which prevents him from making the assumption that the set of options which are admissible relative to the information currently available concerning (i), (ii) and (iii) will be the set of options from which he will choose. In Shackle's view, the agent may assume that he will choose from an admissible set relative to the information available to him concerning (i)–(iii) before the moment of choice. But he should not assume before choice that the information concerning (i)–(iii) at the time and the judgements of

admissibility made accordingly are going to be the choice-constrain-
ing ones. Perhaps some new inspiration will alter these judgements
before the choice is actually made.

> ... you will see that I want to make the term "free will" point in a somewhat
> different direction from that of its meaning in ordinary discourse, where if
> we examined our attitude with exactness we should perhaps be led to define
> the free-willed individual as one who acts or is capable of acting *arbitrarily* in
> the face of a *given* situation. I am proposing instead to say that in his situation,
> his structure of expectations, that he is in some sense free to create, or to
> derive from some unexplained and essentially unpredictable inspiration, but
> that his conduct in the face of any *given* expectational vista, any given set of
> assessments of the possible consequences of specified rival action schemes
> open to him will be non-arbitrary; if you like, that it will be rational. (Shackle,
> 1958: 27)

Thus, Shackle's proposal allows the agent to assume that he will
choose rationally in the sense that he will choose an option which is
admissible relative to the final set of assumptions about (i)–(iii) available to him before choice but prohibits him from taking for granted
that the assumptions about (i)–(iii) currently available to him are that
final set. My proposal allows the agent to suppose that his current
assumptions about (i)–(iii) are the final ones but prohibits him from
assuming that he will choose an admissible option relative to that final
set.

I am not sure that there is a useful way to defend either one of
these proposals as superior to the other. Both have the same virtue –
namely, they allow nonempty applications of principles of admissibility. There is, it seems to me, one consideration which argues in favor
of my proposal over Shackle's, but I myself am not convinced that it
is decisive. It does seem desirable to allow for the nontrivial applicability of criteria for admissibility in contexts where the decision maker
takes for granted that the information about (i)–(iii) he has is the final
version before choice. Shackle's proposal does not allow for this. Mine
does.

Whether one adopts Shackle's solution, mine or some combination
of the two, it will turn out that the deliberating agent cannot, before
choice, predict how he will choose and do so coherently. He does not
have to deny that his choice is constrained by various causal factors to
maintain that he has a choice. But to the extent that he knows what
those factors are and these rule out certain objectively feasible options, the agent regards his scope for choice as having been dimin-
ished. If the agent knows that his choice will conform to certain determinations of admissibility, he is not free, as far as his deliberation
is concerned, to choose anything other than an option whose admissibility has not been ruled out by those determinations. Objectively

speaking, freedom of choice may be compatible with determinism. But from the deliberating agent's point of view, the one crowds the other out.

The "soft determinism" which I have just conceded to be compatible with the view I am advocating does not, however, permit the explanation of the choices which are the outcomes of deliberation (or the actions implementing such choices) by reference to the beliefs and desires of the agents making the choice in accordance with the principles of rational choice. From the point of view of the deliberating agent, such principles cannot be laws. If they were and he knew it, he would be in a position to predict that he would restrict his choice to admissible options relative to his beliefs as to what is given in (i) to be the feasible set, what are the possible consequences of the feasible options given in (ii) and his values and desires as given in (iii). I have denied, in effect, that the agent can know that his choices are constrained by such laws without surrendering the kind of freedom that is presupposed when he evaluates admissibility before choice. Jones' hiring Jane may be caused by his believings and desirings but not when they are so described and not through the operation of criteria of rational choice in terms of which he appraises admissibility.[6]

This conclusion is reinforced by D. Davidson's (1980: 21–42) discussion of weakness of the will. Davidson wants to say that every choice or action done with intention has a reason (where reasons are beliefs and desires). He concedes that what the agent chooses may not be for the best given the agent's beliefs and desires and given the principles of rational choice which, in Davidson's view, determine what is for the best. To admit this much is to concede that the principles of rational choice used to determine admissibility do not always regulate the agent's choices and, hence, cannot function as causal laws.

Davidson does insist, to be sure, that when an agent chooses, he has a reason for his choice. Translating his view into my format, the option chosen may be admissible relative to beliefs and desires which give only a partial characterization of the total information available to the agent. The fundamental principle for Davidson is the principle of continence, which recommends choosing an option which is admissible, all things considered. But an agent who violates the principle of continence will still observe a principle of partial continence involving the choosing of an option which is admissible relative to a partial list of the relevant considerations. In Davidson's (1980: 42) view, we cannot explain why the agent will on some occasions be strong willed and will choose in conformity with the principle of continence and why on some occasions he will invoke only a fragment of his repertoire of beliefs and desires.

By the same reasoning, the agent who, before choice, has calculated the admissible set, all things considered, should not be in a position to predict that he will choose in conformity with such conclusions about admissibility rather than conclusions appropriate to an akratic agent.

The solution to the problem of foreknowledge of self I proposed suggests that even if individuals were never weak willed, the deliberating agent should not take for granted before choice that he will not exhibit weakness of will. This in itself should be good enough reason never to convert the psychological fact to a nomological necessity.

We should not try to draft principles of rational choice into service as covering laws in covering law explanations of human choices or actions. I do not object to their figuring in explanations of human behavior in some other noncausal type of explanation. Nor do I object to causal explanation of human choices or actions in other terms. We value principles of rational choice as criteria for admissibility to be used in deliberation. If they are to be used in a nonempty way, the deliberating agent should not assume that he will choose in conformity with the conclusions about admissibility he has reached or is committed to reaching. Otherwise we deprive the recommendation that agents should choose in conformity with such conclusions its role as a norm guiding deliberation before choice. That in itself ought to be enough to discredit the idea that such principles should be used as laws in explanation.

4.4 The argument thus far

In chapter 1, I argued for Dewey's idea that there are moral conflicts which call for the revision of value commitments through inquiry. This view requires not only a notion of conflict as a form of suspense among values but calls for a recognition of the possibility that rational agents may be compelled to choose without having resolved such conflicts before choice or through the act of will involved in choice. In chapter 2, I compared the conception of value conflict with certain contemporary views of conflict in moral obligations. In chapter 3, I examined conflict in epistemic values and conflict among epistemic values. In these chapters my aim was to suggest that the topic of decision making under unresolved conflict is rather more than a controversial technical chapter in the study of decision theory. Its ramifications affect moral theory and theories of scientific inquiry alike. Further domains in which treatment of unresolved conflict should prove illuminating are considered in chapters 7, 8 and 9.

The current chapter addressed a cluster of questions pertaining to the notion of a feasible option. The topic of feasibility is important here because the value commitments and ways of evaluation are to be applied to sets of feasible options to determine sets of admissible options. It is desirable to keep in mind what assumptions about feasibility must be invoked to ensure that such determinations can be made in a way which does not automatically equate feasibility with admissibility.

With this background, it is appropriate to turn to a more formal characterization of ways of evaluation, value structures and how ways of evaluation and value structures determine admissibility. Chapter 5 provides a characterization of the most general features of the decision theory I favor.

5

Value structures

5.1 Value commitments, value structures and ways of evaluation

Value commitments are constraints on the permissible ways of evaluating feasible options. Such commitments may be moral principles but they need not be so. Professional obligations, economic interests, political loyalties, personal ideals and projects and aesthetic values can all impose constraints on the way feasible options are evaluated in a given decision problem and, hence, may all qualify as value commitments.

Only rarely will a value commitment be so powerful as to restrict ways of evaluating feasible options in a given decision problem to a single way. If Jones has borrowed money from Smith and faces the question of paying her back, he may have the choice of repaying in cash, repaying by check or not repaying at all. Assuming that Jones endorses the obligation to repay his debts as a value commitment, he is constrained to rank repaying by cash over not repaying and repaying by check over not repaying. But his obligation does not constrain him in any way regarding the choice between check and cash. It is not that his value commitment ranks the two options together. Rather it leaves open the way that repaying by cash and by check are to be ranked vis-à-vis one another.

For this reason, it is not useful in systematic discussions to think of value commitments as applying directly to the determination of what ought and what ought not to be done even though moral principles and other value commitments are often couched in the language of the obligatory or permissible character of acts. I suggest that it is more useful to proceed in the way I proposed in chapter 1 and regard value commitments as constraints on ways of evaluating feasible options in decision problems falling within their domains of applicability. In this way, an agent's value commitments determine a system of *permissible* ways of evaluating the options in the feasible set U.

I call the set $V(U)$ of such permissible ways of evaluating the elements of U the *value structure* determined by the agent's value commitments covering the given decision problem. This value structure determines those options which are *V-admissible*. Given his value commitments, the agent is obliged to restrict his choice to a V-admissible option and is permitted to choose one of these.

This way of formulating matters may seem excessively roundabout, and for many purposes it no doubt is. But the customary practice of formulating value commitments as constraints on what ought to be done or what is permitted tends to simplify in a way which tacitly presupposes that all evaluations of three or more alternatives are reducible to all possible binary comparisons which can be concocted for the set. I shall question the binary character of the rational valuation of feasible options. To develop the argument, however, care must be taken not to beg the question one way or the other. Hence, the ordinary ways of formulating value commitments which give the appearance, at least, of begging this question should not be deployed. At the expense of artificiality, technical devices will be exploited which avoid prejudging the issue of binariness.

Another advantage of utilizing the distinction between value commitments, value structures and ways of evaluation to determine V-admissibility and, hence, what ought to be done is that it provides a useful means of distinguishing between decision problems where the constraints imposed by distinct value commitments are consistently applicable and decision problems where they are not. If no ways of evaluation are permissible, then no feasible options can be V-admissible. Value commitments which lead to such an impasse fail to serve their primary function and the claim that they are jointly applicable to the given decision problem ought to be considered inconsistent.

According to the proposal made in chapter 1, in such cases the agent should remove the inconsistency generated by applying his value commitments jointly to the problematic choice by shifting to a value structure which recognizes ways of valuation permitted by each of the competing value commitments to be permissible. This implies that for any given competing value commitment, if a feasible option is obligatory according to it, it will be V-admissible when the shift is made to a state of suspense.

According to this view of value conflict, when an agent is in suspense among rival value commitments, inconsistency is avoided but the conflict remains unresolved precisely because several different ways of evaluating feasible options remain permissible. This characterization will be refined in some respects as the discussion proceeds. In any case, for the time being, we shall turn away from value commitments and focus on decision problems where the agent knows that the feasible options belong to some definite set U. An effort will be made to characterize ways of evaluation and, with the aid of such characterizations, the value structures which contain ways of evaluation as elements. On this basis, a general formulation of criteria of admissibility will be introduced which will serve as the core of the approach to decision making under unresolved conflict proposed in this volume.

5.2 Ways of evaluation

A value structure $V(U)$ for a set U of feasible options is a set of permissible ways of evaluating the feasible options in U as better or worse. How should the elements of the value structure, the so-called ways of evaluation, be represented?

An obvious suggestion is to characterize such ways by orderings of the elements of U which secure that for every pair of options x and y in U, x is ranked over y, y over x or they are ranked together. As long as U is finite, this proposal guarantees that given any permissible way of evaluation in $V(U)$, there is at least one element of U which is optimal according to it. Hence, as long as the set of permissible ways of evaluation is not empty, the set of V-admissible options (options which are optimal according to at least one permissible way of evaluating elements of U) will be nonempty. Attractive as this suggestion seems to be, it characterizes value structures in a way which is too crude to capture some important distinctions.

Return to the predicament of Jones, the office manager. He wants to hire a secretary who is a good typist and a good stenographer as well. He has two value commitments imposing constraints on the permissible ways of evaluating his options. According to one such commitment, the candidates for the job should be assessed exclusively in terms of proficiency in typing. According to the other, they should be evaluated in terms of their stenographic capabilities. We have supposed that the first way of evaluation ranks Jane over Dolly over Lilly, whereas the second ranks Lilly over Dolly over Jane. Conflict sets in so that Jones should recognize as permissible all ways of evaluation permissible according to one or the other of the value commitments as well as ways of evaluation which are potential resolutions of differences between the ways generated by the different value commitments.

Recall, however, that we noticed a difference between two versions of Jones' predicament. According to one version, Dolly was nearly as good a typist as Jane and nearly as good a stenographer as Lilly. This suggests that the value structure representing suspense between the two value commitments acknowledges as permissible a way of evaluation recognizing hiring Dolly as optimal, for when hiring Dolly is a second-best option according to both of the rival commitments, presystematic judgement seems to suggest that it is admissible as an expression of a compromise between the competing desiderata.

The situation is different when hiring Dolly is second worst – i.e., when Dolly is almost as bad a typist as Lilly and as poor a stenographer as Jane. There should then be no permissible way of evaluating the options ranking the hiring of Dolly as optimal and, hence, recognizing that option to be V-admissible.

If ways of evaluation are characterized by weak orderings of the feasible options, however, there is no procedure for distinguishing the case where hiring Dolly is second best according to the two initial value commitments from the case where hiring Dolly is second worst. The set of V-admissible options ought to be the same in both variations of the predicament. On the assumption that this conclusion is misguided, permissible ways of evaluating feasible options should be sensitive to differences in values of such options and not merely to their ranking as better and worse.

Another argument can be mustered against representing ways of evaluation by orderings as better or worse. Suppose that Jones is offered the opportunity of tossing a fair coin and letting the outcome decide whether he hires Jane or Lilly. This is a fourth feasible option distinct from the other three we have mentioned.

Suppose further that Jones does not care whether he hires Jane directly or as the outcome of gambling, no matter which permissible way of evaluating feasible options is being used to assess the feasible options. We assume the same holds for hiring Lilly as well. This means that in the context of this decision problem, Jones has neither a taste nor an aversion for gambling.

Once more we can consider a second-best and a second-worst version of Jones' predicament. When hiring Dolly is second best both according to typing and according to stenography, the "mixed option" of deciding whether to hire Jane or Lilly depending on the outcome of the toss of the fair coin should be ranked below hiring Dolly regardless of which desideratum is considered. In contrast, when hiring Dolly is second worst with respect both to typing and to stenography, the mixed option should be superior to hiring Dolly in both respects.

We should not expect that the feasible options will include all mixtures of feasible options (where a mixture of feasible options is a way of selecting one of a given list of "pure" feasible options according to a stochastic process determining a definite chance or statistical probability for each pure option on the list). Indeed, there is no a priori reason that the feasible options should contain any mixtures. Furthermore, even if such mixed options are feasible, no agent is obliged, as a rational agent, to have or to lack a taste or aversion for gambling.

Nonetheless, cases do arise where mixed options are feasible and the agent has a neutral attitude towards gambling. Our theory should allow for such cases. When the mixed option is a mixture of finitely many "pure" options, the value of the mixture should, I assume, be determined by the values of the pure options. Given this assumption, the difference just noted between the variation of Jones' predicament where hiring Dolly is second best and that where it is second worst could not obtain were we to evaluate the feasible options only as better or worse according to some ranking, for the distinction between second best and second worst would lose all relevance.

Two arguments have been mustered to suggest that ways of evaluating feasible options should not be equated with rankings of these options but with assessments sensitive to differences in values attributed to these options. One argument considers how potential resolutions of conflict among permissible ways of evaluation are to be determined. The second argument examines the evaluation of mixed options in terms of the assessments of the pure options ingredient in the mixtures. These considerations suggest that a way of evaluating feasible options in U be represented by a real-valued function $v(x)$ defined over U together with all positive affine transformations of $v(x)$. (A positive affine transformation of v is a function of the form $av + b$, where a is positive.) When numerical resprentation is unique up to a positive affine transformation, differences in value are numerically determined up to the choice of a unit. Numerical representation of the values of the options themselves (as opposed to differences in value) require choice of a o point as well as a unit.

Perhaps the strongest argument for favoring this means of representing ways of evaluating feasible options over the ordinal method is that it does not preclude our representing the point of view of the ordinalist. The ordinalist position is equivalent to the requirement that if v represents a permissible way of evaluating the elements of U, so does every positive monotonic transformation of v (i.e., every other v-function preserving the order induced by v). The intervalist position I have just been advocating recommends that if v represents a permissible way of evaluating elements of U, so does every positive affine transformation. The ordinalist position imposes stricter requirements on the set of v-functions permissible according to a value structure than does the intervalist view. Thus, the *onus probandi* is on the ordinalist to explain why the ordinalist position is to be favored over the intervalist characterization of ways of evaluation.

It may be asked why ways of evaluation are represented by an intervalist approach. This view assumes that two v-functions which are positive affine transformations are representations of the same way of evaluation or, equivalently, that if v is permissible so is every positive affine transformation of it. Perhaps this assumption is debatable and we should move to a weaker position.

I have no way of ruling out this possibility and will not try. But I do not think any issue of substance to be considered in this volume depends upon endorsing the intervalist conception of ways of evaluation I advocate over a weaker view. If such an issue is raised, the matter will have to be reconsidered. For the duration of this discussion, however, I shall use the intervalist approach.

To avoid confusion, it should be emphasized that endorsing an intervalist conception of ways of evaluation is not to endorse the view that a rational agent's values are representable by a real-valued function unique up to a positive affine transformation. This form of intervalism combines an intervalist conception of ways of evaluation with the condition that the value structure of a rational agent recognize one and only one way of evaluation as permissible. Since I reject the latter condition, nothing I have said in favor of intervalism implies this stronger and objectionable version.

5.3 The mixture property

Sometimes the set U of feasible options will contain mixtures of options in U and sometimes will be restricted to options none of which are mixtures of any other options in U. One option y is a mixture of finitely many other options $x_1, x_2, \ldots, x_n$ when there are n nonnegative numbers $p_1, p_2, \ldots, p_n$ summing to 1 such that y is the gamble in which option x_i is selected with objective statistical probability or chance equal to p_i. When a mixed option is available, it is neutral for the agent if and only if the agent is indifferent between selecting x_i as an outcome of exercising the mixed option and choosing it directly.

Given a way of evaluating the options $x_1, x_2, \ldots, x_n$ in a mixed option y which is neutral for the agent, the value of y, as I assumed in 5.2, ought to be determined uniquely by the values of the x_i's and the chances associated with them in the mixture. Hence, given a way of evaluation for elements of a set of feasible options U, the way of evaluation for U is completely determined by the way of evaluation for those elements in the subset which are not themselves neutral mixtures of any other elements of U.

I shall call such elements of U the *pure* options in U. The terminology deviates slightly from customary practice. Pure options are normally taken to be options which are not mixtures of other options regardless of whether the mixtures are neutral or not. According to my usage, a pure option may be a mixture of other feasible options provided that it is not a neutral mixture. The point is that once we see that the value of the option is not uniquely determined by the values and chances of the ingredients of the mixture, we treat the value of the option as an independent variable for the purpose of determining the values of other feasible options which are neutral mixtures of finite subsets of elements of U.

Thus, I am assuming that given any feasible set U of options (which may be finite or infinite), there is a set U_p (which may be finite or infinite) contained in U consisting of all pure options in U in the sense just defined. Let $M(U_p)$ be the set of all possible neutral mixtures of finite subsets of U_p. Since a pure option is a neutral mixture of itself, U must itself be a subset of $M(U_p)$. My contention is that a way of evaluation for U restricted to the pure options in U_p is extendable in a unique way to all elements of $M(U_p)$. If we then take the restriction of this extension to the elements of U, we have shown how the full evaluation for elements of U can be recovered by starting with the restriction of that evaluation to elements of U_p.

Let us use Jones' predicament once more to illustrate the points being made. In the versions introduced in 5.2, Jones has the option of letting the outcome of a toss of an unbiased coin decide whether he ends up hiring Jane or hiring Lilly as a fourth alternative to the other three options. If Jones has a taste or an aversion for gambling, all four options, including the last one are pure in the sense I am using. Hence, $U = U_p$. $M(U_p) = M(U)$ and consists of all neutral mixtures of the four options in U which might be constructed (even though they may not be and, in this case, are not feasible for Jones). In particular, it includes a 50–50 gamble determining whether Jane or Lilly is hired, where the gamble is neutral for Jones. Since Jones has a taste or an aversion for the gamble he is offered, it cannot be equated with this hypothetically envisaged mixture.

Any way of evaluating v over the elements $U = U_p$ determines, I claim, a way of evaluation over the elements of $M(U)$ which is an extension of v. Of course, in this case, the result is not especially useful to us, for the particular way of evaluation we are considering for the pure options in U_p is identical with the way of evaluation for the set of options actually feasible for Jones.

Contrast this situation, however, with one where Jones has no aversion or taste for gambling. The gamble is neutral for Jones and, hence, qualifies as a mixed option rather than a pure one. It is an element in the set of feasible options U but not in the set of pure feasible options U_p. Hence, it may be of some interest to derive the v-function for U from that for U_p.

I have assumed that the v-function defined for U_p can be uniquely extended to $M(U_p)$ but nothing has been said thus far concerning the principles governing the extension.

The *expected v-value of a mixture* of the elements $x_1, x_2, \ldots, x_n$ with corresponding chances $p_1, p_2, \ldots, p_n$ is equal to $\Sigma\ p_i v$ A v-function has the *mixture property* if and only if the v-value assigned to every *neutral* mixture in $M(U_\mathrm{p})$ is its expected v-value according to the v-function as defined over the elements of U_p.

Assume that every v-function representing a way of evaluating elements of U has the mixture property. It is easy to see that we can start with the restriction of that function to elements of U_p and determine the values for all elements of $M(U_\mathrm{p})$. It is also easily seen that the positive affine transformation of a v-function defined over U_p will extend to $M(U_\mathrm{p})$ in a manner preserving the order induced on this set by the given v-function. More importantly, any two v-functions possessing the mixture property which order the elements of $M(U_\mathrm{p})$ in the same way are positive affine transformations of one another. Thus, if we are concerned with the ordering of all neutral mixtures of a given set on the basis of the way of evaluation for that set and with discriminations no finer than this, numerical representations unique up to a positive affine transformation characterize ways of evaluation in just the right way.

There is no way to prove that numerical representations of ways of evaluation ought to exhibit the mixture property except by postulating other, perhaps controversial, assumptions which entail it. Although studying such postulates may be helpful for understanding the theory underlying the requirement, an appeal to such postulates in efforts to convince the skeptical will depend for success on the idiosyncracies of the skeptics being addressed. If determined enough, a skeptic can question the postulates just as easily as the requirement itself. For my part, I am content to assert the mixture property and to point out how relatively weak it is in the form in which I am committed to it.

The mixture property implies that under the conditions specified, the neutral mixtures in $M(U_\mathrm{p})$ should be evaluated in accordance with their expected values. If we use "utility" in a generous enough sense so that we think of utility as representing any kind of value and not specifically the net of pleasure over pain, endorsing the mixture property principle seems suspiciously like endorsing the principle of maximizing expected utility; and there are many difficulties with that principle.

For one thing, the principle of maximizing expected utility or v-value suggests that the agent is free of value conflict and allows only one way of evaluating options to be permissible. I have already questioned this assumption and will continue to do so. However, I have not presupposed here that rational agents are free of conflict. We have been discussing how ways of evaluation should be individuated and represented. In saying that a way of evaluation should always have the mixture property, I am claiming that were that way of evaluation uniquely permissible, the options in U would be ranked in accordance with increasing expected v-value or, if one likes, expected utility. But the antecedent of this conditional has not been affirmed.

Another common objection focuses on the widespread phenomenon of taste for or aversion to risk. Agents are often not neutral towards mixed options. Hence, mixed options quite frequently cannot be assessed in conformity with expected v-value. But my version of the mixture condition does not require that they should.

A third objection concerns situations where agents are called upon to make calculations of expected value without grounding their judgements of probability in knowledge of chances. Thus, if Jones is told he is being offered a lottery in which the outcome is hiring Jane or hiring Lilly but is not told what the chances of either eventuality are, he cannot determine probability weights to use in computing expectations on the basis of his knowledge of chances.

Some authors would insist that rational agents willy-nilly are committed to some system of personal probability judgements which may be used to compute expectations even though they are not derivable from knowledge of chances. Others deny that anyone can legitimately assign numerically definite probabilities under such circumstances.

My own view is more tolerant than either of these (see Levi, 1980a, and chapter 7). In the situation we envisage, however, the chances involved in the mixtures in $M(U_p)$ are hypothesized to be known to the decision maker, and no additional information is available to him which might disturb the "direct inference" from knowledge of chances to personal probabilities. Under these conditions, the objection to the mixture principle no longer applies.

Thus, my appeal to the mixture property is extremely weak. Even so, a determined enough skeptic may continue to reject the appeal to expected values implicit in it. This book is not addressed to such skeptics. I think the hedges I have placed on the use of mixture property have rendered it sufficiently weak to make it noncontroversial to those who do more than nurse their skepticism to keep it warm.

5.4 Potential resolutions

The value structure $V(U)$ for a set of feasible options U is represented by the set of permissible ways of evaluating elements of U. Since each permissible way of evaluating elements of U is itself represented by a set of functions (namely, some real-valued function v and all positive affine transformations of it), $V(U)$ can also be represented by the union of the sets of v-functions associated with each permissible way of evaluation. It is then representable as a set of permissible v-functions.

In 5.1, I assumed that if two ways of evaluation are permissible, so are all ways of evaluation which are potential resolutions of the differences between them. In this section, we shall consider the formal relation between a pair of v-functions and a v-function representing a potential resolution of the conflict between the ways of evaluation represented by the members of the initial pair.

The principle I shall endorse is given as follows:

The weighted average principle:
If $v_1, v_2, \ldots, v_n$ (n finite) are v-functions permissible in $V(U)$ which are not positive affine transformations of one another (and, hence, represent distinct ways of evaluation), then for every n-tuple $\langle w_1, w_2, \ldots, w_n \rangle$ of nonnegative weights which sum to 1, the weighted average $\Sigma w_i v_i$ is also permissible.

The determined skeptic can resist this principle just as easily as he can resist the universal applicability of the mixture property. For what it is worth, however, the weighted average principle may be derived from the following conditions on potential resolutions of conflict.

Since the set U may be finite or only countably infinite, we cannot assume that for every pair of real numbers r and s, there is an element x of U such that $v_1(x) = r$ and $v_2(x) = s$. However, we can embed the set of feasible options U in a set $N(U)$ of hypothetical options such that for every pair $\langle r,s \rangle$ of real numbers there is an element of $N(U)$ such that $v_1(x) = r$ and $v_2(x) = s$. Moreover, any v-function representing a potential resolution of a conflict between v_1 and v_2 is defined over the same domain.

Assumption L_1

If $v(x)$ is a potential resolution of conflict between $v_1(x)$ and $v_2(x)$, for each x in $N(U)$ the value of $v(x)$ should be uniquely determined by the values of $v_1(x)$ and $v_2(x)$ independently of the values assigned other elements of $N(U)$ by the two v_i-functions.

Assumption L_2

If $v_1(x)$ is at least as great as $v_1(y)$ and $v_2(x)$ is at least as great as $v_2(y)$, $v(x)$ is at least as great as $v(y)$.

Assumption L_3

Let $v(x)$ be at least as great as $v(y)$. In N(U) (but not necessarily in U), there must be options w and z such that $v_1(w) = v_1(x) + c$, $v_2(w) = v_2(x) + d$, $v_1(z) = v_1(y) + c$ and $v_2(z) = v_2(y) + d$; $v(w)$ must be at least as great as $v(z)$.

By adapting an argument of D. Blackwell and M. A. Girshick,[1] it can be shown that these three assumptions imply that v must be a weighted average of v_1 and v_2. This argument generalizes to potential resolutions of conflicts among any finite number of ways of evaluation.

M. Fleming (1952) and J. Harsanyi (1955) have argued that aggregate social welfare evaluations of alternative public policies should be weighted averages of the welfare values for each citizen and have done so in a way which can be readily adapted to defend the claim that a potential resolution of value conflict ought to be a weighted average of conflicting ways of evaluation. Harsanyi's procedure relies on the requirement that v-functions representing ways of evaluation have the mixture property.

If a potential resolution of conflict ought to be representable as a weighted average of the ways of evaluation in conflict and if, as I have assumed, all potential resolutions of conflict among permissible ways of evaluation ought to be permissible, a value structure ought, in general, to exhibit the following three properties (Levi, 1980a: 94–95, 164–182):

1. $V(U)$ ought to be nonempty (valuational consistency).

2. $V(U)$ ought to be closed under positive affine transformation. That is to say, every positive affine transformation of a permissible v-function ought also to be permissible.

3. $V(U)$ ought to be convex. Every weighted average of a finite collection of v-functions ought also to be permissible (valuational convexity).

5.5 Cardinal and ordinal conflict

I have argued that we should think of numerical representations of value which are not positive affine transformations of one another as representatives of distinct ways of evaluating options in U even if they order the elements of U in the same manner. Although this approach is advantageous when one is evaluating neutral mixtures and characterizing potential resolutions, it yields a disconcerting result.

Suppose an agent's value structure $V(U)$ allows all and only those v-functions which rank the elements of U in the same way to be permissible. That is to say, one and only one value ranking of elements of U is permissible. Utilizing the distinctions I have introduced, we should say that the agent's value structure suffers from conflict. This runs counter to presystematic practice. There is no conflict in identifying those options which are noncontroversially optimal. There does not appear to be pressure for a moral struggle of the second kind in the sense discussed in chapter 1.

To be sure, when we add neutral mixtures of options in U to the set of feasible options, conflict is revealed. But if no such mixtures are feasible, there appears to be no need to consider this. Thus, the considerations which warrant characterizing ways of valuation by real-valued functions unique up to a positive affine transformation generate a terminological tension with the considerations suggesting that if an agent has a ranking of his feasible options there is no conflict.

It should be emphasized that the tension is terminological rather than substantial. The considerations in favor of real-valued representations are as cogent as ever. Yet it remains the case that the pressure to resolve conflict diminishes when one can rank the feasible options. There is no contradiction here – only two senses of conflict. I shall call one *cardinal conflict* and the other *ordinal conflict*. When all the permissible v-functions in $V(U)$ generate the same ranking of elements of U, that ranking is uniquely permissible and the value structure is free of ordinal conflict even though cardinal conflict is present. If the permissible v-functions generate several rankings, all these rankings are permissible. Both cardinal conflict and ordinal conflict are present. Cardinal conflict is absent if and only if all permissible v-functions are positive affine transformations of one another.

5.6 V-admissibility

The set of v-functions permissible according to the agent's value structure $V(U)$ determines a set of permissible value rankings of the elements of U. Relative to each one of these rankings, there is a subset of U consisting of options in U which are optimal according to that ranking. When there is freedom from ordinal conflict, of course, there is only one permissible value ranking and, hence, the set of optimal options is noncontroversial.

When there are two or more permissible rankings, the set of options optimal according to one need not coincide with the set of options optimal according to another. It is in such contexts that unresolved conflict becomes poignant. If the conflict remains unresolved, then no option which is optimal according to some permissible ranking has been ruled out for choice according to the given value structure. In this sense, all such options are *V-admissible*.

To say that an option is V-admissible is not to say that it is best according to the agent's values. Rather it implies that the option is best according to some way of evaluation which the agent has not ruled out of consideration as impermissible.

5.7 Lexicographically ordered value structures

Recall once more the case of Jones, the office manager. He faces the three options of hiring Jane, Dolly or Lilly. The typing scores are 100,

91, 90 and the stenography scores are 90, 91, 100 respectively. As-suming, for the sake of simplicity, that these two sets of scores are v-functions representing distinct ways of evaluation, Jones' value struc-ture is the set of positive affine transformations of the "convex hull" (the set of weighted averages) of the typing scores and the stenogra-phy scores. There is no v-function which represents a weighted aver-age yielding a ranking according to which hiring Dolly is optimal. Hiring Jane and hiring Lilly are both V-admissible.

As for Jones' professional commitments to seeking a good typist and a good stenographer, there is nothing more to say. If Jones must decide, he should restrict his choice to hiring Jane or hiring Lilly. However, there is no reason for him not to ground his choice between the V-admissible options in other values which he has not yet taken into account. Recall that Jones is committed in his professional capac-ity to hiring the best typist-stenographer he can. He himself would also like to have an attractive woman functioning as secretary, but his commitment to his professional obligations prohibits his taking this into account at the beginning of his deliberation. Yet once he recog-nizes that his professional obligations fail to render a verdict between hiring Jane and hiring Lilly, he might let his predilections for femi-nine pulchritude determine his choice.

As pointed out in chapter 1, the secondary considerations invoked by Jones need not be as male chauvinist as this. Jones might insist that in hiring a secretary, the professional requirements are paramount but that when the professional requirements are no longer decisive, he should favor the hiring of a member of an ethical or racial minor-ity which is, by some criterion or other, disadvantaged.

Of course, there is the possibility that in invoking secondary consid-erations, Jones will be conflicted between his interest in feminine pul-chritude and ethnic and racial equity. Thus, Jones may be committed to a secondary value structure for the elements of U. This structure, like the primary one, is representable by a nonempty, convex set of real-valued v-functions closed under positive affine transformations. However, the secondary structure is not applied to assess the admis-sibility of options of U. Rather, given the set of options which are V-admissible according to the primary value structure and the restric-tion of the permissible v-functions in the secondary value structure to these options, a system of secondarily V-admissible options is defined.

This process may be iterated any finite number of times. There may be a hierarchy $V_1(U)$, $V_2(U)$, ..., $V_n(U)$ of value structures. The V_i-admissible options are those options optimal among the V_{i-1}-admis-sible options according to at least one permissible ranking in $V_i(U)$ restricted to the V_{i-1}-admissible options. An option is admissible rel-ative to such a hierarchy if and only if it is V_n-admissible.

According to the view I am proposing, a rational agent's value commitments constrain a hierarchy of value structures and not merely a single value structure. Conflict may be manifested at the ith level of the hierarchy but be absent at the jth, or it can be present (or absent) at both levels.

Even when there is no conflict at the first-level value structure, there can be a role for the second level value structure, for two options may be optimal according to the uniquely permissible ranking at the first level and, hence, both V_1-admissible. A second-level value structure may then be invoked, if it is defined, to break the tie for optimality.[2]

Given a hierarchically ordered system of value structures, it is possible to determine a set of admissible options for the set U. In a very general way, therefore, the account just outlined offers a criterion for rational choice under unresolved conflict: Restrict choice to the set of admissible options relative to the hierarchy of value structures to which one is committed.

Of course, much more should be said to fill out this idea. I will not explore all the issues meriting consideration in this volume. The next chapter will, however, address a point discussed briefly at the beginning of this chapter. The scheme outlined here seems extremely complex and roundabout. Perhaps the complexity is a tempest in a teapot; perhaps the recommendations yielded by following the lines of reasoning favored here can be simplified in a manner which reveals that the alleged phenomenon of decision making under unresolved conflict is an illusion.

I do not think this is so. In the next chapter, the technical architecture sketched here will be elaborated in a way which will explain why.

6

Values revealed by choices

6.1 Choice and preference

An agent choosing between options x and y in a state of unresolved conflict might recognize as permissible three distinct value rankings: x better than y, x equal in value to y and y better than x. If the agent's value structure did acknowledge the permissibility of all three rankings, both x and y would be V_1-admissible, and if there were no secondary or still higher level value structure, both options would be admissible.

This way of describing the agent's predicament may seem misleading. According to a widely held opinion, if both options are admissible for the agent, he should be considered indifferent between them and both options counted as optimal for him. What in my accounting is regarded as unresolved conflict is nothing more than a situation where two options are best.

Suppose, however, that, in the way of speaking I have been using, the agent has a secondary value structure. Although both x and y are, as before, V_1-admissible, x is rated over y according to the secondary structure and, hence, is uniquely admissible. Here too it may seem that what I consider to be a decision problem under unresolved conflict is better seen as a choice situation where the agent ranks x over y and x is counted as uniquely optimal.

According to this rival way of describing matters, an agent's rating of alternatives is determined by how he would choose between any given pair of options or by determining for each pair which is and which is not admissible for the agent. If both are, they are ranked together. If one is admissible and the other not, the agent's strict preference for the admissible option has been "revealed".

There are other schemes different from the one just sketched for revealing preferences by hypothetical choice or judgements of admissibility. If U is the feasible set, one might say that x is revealed weakly preferred to y if and only if there is some nonempty, finite subset S of U containing x and y such that x would be admissible for the agent were S the agent's feasible set. Option x is revealed indifferent to y if x is revealed weakly preferred to y and vice versa. Otherwise x is revealed strictly preferred to y. This way of revealing the agent's evaluations of options as better or worse may sometimes yield a result which is different from the one previously described in which only pairwise choices are considered. However, both alternatives give an account of the evaluation of feasible options as better or worse (or of "preference") which appears to deny that there is any conflict between alternative ways of ranking options as better or worse and which can be obtained by taking the determinations of admissibility my scheme generates. To those who favor representing an agent's evaluation of options in this way, my proposals may appear to raise a terminological tempest in a teapot which can only mislead.

The issues under dispute here are not merely terminological. Those who advocate characterizing "preference" or comparisons of options with respect to value in terms of revelation in actual or hypothetical choice situations take for granted that the comparisons which emerge ought to be such that the admissible options and those which are optimal according to the revealed preference ranking coincide. To guarantee that this condition (and others related to it) will be satisfied, judgements of admissibility will also have to meet certain requirements.

The account of admissibility I have been sketching does not impose these requirements. Those who insist on revealed preference models of evaluation impose stronger restrictions on rational agents than those who allow for decision making under unresolved conflict require. These stronger restrictions are as controversial as the insistence that rational agents have resolved their conflicts by the moment of choice. Far from showing that the proposals made here are misleading exercises in terminological reform, doctrines of revealed preference exploit their terminological practices to beg the question against those who wish to recognize the rationality of decision making under unresolved conflict.

In this chapter, I shall rehearse some familiar technical points concerning revealed preference and then show how the approach to the assessment of admissibility I favor deviates from common shibboleths of decision theory derived from uncritical commitment to value rankings reducible to revealed preference rankings.

6.2 Value preference

In order to explore how the theory of decision making under unresolved conflict I am proposing differs in nontrivial ways from decision theories where value structures are reducible to rankings generated by revealed preference, it will prove helpful to begin by examining those cases where revealed preference is obviously most at home – to wit, where the value structure, on my representation, is free of ordinal conflict so that exactly one value ranking is permissible.

Optimality relative to such a value ranking is defined by reference to how the alternatives in U are compared in the ranking. Three types of relations emerge from such a ranking:

x is weakly preferred to y in value (xRy) if and only if x is rated at least as good as y.

x is strictly preferred to y in value (xPy) if and only if x is rated better than y.

x is indifferent in value to y (xIy) if and only if x is rated equal in value to y.

By using the term "preference", I do not imply that agent X is comparing elements of U with respect to his anticipated satisfactions or desires. The ranking may be induced by X's moral, professional, economic or aesthetic commitments. And, of course, if X is an institutional agent, the notion of satisfaction makes little sense altogether.

6.3 Robust preference

If agent X's value structure $V(U)$ were free of ordinal conflict, the uniquely permissible ranking of the elements of U should enable X to compare the options in U with respect to whether they are better or worse or equal in value in a manner which satisfies the requirements of revealed preference theorists. For any finite, nonempty subset S of U, there should be a nonempty subset of S consisting of the best or optimal elements of S relative to those comparisons; and those options should be the V-admissible options relative to the value structure $V(S)$, which is the restriction of $V(U)$ to the elements of S.

To exploit information concerning the options which would be V-admissible were the feasible options restricted to S rather than the more inclusive set U to ascertain the value structure for U, we must assume that the agent would not revise his valuations of the elements of S were he to realize that he was not free to choose from U but was confined to the subset S.

This assumption is taken to be part of the conditions built into the hypothetical choice situation used to probe value structures and thereby "reveal" preference. It does *not* require us to insist that a rational agent should use the restriction of his value structure for U to the set S if he finds out that his feasible set is not U but S. In this volume, I try to avoid discussion of considerations which warrant revisions of one's value structure and value commitments although, as I explained in chapter 1, the topic of decision making under unresolved conflict, which is the focus of our discussion, presupposes the urgency of an account of such revisions. In any case, the assumption of robustness which is built into the hypotheses of the counterfactuals about restrictions of the feasible sets when one is discussing revealed preference is neutral with respect to the legitimacy of revisions of value structures when the feasible set has been altered.

Under the assumption of robustness, the value structure $V(U)$ may be used to define a set function $C[S,V(U)]$ for every finite nonempty subset S of U whether or not $V(U)$ is free of conflict. The value of this function for given subset S consists of those elements of S which are V-admissible in S according to the value structure $V(S)$, which is the restriction of $V(U)$. The restriction of $V(U)$ to S is the set of permissible v-functions in $V(U)$ where each function is restricted to those elements of U which are members of the subset S. If $V(U)$ is free of ordinal conflict, each restriction $V(S)$ of $V(U)$ should also be free of ordinal conflict and $C[S,V(U)]$ should be the set of options which are optimal in S according to $V(S)$.

The next task is to focus on some of the presuppositions built into common conceptions of optimality.

6.4 Optimality

Let S be a nonempty, finite subset of U and consider some value ranking over U characterizable by means of relations of weak preference, strict preference and indifference.

The following two conditions are each necessary and jointly sufficient for the optimality of x in S:

(i) For every y in S, y is optimal in S if and only if $y\mathbf{I}x$.
(ii) For every y in S, y is not optimal if and only if $x\mathbf{P}y$.

These conditions do not, of course, define optimality, for the notion of optimality appears in both (i) and (ii). Still the necessity and joint sufficiency of (i) and (ii) may be taken as a condition of adequacy of any characterization of optimality.

This condition of adequacy entails that the following is a necessary condition for the optimality of x in S.

(iii) For every y in S, $x\mathbf{P}y$ or $x\mathbf{I}y$.

Converting (iii) to a sufficient as well as a necessary condition for the optimality of x in S yields a noncircular definition of optimality.

A. K. Sen (1970a: 10), among many others, adopts the following requirement as necessary and sufficient for the optimality of x in S relative to a given value ranking (Sen speaks of "best" elements in S rather than "optimal" elements):

(iv) For every y in S, xRy.

This definition of optimality is equivalent to the one built on the necessity and sufficiency of (iii) provided that strict preference and indifference are related to weak preference in the customary way characterized by the following requirements:

Ia. xIy → xRy & yRx
Ib. xPy → xRy & ~yRx
IIa. xRy & yRx → xIy
IIb. xRy & ~yRx → xPy

I can see no objection to taking (iv) as necessary and sufficient for the optimality of x in S provided that the relations in the value ranking satisfy conditions I and II and provided, in addition, that *satisfaction of (i) and (ii) remains necessary and sufficient for the optimality of x in S.*

Sen (like most authors who discuss value or preference rankings) explicitly endorses I and II; but he is prepared to permit the definition of optimality in terms of weak preference utilizing (iv) or in terms of strict preference and indifference utilizing (iii) even when there is no assurance that (i) and (ii) remain individually necessary and jointly sufficient for the optimality of x in S. This becomes apparent when Sen addresses the question of identifying necessary conditions jointly sufficient for a value ranking guaranteeing the existence of an optimal element in every finite, nonempty subset S of U. These conditions will be discussed shortly, and it will then be explained why Sen's conception of optimality does not require satisfaction of (i) and (ii) when x is optimal in the sense he is exploring.

I propose to understand optimality in a sense which follows Sen in endorsing (iv) as necessary and sufficient for optimality. Unlike Sen, however, I shall assume that (i) and (ii) are each necessary and jointly sufficient for the optimality of x in S. I shall call an element of S which is optimal in Sen's sense *quasi optimal.* As will emerge in the technical elaboration, in order for a comparison of elements of U with respect to better or worse to determine a nonempty set of optimal elements for every finite, nonempty subset S of U, U must be weakly ordered.[1] (This condition is, of course, sufficient as well as necessary.) Weak ordering of U is not necessary for quasi optimality. Thus, every finite, nonempty subset S of U may have quasi-optimal elements even though there is no uniquely permissible weak ordering of the elements of U. I prefer to understand optimality in a way which implies that when there is ordinal conflict in U, there is some finite, nonempty subset of U in which there are no optimal options.

To understand the technicalities, observe that assumptions I and II imply that strict preference is asymmetrical whereas indifference is symmetrical:

IIIa. $xPy \rightarrow {\sim}yPx$
IIIb. $xIy \rightarrow yIx$

If the set of optimal options in S is to be nonempty, then optimal x in S must, according to (iv) be weakly preferred to itself and, hence, by conditions I and II be indifferent to itself. Condition Ib implies that strict preference is irreflexive so that the following conditions hold:

IVa. ${\sim}xPx$
IVb. xIx
IVc. xRx

If the set of options optimal in S is to be nonempty for every nonempty, finite subset S of U according to the value ranking, it must be the case that for every x and y in U either x is weakly preferred in value to y or y is weakly preferred in value to x. Weak preference must be complete. This leads to the following condition:

Va. Weak preference is complete: $xRy \lor yRx$.

Condition Va together with I and II entails the following:

Vb. Strict preference and indifference are connected. $xPy \lor xIy \lor yPx$.

The necessary conditions thus far identified for guaranteeing optimality of some element of S for every nonempty, finite subset S of U are not jointly sufficient. However, given the reflexivity and completeness of R as conditions IV and V require, the following condition is necessary and sufficient for guaranteeing the existence of a quasi-optimal element in every nonempty, finite subset S of U (Sen, 1970a: 16, lemma 1*1):

VI. Acyclicity of weak preference: If there are n elements y_1, y_2, ..., y_n in U such that for each i greater than or equal to 1 and less than or equal to $n - 1$, $y_i P y_{i+1}$, $y_1 R y_n$.

Thus, given conditions I and II, conditions IVc, Va and VI are each necessary and jointly sufficient for the existence of a quasi-optimal element in every finite, nonempty subset S of U.

However, as we have mentioned previously, all these conditions may be satisfied even though conditions (i) and (ii) are not satisfied by optimal x in S. The following two examples illustrate the point:

Case 1: xIy & yIz & xPz

Case 2: xPy & yPz & xIz
In both cases, U is the set $\{x,y,z\}$.

Because of condition (iv), x and y but not z are quasi-optimal in case 1. Yet z is indifferent to y. Neither (i) nor (ii) is satisfied by x and y

even though they count as quasi-optimal. Option x alone is quasi-optimal in U in case 2 even though neither (i) nor (ii) is satisfied. Yet all of the conditions in I–VI are satisfied in both cases. Thus, the conditions Sen considers necessary and sufficient to guarantee nonempty sets of optimal options relative to finite, nonempty subsets of U fail to guarantee that optimal options satisfy (i) and (ii).

To avoid terminological confusion, I have reserved the notion of an option being optimal in nonempty subset S of U for elements of S which satisfy (iv) and, in addition, meet requirements (i) and (ii). If (iv) is satisfied but (i) and (ii) are not, the option is quasi-optimal.

Conditions I–VI are individually necessary and jointly sufficient for the existence of quasi-optimal elements in every finite, nonempty subset S of U; but they are not jointly sufficient for the existence of optimal elements in every such S. Condition VI must be strengthened to the following transitivity requirement:

VIIa. $xPy \ \& \ yPz \rightarrow xPz$
VIIb. $xIy \ \& \ yIz \rightarrow xIz$
VIIc. $xRy \ \& \ yRz \rightarrow xRz$

Observe, however, that I–VII are individually necessary and jointly sufficient for weakly ordering the elements of U by the weak preference relation R. When a value structure is free of ordinal conflict, this means, according to previous explanations, that only one weak ordering with respect to better or worse is permissible according to the value structure. I have sought to construe the notion of optimality so that only in such cases of freedom from ordinal conflict in the value structure may we say unequivocally that for every nonempty, finite subset S of the feasible options in U, there exists at least one optimal option. Sen's equation of optimality with what I call "quasi optimality" allows for the existence of optimal options in every nonempty, finite subset S even when there is no uniquely permissible weak value ranking of the elements of U.

To what extent do these differences in the conceptions of optimality favored by Sen and myself represent terminological decisions and to what extent are substantive issues involved? The answer depends on how the relations of weak and strong preference in value and indifference are to be interpreted relative to underlying value structures. There are two broad approaches to explore. According to one, we are to begin by identifying relations of categorical preferences which represent those comparisons with respect to better or worse which are the same for all permissible rankings according to the value structure and then to define optimality relative to that system of preferences. The alternative approach is to invoke criteria of admissibility relative to a value structure to define relations of revealed preference and then to define optimality. In the next section categorical preferences will be explored, and in the section following revealed preferences will be discussed.

It turns out that categorical preference relations always satisfy condition VII so that if quasi optimality is employed, we cannot attribute violations of (i) and (ii) to breakdowns in transitivity. Rather violations will be attributable to violations of V – completeness and connectedness. These, in turn, can occur only if there is ordinal conflict in the underlying value structure. And if there is such ordinal conflict, then there will be finite, nonempty subsets S of U for which there will be no quasi-optimal options. In short, we can guarantee the existence of quasi-optimal options in every finite, nonempty subset S of U when quasi optimality is defined relative to categorical preferences if and only if the underlying value structure is free of ordinal conflict. But then quasi optimality is equivalent to optimality simpliciter.

This brings us to the possibility of interpreting quasi optimality in terms of revealed relations of preference. In 6.6 I shall show that it is possible to use criteria for admissibility and value structures allowed by my approach to define revealed preference relations satisfying I– VI but not VII, as illustrated by the formal cases 1 and 2. These revealed preference relations cannot, of course, be understood to characterize permissible value or preference rankings relative to which admissibility is determined. And optimality defined according to Sen's procedure relative to the revealed preference relations will not coincide in all cases with admissibility. I am not denying the possibility of revealed preference relations like those given in cases 1 and 2 arising. The substantive point is that the revealed preference relations do not in general characterize a sense of optimality according to which all options which are optimal relative to a value structure are V-admissible relative to that value structure – i.e., not prohibited by that value structure.

The upshot of all of this is that either Sen's notion of quasi optimality is generated by categorical preference relations in a way which makes it coincide with optimality in cases where all finite, nonempty subsets S of U have quasi-optimal elements (i.e., where the value structure is free of ordinal conflict) or it is generated by relations of revealed preference which yield criteria for admissibility deviating from those I favor.

Sen mentions another sense in which one might speak of optimal options (Sen calls them "maximal") according to which x is optimal in S if and only if there is no y in S strictly preferred to x. According to this conception, we may guarantee the existence of optimal options in every finite, nonempty subset S of U even when the ranking of U is incomplete (Sen, 1970a: 9–10). H. Herzberger (1973: 198–199) has explicitly advocated focusing on this sense of optimality because of its liberality. Optimality in this sense is not built on relations of revealed preference directly, for such relations as customarily defined are complete. Rather they are based on preferences which generate quasi orderings. I shall show how one can generate what I shall call "categorical quasi orderings" in cases where value structures reveal ordinal conflict and shall show that distinct value structures may generate the same categorical quasi ordering and, hence, the same system of optimal options in Herzberger's liberal sense. Yet the V-admissible options may be different relative to the two value structures. Thus, the liberal sense of optimality may prove to be illiberal in that it overlooks discriminations which a finer grained analysis reveals.

6.5 Categorical Preference

Conflict is rarely total. Even when a value structure is ordinally conflicted, the comparison of some options in U may be free of controversy. Thus, x might be strictly preferred in value to y according to all permissible value rankings. From X's point of view, all relevant considerations favor ranking x as strictly better than y. In that case, x is *categorically strictly preferred* to y according to X's value structure $V(U)$. Similarly, x is *categorically indifferent* to y if and only if x is ranked together with y according to every permissible value ranking. Finally, x is *categorically weakly preferred* to y if and only if x is weakly preferred in value to y according to every permissible value ranking. These categorical preference relations always satisfy conditions I, IIa, III, IV, VI and VII of 6.4.

However, when the value structure $V(U)$ suffers from ordinal conflict, IIb and V may be violated. Such violations can arise in two important ways. One possibility emerges when xPy according to some permissible value rankings, xIy according to others and yPx according to still others. In that case, x is neither categorically preferred to y nor vice versa. Condition Va is violated. In the domain consisting of x and y, IIb is trivially satisfied. Another possibility arises when xPy according to one permissible ranking and xIy according to others, whereas there is no permissible ranking according to which yPx. In that case, x is categorically weakly preferred in value to y without being categorically strictly preferred or categorically indifferent to y. Condition Va is satisfied, but IIb and Vb are violated. The first case illustrates what might be called *disconnected incompleteness,* whereas the second illustrates *disconnected completeness.*

Most students of social choice and economic welfare endorse the view that if society's clients or citizens agree on how they compare social policies x and y, society should join the consensus.[2] In effect, society's permissible value rankings are required to agree with those unanimous or "Paretian" comparisons so that categorical and Paretian comparisons coincide.

However, the conception of a categorical preference in value should be distinguished from a Paretian comparison. Categorical comparisons are noncontroversial according to all permissible value rankings in a value structure. Paretian comparisons are noncontroversial according to rankings of the social states with respect to the "welfares" of the individual citizens (where "welfare" is intended to be left open to diverse interpretations). Individuals and institutions may endorse value commitments which are social welfaristic and thereby restrict their value structures so that their categorical comparisons are compatible with Paretian comparisons. But an agent need not be social welfaristic in the requisite sense to be consistent, coherent or rational in the weak sense I am elaborating.

If there is sufficient ordinal conflict in $V(U)$, categorical preferences in value are disconnected and incomplete. Social welfarists who insist that categorical preference coincide with Paretian preference in social choice are well aware of this point. But such authors often feel the pressure to remove the incompleteness and disconnectedness so that they can guarantee the existence of options which maximize social welfare while preserving the Paretian comparisons.

Returning to the more general question of categorical comparisons, it is useful to consider weak orderings which are compatible with the categorical quasi ordering relative to $V(U)$ to be *extensions* of that categorical quasi ordering. Consider any two permissible v-functions over U in $V(U)$ which rank x and y together. Any weighted average of these functions must do likewise. Similarly, if both functions rank x over y, so does any weighted average; and if both functions rank x at least as high as y, so does any weighted average. Thus, any potential resolution of two ways of evaluating elements of U must induce a ranking of the elements of U which is an extension of the categorical quasi ordering relative to $V(U)$. Hence, all permissible value rankings are extensions of the categorical quasi ordering. I shall call this principle the *categorical extension condition*.

The categorical extension condition is a constraint on value structures. It is a trivial consequence of the way value structures and ways of evaluation have been characterized. The status of the converse of the categorical extension condition is not so trivial. The *converse categorical extension condition* is satisfied by a value structure $V(U)$ if and only if all extensions of the categorical quasi ordering generated by $V(U)$ are permissible according to $V(U)$.

Value structures as I have defined them need not satisfy the converse categorical extension condition. Let us return to the version of Jones' predicament in which Dolly is nearly as bad as Lilly as a typist and nearly as bad as Jane as a stenographer. None of the three options is categorically comparable to any other. Hence, any possible weak ordering of the three alternatives is an extension of the categorical quasi ordering according to $V(U)$. If the converse categorical extension condition were applied to this case, all such extensions would be permissible ways of ranking the alternatives. There would, in particular, be rankings rating the hiring of Dolly as optimal.

However, the set of weighted averages of v-functions which rate hiring Dolly second worst in typing and also in stenography (while rating hiring Jane and hiring Lilly best and worst in typing and worst and best in stenography respectively) fails to allow for any permissible ranking which rates hiring Dolly optimal. As we have seen, this result conforms with presystematic precedent. If this precedent is to be preserved, the converse categorical extension condition has to be rejected.

The breakdown of the converse categorical extension condition in this case illustrates the relevance of discriminating among numerical representations of ways of evaluating elements of U which are not positive affine transformations of one another even though they order elements of U in the same way – a point already emphasized in 5.2.

The categorical preferences in value relations generated by a value structure fail to induce a weak ordering of the elements of U except when the value structure is free of ordinal conflict. They do induce a so-called quasi ordering.

In 6.4, I proposed to restrict the use of "optimal" to options in set S where not only is (iv) necessary and sufficient for optimality but (i) and (ii) are each necessary and jointly sufficient for optimality. This is guaranteed, in general, by requiring that the preferences relative to which optimality is assessed constitute a weak ordering. Since categorical preferences fail to induce such an ordering in cases of ordinal conflict in the value structure, the existence of optimal options in every finite, nonempty subset S of U cannot, in general, be secured.

Even so, there is some advantage in exploiting a conception of optimality relative to categorical preference relations satisfying (iv) even though it fails to satisfy (i) and (ii). If an option is optimal in the sense I use relative to all permissible rankings in the value structure for S, it is categorically weakly preferred to all options in S. Such *categorically optimal* options in S are optimal in a sense which is a useful generalization of the notion of optimality. I shall sometimes call them *V-optimal* relative to $V(S)$.

V-optimality is quasi optimality in the sense of 6.4 when categorical relations are used in formulating condition (iv). But since all the permissible value rankings in a value structure which defines categorical preference relations satisfy I–VII, the categorical preference relations of weak and strict preference and of indifference are transitive and, hence, satisfy VII. The completeness condition Va, the connect-edness condition Vb and the condition IIb may be violated. (If IIb is violated, so is Vb. The converse is not always true.) The reason that conditions (i) and (ii) are not satisfied is that there is incompleteness or disconnectedness and not failure of transitivity; and precisely the same reasons explain why the existence of V-optimal elements in every finite, nonempty subset S of U is not guaranteed. When quasi opti-mality is V-optimality, the idea seems to be a useful generalization of optimality as I favor understanding it. V-optimal options in S (when they exist) are those options in S which are noncontroversially optimal – optimal in S according to all permissible rankings. One must be careful even here. If x is strictly preferred to y according to one per-missible ranking and ranked with it according to another, both are V-admissible in the set $\{x,y\}$. Yet x is categorically weakly preferred to y whereas y is not categorically weakly preferred to x. Option y is not V-optimal, whereas x is. The criterion of V-admissibility does not always agree with the criterion of V-optimality even in those cases where there are V-optimal options.

Although some instances of quasi optimality can be explained as cases of categorical optimality when the value structure suffers from ordinal conflict, cases 1 and 2 are not examples of this. Indeed, both cases illustrate breakdowns of transitivity rather than completeness or disconnectedness. The relations mentioned in these cases cannot be construed as categorical preference relations. The interesting exam-ples of quasi optimality of the sort explored by Sen must be inter-preted in terms of value structures in a different way. As we shall see in the next section, relations of revealed preference will serve.

However, the sense of optimality which Sen called "maximality" and which Herzberger regarded as the "liberal" conception of optimality may be interpreted easily in terms of categorical preference relations. An option in S is *V-noninferior* if and only if there is no option in S categorically strictly preferred to it. There is at least one V-noninfer-ior element in every finite, nonempty subset S of U. Yet when ordinal conflict in a value structure is severe enough, there will be some such S for which there is neither an optimal nor a V-optimal option.

This in itself is not great news to those who take conflict seriously, for it is to be expected that when the conflict is sufficiently severe there will, in general, be no option which is for the best all things con-sidered. To this extent, the "liberality" Herzberger is advocating is in tune with my approach, although his terminology differs from that which I would use. Nonetheless, what is crucial here is the criterion for determining the set of options from which an agent is allowed to choose in cases where decision making is under unresolved conflict. Herzberger proposes to endorse V-noninferiority as the criterion of admissibility relative to the conflicted value structure.

Were the converse categorical extension condition supposed to be satisfied, then my criterion of V-admissibility would coincide with V-noninferiority. But when that condition fails, some V-noninferior options fail to be V-admissible and, hence, ought not to be chosen. In the case where hiring Dolly is a second-worst option and where only professional considerations are being taken into account, hiring Dolly is V-noninferior but not V-admissible.

Thus, in one sense, Herzberger's liberality is too liberal. It recognizes as admissible options which ought to be ruled out. And it does so because, in another sense, his approach is not liberal enough. By (tacitly) presupposing the applicability of the converse categorical extension condition, Herzberger's approach prohibits making the distinction between value structures where hiring Dolly is second best and where hiring Dolly is second worst.

6.6 Revealing preference

According to the approach I have been proposing, a system of value structures hierarchically structured is used to determine a set of admissible options for each finite, nonempty subset S of U. The question was raised in 6.1 whether one could construct a system of "revealed" preference relations by starting with the criterion of admissibility generated according to the proposals I have made and then redefine admissibility as optimality relative to the revealed preference relations. To the extent that one can answer this question affirmatively, the emphasis I have placed on the importance of decision making under unresolved conflict may be dismissed as needless verbal byplay.

Given a *choice function* $C(S)$ defined for all finite, nonempty subsets of U and taking as values nonempty subsets of the arguments, *weak revealed preference* $x R_c y$ may be defined as follows:

A: $x R_c y$ if and only if there is a finite, nonempty subset S of U such that x and y are members of S and x is a member of $C(S)$.

Revealed strict preference P_c and revealed indifference I_c are defined in terms of R_c:

B: $x P_c y$ if and only if $x R_c y$ & $\sim y R_c x$.

C: $x I_c y$ if and only if $x R_c y$ & $y R_c x$.

These relations satisfy conditions I–VI of 6.4.[3] The results cited from Sen in 6.4 show that relative to R_c there is for every finite, nonempty subset S of U, a set of quasi optimal options satisfying condition (iv). Let us call such options *revealed optimal* relative to the choice function C. The set of revealed optimal options for the set S shall be represented as $C^*(S, R_c)$. The C^* gives us a new criterion of admissibility generated by the original choice function C. If we are going to regard the valuations represented by the revealed preference relations as the values which are being maximized by the agent using the original choice function C, consistency requires that $C^*(S,R_c) = C(S)$. When and only when this condition is satisfied should we accept the claim that the options quasi optimal according to the revealed preference ranking are the options admissible for the agent.

A choice function C is *normal* if and only if $C(S) = C^*(S,R_c)$.[4] In addition to requiring that the choice function generated by the revealed preference relations be normal, we should expect that the revealed preference relations given by A, B and C should satisfy the requirements for generating a weak ordering over U as specified by I–VII of 6.4. If these relations fail to satisfy all these requirements, then we cannot say that relative to these relations ordinal conflict is resolved.

Thus, to sustain the thesis that there is no ordinal conflict in revealed preference, the choice function used to define the revealed preference relations must itself satisfy certain requirements. If it could be shown that criteria for admissibility as I have proposed them relative to a hierarchy of value structures exhibiting ordinal conflict define choice functions meeting these requirements, the existence of unresolved conflict would, indeed, cease to be interesting.

I shall first consider a value structure in a hierarchy containing only one level so that admissibility coincides with V-admissibility as characterized by $C[S,V(U)]$. It will be shown that when $C(S)$ is equated with $C[S,V(U)]$, the system of revealed preference relations generated does not, in general, determine a weak ordering of the elements of U. Furthermore, $C(S)$ will, in general, fail to be normal. Finally, when admissibility is characterized by means of a lexicographically ordered series of criteria of V-admissibility relative to a hierarchy of value structures as outlined in 5.7, it will be shown that still additional requirements necessary for normality can be violated.

These results should establish decisively that the account of decision making under unresolved conflict cannot be characterized adequately in terms of conceptions of revealed preference. Those who insist on advocating such conceptions as fundamental to accounts of rational choice are thereby ruling out in advance all possibility of decision making under unresolved conflict. They are not showing that those who insist on the rationality of such decision making are engaged in needless verbal circumlocutions which are reducible to more orthodox approaches relying on notions of revealed preference. They are merely begging the question as to whether such decision making is rational.

By pointing this out I am not, of course, refuting the thesis that preference is to be defined in terms of revealed preference. The best way to do that is to construct an account of decision making under unresolved conflict and explore its applications. But it is important to deflate the question begging pretensions of revealed preference theory.

Before we turn to the technical elaboration of the claims made above, notice should be taken of the fact that the conceptions of revealed preference defined by means of A, B and C are not the only ones which have been proposed.[5] I will not review all of them here. One of them, however, should be mentioned:

Option x is *revealed basically weakly preferred* to y ($x\bar{R}_c y$) relative to the choice function $C(S)$ if and only if x is in $C(\{x,y\})$. (Revealed basic indifference and strict preference may be defined in the usual way.)

The conception of basic weak revealed preference focuses attention on pairwise choices between options. It automatically satisfies conditions I–V. But unlike revealed preference, basic revealed preference may not satisfy the acyclicity condition VI. Thus, there is no guarantee that one can represent the valuations expressed by basic preference relations so that there will always be a quasi-optimal option. Revealed basic preference is, in general, a less likely candidate for ordering of options in terms of revealed preference which eliminates recognition of conflict than is the revealed preference relation R_c. However, under special circumstances, $\bar{R}_c = R_c$. Under these circumstances, revealed basic preference rankings secure an optimum in every finite, nonempty subset of U. If we could show that the criteria for admissibility proposed here generate choice functions meeting these conditions, basic revealed preference would serve as well as revealed preference to eliminate conflict. I shall show that the criteria for admissibility proposed here allow for cases where conflict in values becomes so severe that basic revealed preference and revealed preference cannot be equated. And when they can be equated, I shall show, as promised before, that the choice function may fail to be normal. Invoking basic revealed preference is no more useful than invoking revealed preference as a means of eliminating conflicted value structures and, in some instances, turns out to face more substantial difficulties. Since many moralists and decision theorists tend to suppose that attention may be focused on pairwise choices and that other decision problems can be fully understood if pairwise choice is, the difficulties of focusing on binariness should, perhaps, be emphasized.

6.7 Normality

Certain properties which choice functions may or may not possess should be introduced. Having these properties is relevant to the satisfaction of conditions like normality, to the equivalence of revealed preference and revealed basic preference and to the transitivity of revealed preference.[6]

Definition 1: Choice function C exhibits *property* α if and only if for all finite, nonempty subsets S and T of U such that S is contained in T, if x is a member of S and of $C(T)$, x is a member of C(S).

Definition 2: Choice function C exhibits *property* β if and only if for all finite, nonempty subsets S and T of U such that S is contained in T, if x and y are both members of $C(S)$, then if y is a member of $C(T)$, so is x.

Definition 3: Choice function C exhibits *property* γ if and only if for any class M of nonempty finite subsets of U, if x is a member of $C(S_i)$ for all S_i in M, x is a member of $C(\cup\ M)$ where $\cup\ M$ is the union of sets in M.

Definition 4: Choice function C exhibits *property* ϵ if and only if for every S which is a subset of T, $C(T)$ is not a proper subset of $C(S)$.

Recalling the definitions of revealed weak preference and revealed basic weak preference given in 6.6, it should be obvious that $x\bar{R}_c y$ implies $xR_c y$. To obtain the equivalence of $\bar{R}_c$ and R_c, the converse must hold as well. But our definitions then show that the converse is entailed by the choice function's satisfying property α.

Theorem 1: If $C(S)$ has property α, $\bar{R}_c = R_c$.

We have already noted that R_c by definition satisfies condition VI – i.e., acyclicity. Theorem 1, therefore, yields the following corollary:

Corollary 1: If $C(S)$ has property α, $\bar{R}_c$ is acyclic.

Thus, as long as property α is satisfied by the choice function characterizing admissibility, revealed preference and revealed basic preference are equivalent. Moreover, for every finite, nonempty subset S of U, there will be at least one quasi-optimal option in S in the sense of 6.4 relative to the revealed basic preference relation as well as the revealed preference relation. However, as we have noted, such revealed quasi optimality need not satisfy conditions (i) and (ii). Furthermore, even when the choice function has property α, there is no guarantee that the choice function is normal. Proof of the following theorem (as well as theorem 3 succeeding it) is given in Sen (1977).

Theorem 2: $C(S)$ is normal if and only if it has properties α and γ.

Thus, even if we have a choice function satisfying property α (so that there is a notion of quasi optimality relative to revealed preference which is equivalent to quasi optimality relative to revealed basic preference and which is such that the existence of quasi-optimal options is guaranteed for all finite, nonempty subsets of U), we still have no guarantee that the criterion of revealed quasi optimality will be equivalent to the criterion of admissibility characterizing the choice function $C(S)$ with which we began unless property γ is present as well.

But even satisfaction of α and γ will not establish that quasi-optimal options are optimal. The relation of revealed preference must be transitive and, hence, generate a weak ordering of the elements of U. The conditions under which this happens are given in the following theorem:

Theorem 3: $C(S)$ is normal and R_c is transitive if and only $C(S)$ has properties α and β.

Mention should also be made of another general result. Satisfaction of α guarantees that revealed basic preference as well as revealed preference is acyclic. However, the question may arise as to when a choice function generates so-called quasi-transitive revealed preference relations – i.e., relations satisfying condition VIIa (transitivity of strict preference) but not necessarily VIIb or VIIc (transitivity of indifference or weak preference).

Theorem 4: If $C(S)$ satisfies α and ϵ, R_c is quasi-transitive.[7]

These results hold for any choice function. Our concern here is with choice functions which are defined by criteria of admissibility relative to value structures along lines developed previously in this volume.

In 6.8, choice functions defined by criteria of admissibility relative to a hierarchy of value structures consisting of exactly one value structure will be examined. In 6.9, I shall turn to the more general case where the hierarchy of value structures contains more than one value structure and the lexicographical version of V-admissibility determines the set of V-admissible options.

6.8 Revealed preference according to V-admissibility

Given a single value structure $V(U)$, the criterion of V-admissibility defines a choice function $C[S,V(U)]$, which we shall abbreviate $C_v(S)$.

Theorem 5: $C_v(S)$ satisfies property α.

Proof: Let x be a member of $C_v(T)$ and let S be a proper subset of T. There is a permissible value ranking in $V(U)$ relative to which x is optimal in T. Since that value ranking is a weak ordering of T and, hence, of S, x is optimal in S according to that ranking. Hence, x is in $C_v(S)$.

Theorem 6: For every finite, nonempty set S of U, there is a weak ordering of U which is an extension of the categorical quasi ordering according to $V(U)$ such that all and only V-noninferior elements of S are ranked together and ranked optimal.

Proof: If x and y are V-noninferior in S, there is some permissible ranking which ranks them together. If z is not V-noninferior, there is at least one V-noninferior option which is categorically strictly preferred to z. Hence, no extension of the categorical quasi order can rank all the V-noninferior options together and rank z with them. But all V-noninferior options may be ranked together. If they are, the extension of the categorical quasi ordering which is developed must render them optimal.

Comment: It is not claimed that the weak ordering of U which is the extension of the categorical quasi ordering of U that guarantees the optimality of all and only V-noninferior options in S will be the same extension of the categorical quasi ordering of U that guarantees the optimality of all and only V-noninferior options in some different finite subset S' of U.

Theorem 7: If the converse categorical extension condition is satisfied by $V(U)$, $C_v(S)$ is the set of V-noninferior options in S.

Proof: The definition of V-admissibility trivially implies that all V-admissible options are V-noninferior. To obtain the converse, assume that the converse categorical extension condition is satisfied. Then the weak ordering which by theorem 6 is an extension of the categorical quasi ordering and counts all and only the V-noninferior options in S as optimal in S is permissible according to the value structure $V(S)$. Hence, all V-noninferior options in S are V-admissible in S.

Theorem 8: If the converse categorical extension condition is satisfied, $C_v(S)$ has property γ.

Proof: Let x be V-admissible in S_i for every S_i in class M of finite, nonempty subsets of U. Since every y in the union $\cup\, M^*$ of the sets in M is in S_i for some i, there is some extension of the categorical quasi ordering of U according to which x is weakly preferred to y. Hence, x must be V-noninferior in $\cup\, M$. By theorem 7, x must be V-admissible in $\cup\, M$.

Theorem 9: If the converse categorical extension condition is satisfied, $C_v(S)$ is normal.

Proof: Theorems 2, 5 and 8.

Thus, under the assumption of the converse categorical extension condition, it is possible to construct a system of revealed preference relations and a system of revealed basic preference relations which (a) are equivalent, (b) guarantee the acyclicity of the revealed basic weak preference and (c) establish the normality of the choice function. Under the converse categorical extension condition, V-admissible options coincide with revealed quasi-optimal options. There is no guarantee, however, that the quasi-optimal options are also optimal.

To guarantee that the V-admissible options are not merely quasi-optimal but optimal as well, the relation of revealed weak preference must be transitive. Theorem 3 asserts that the choice function will generate a transitive revealed preference relation as well as be normal if and only if it has properties α and β. (Of course, if it is normal, theorem 2 implies that it has property γ as well.)

Theorem 10: There are value structures satisfying the converse categorical extension condition such that C_v lacks property β.

Proof: Let $V(S)$ recognize the following rankings as permissible:

 (a) x over y equal to z
 (b) x equal to y over z

By the converse categorical extension condition, the following ranking ought also to be permissible:

 (c) x over y over z

No other ranking need be permissible according to the value structure. In a pairwise choice between y and z, both y and z are V-admissible. But in a three-way choice between x, y and z, x and y but not z are V-admissible. This violates β.

The value structure exhibited in the proof of theorem 10 generates a revealed preference relation satisfying case 1 of 6.4. Options x and

y but not z are quasi-optimal but violate (i) and (ii) of 6.4 and, hence, are not optimal. The point may not seem to matter much, for the quasi-optimal options do coincide with the V-admissible options. But everything depends here on the converse categorical extension condition being satisfied. When this condition is violated (and we have already shown that there is good reason to allow it to be violated), γ as well as β may be violated. This means that normality is not always satisfied and that some quasi-optimal options need not be V-admissible.

Recall that the converse categorical extension condition is violated in cases like Jones' predicament where one of three options is second worst according to two desiderata which conflict concerning which of the other options is ranked best and which worst. Suppose, as before, that Dolly is second worst in both categories. Let x be the option of hiring Jane, y the option of hiring Dolly and z the option of hiring Lilly. v_1 represents the values of the options when typing alone is taken into account, and v_2 represents the values of the options when stenography alone is considered. We assume that $v_1(x) - v_1(y)$ is greater than $v_1(y) - v_1(z)$ which is greater than o. Likewise, $v_2(z) - v_2(y)$ is greater than $v_2(y) - v_2(x)$, which again is positive. If we regard all possible weighted averages of two functions satisfying these conditions as permissible, the following are the sole permissible value rankings:

(a) x over y over z
(b) x over y equal to z
(c) x over z over y
(d) x equal to z over y
(e) z over x over y
(f) z over x equal to y
(g) z over y over x

All three options are categorically noncomparable. Yet there are rankings of them which are not permissible. This violates the converse categorical extension condition.

In a three-way choice, x and z are V-admissible; y is not. Yet both x and y are V-admissible in a pairwise choice between x and y. Similarly, both y and z are V-admissible in a pairwise choice between y and z. Clearly γ is violated in addition to β. Hence, the revealed preference relations not only fail to generate a transitive weak preference but fail to generate a normal choice function. There are options revealed quasi-optimal and revealed basically quasi-optimal which are not V-admissible. In our example, option y (hiring Dolly) is revealed quasi-optimal (and revealed basically quasi-optimal) in the three-way choice but is not V-admissible.

In order to secure the existence of quasi optimal options relative to revealed preference and revealed basic preference relations, all that is required is that these relations satisfy condition VI – i.e., acyclicity. Because the choice function defined by V-admissibility satisfies property α, not only is revealed preference acyclic but so is revealed basic preference. But we can say something stronger than this:

Theorem 11: C_v has property ϵ.

Proof: Let S and T be finite subsets of U, and S a subset of T. Given any permissible ranking of the elements of U, the set of optimal options in T cannot be a proper subset of the optimal options in S. The V-admissible options in T (in S) form the union of the options optimal according to all permissible rankings. Hence, the V-admissible options in T cannot be a proper subset of the V-admissible options in S.

Theorem 12: The revealed preference and revealed basic preference relations generated by V-admissibility are quasi-transitive – i.e., satisfy VIIa.

The breakdown of normality which can occur in cases where we have conflict but one option is counted as second worst according to all criteria ought to undermine severely the usefulness of revealed preference relations as representations of an agent's valuations. To be sure, revealed preference (revealed basic preference) satisfies VIIa so that strict revealed (revealed basic) preference is transitive (even though this virtue is sullied by the breakdown of transitivity of revealed [revealed basic] indifference). But quasi optimal options will not in general coincide with the V-admissible options. Hence, V-admissibility cannot be reduced to quasi optimality relative to revealed (revealed basic) preference and *a fortiori* cannot be reduced to optimality relative to such preference.

Of course, one might insist, as a condition on rationality, that choice functions be normal. To do so, however, is to rule out value structures violating the converse categorical extension condition, not, so it seems, because there is anything incoherent in value structures of this sort (they seem commonplace enough) but because of a commitment to the importance of conceptions of revealed preference.

Assuming as I have done that value conflict can be sufficiently severe to lead to violations of the converse categorical extension condition, the following theorem has been established:

Theorem 13: There are value structures relative to which C_v lacks property γ and, hence, fails to be normal.

6.9 Lexicographical V-admissibility

Let us turn now to a situation where the agent's valuations of the feasible options are representable by a lexicographically ordered series of value structures $V_1, V_2, \ldots, V_n$. Admissibility is determined according to the lexicographical V-admissibility rule described in 5.7. Let the choice function defined in terms of lexicographical V-admissibility be C_L.

Even when there are several value structures in the hierarchy, it can turn out that the higher level value structures fail to rule out any V_1-admissible options for any nonempty subset S of U so that lexicographical V-admissibility collapses into V_1-admissibility. When this is the case, all the theorems previously established apply.

New results emerge when higher level value structures are capable of rendering verdicts between V_1-admissible options. In particular, C_L can violate property α.

Consider still again Jones' predicament, where hiring Dolly is second worst according to considerations of typing and of stenographic skills. Suppose that Jones ignores considerations like feminine pulchritude and membership in a disadvantaged minority group as long as he is able to reach a verdict on professional grounds (i.e., typing and stenographic skills of the applicant) but is prepared to invoke one or the other (or both) of these secondary considerations if he is unable to decide on the basis of professionally relevant considerations. In 1.6, it was pointed out that in this type of situation, if Dolly ranks over Jane, who ranks over Lilly with respect to these secondary considerations, the choice function C_L defined by admissibility will violate property α.

Theorem 14: There are hierarchies of value structures according to which C_L lacks property α.

In 1.4, I noted that most authors interested in rational decision making would require possession of property α as a condition of adequacy of any acceptable choice function. I contended there and reiterate here the view that indiscriminate endorsement of property α condemns as inconsistent or irrational examples of reverse discrimination like the one which can be generated from Jones' predicament. Whether such practices are morally or politically acceptable may be open to debate, but any account of rational choice which rules out such practices as incoherent or irrational is itself, in my view, unacceptably dogmatic.

Some critics complain that permitting choice functions defined according to my criteria of lexicographical V-admissibility leads to violations of transitivity.[8] The trouble with such objections in the first instance is their obscurity. Clearly all the permissible value rankings in a value structure have transitive weak preference (strict preference and indifference) relations. Categorical weak preference (strict preference and indifference) is also transitive. We have also seen that as long as the lexicographical hierarchy contains only one value structure, strict revealed (revealed basic) preference remains transitive even though revealed (revealed basic) indifference does not. In the more general case we are now considering, strict revealed preference is no longer transitive. However, revealed preference is by definition acyclic.

Revealed basic preference fails to satisfy even this requirement. The following examples illustrate this point: Suppose the scores on the typing test for the three applicants for the job offered by Jones are 100, 90 and 95 for Jane, Dolly and Lilly respectively, and 90, 95 and 100 are the scores on their typing tests. Dolly is no longer second worst according to both tests. She is worst in typing but in the middle in stenography. If we consider these scores to be v-functions and take the convex hull of all of these to be the value structure, we obtain a criterion of V-admissibility which violates β but obeys γ. Suppose Dolly is more underprivileged than Jane, who is more deprived than Lilly. Lexicographical V-admissibility specifies that Jane is uniquely admissible in the three-way choice, Dolly in a pairwise choice with Jane, Lilly in a pairwise choice with Dolly, whereas Jane is chosen over Lilly. Clearly strict revealed preference is no longer transitive. However, as promised, condition VI remains satisfied. In contrast, if we consider revealed basic preference, Dolly is strictly preferred to Jane, Jane to Lilly and Lilly to Dolly. Not even acyclicity (condition VI) is satisfied.

My point in rehearsing all of this is, in part, to emphasize the ambiguity in the charge that the criterion of lexicographical V-admissibility leads to intransitivities. Unless one specifies the sense of preference relative to which intransitivity is charged, the charge is not even clearly formulated.

Consider then the complaint that strict preference is not transitive. Unless we demand that admissibility be reduced to optimality or quasi optimality relative to revealed basic preference, this intransitivity is innocuous. And if we demand that admissibility be reduced to quasi optimality relative to revealed (revealed basic) preference, we have already decided not to endorse the criterion of lexicographical V-admissibility. The breakdown of intransitivity cannot itself decide anything.

Recall that even when we rest content with a criterion of V-admissibility and do not seek to invoke secondary and higher order value structures to cut down the admissible options, admissibility does not coincide with quasi optimality relative to revealed basic preference. Those who mean to insist on equating admissibility with such quasi optimality and with V-admissibility as well will have to insist on the converse categorical extension condition. If they do not insist on this, then the fact that revealed (revealed basic) strict preference is transitive in this case does not appear to render V-admissibility preferable as a criterion of admissibility to lexicographical V-admissibility. Revealed (revealed basic) preference is an epiphenomenon and not a fundamental determinant of the admissibility of options. Whether transitivity is satisfied is a matter of no importance once normality is gone.

6.10 Conclusion

My purpose in this chapter has not been to demonstrate the superiority of the criteria of admissibility proposed here to more conventional views. To the contrary, I have been concerned to show how extensively the proposals I am advocating deviate from such views and to indicate what sorts of phenomena those who insist on the reducibility of notions of admissibility to quasi optimality or optimality relative to revealed (revealed basic) preference have to dismiss as manifestations of incoherence, inconsistency or irrationality. No matter what bad names one uses, I mean to suggest that on some occasions, properties α, β, and γ may all be violated legitimately.

This does not mean that anything goes. Although the criteria for admissibility proposed here are less demanding than customary approaches in some respects, they remain restrictive in others. I have no proof that these restrictions, weak though they are, are obligatory. The best one can do is to explore the ramifications of employing the approach I am advancing in diverse contexts.

A further step in this exploration will be taken in chapter 7. I shall summarize a treatment of decision making under uncertainty already elaborated (Levi, 1980a) in order to show how uncertainty contributes to conflict which may go unresolved at the moment of choice. What is new here is the attempt to integrate the views I have previously published about decision making under uncertainty into a larger framework designed to accommodate both unresolved conflict derived from uncertainty and that derived from the tensions among competing value commitments. To illustrate the impact of this larger framework, some attention will be devoted to phenomena sometimes question beggingly called "preference reversal" exemplified by responses to problems posed many years ago by D. Ellsberg and M. Allais.

Another illustration of the usefulness of the framework being proposed here will be developed in chapters 6–11. Chapter 8 will discuss the relation between the rationality of decision making under unresolved conflict and social agency. Chapters 9–11 will explore a broad class of value commitments including assorted versions of utilitarianism, Rawlsian approaches to distribution and Arrovian approaches to social choice to show how the analytical framework proposed here can systematize and refine many of the insights already put forth in that literature and can undermine the still widespread prejudices against decision making under unresolved conflict.

7

Uncertainty as a source of conflict

7.1 Uncertainty

Moral struggles of the second kind are generated by decision problems in which the feasible options are evaluated according to different value commitments in incompatible ways. I have argued that such predicaments call for suspending judgement concerning the applicability of the competing value commitments and evaluating the feasible options with the aid of a value structure which mirrors this unresolved conflict.

Conflict in value structures can arise without being directly generated by conflicts among value commitments. For example, a physician may be convinced (rightly or wrongly) that abortion is wrong except when it will prevent the death of the mother or serious physical harm to her. This value commitment may be used to evaluate feasible options open to the physician, provided that the physician can make a sure determination of the prospects of the mother being seriously harmed by seeing the baby through to term. There is no conflict between the physician's value commitment and other commitments he endorses.

Difficulties arise, however, if the physician does not know whether the mother will die if the baby is carried through to term. In that event, the physician will not know whether performing an abortion or refraining from doing so is the option mandated by his value commitment. There is no conflict between his value commitments. Still the physician does not know how to apply his value commitment to the feasible options under the descriptions according to which they are optional for him.

The value commitment considered in this example is one which many authors would take to be distinctively moral. I myself am disinclined to place too much weight on a distinction between moral value commitments and prudential, self-interested, utilitarian, aesthetic, economic or social value commitments. But the importance of the distinction need not be disputed here. Even though the value commitment is a moral one, uncertainty can generate value conflict. Furthermore, it does not matter whether or not the value commitment is agent centered. In these respects, moral and agent-centered value commitments do not differ from value commitments more widely regarded as "consequentialist".

In this chapter, I shall summarize and, in some respects, elaborate upon an account of decision making under uncertainty which will enable us to represent the ways in which uncertainty can generate conflict in value structures even when there is no conflict between value commitments.

The chief ideas presented in this chapter are derived from the approach developed in Levi (1980a). The emphasis, however, is different. In my previous book, the focus was on the revision of knowledge and probability judgement. The account of decision making under uncertainty was ancillary to that concern. In this discussion, attention is directed to unresolved conflict. This leads to a consideration of uncertainty as a contributor to such conflict. Even so, the interested reader may want to look at Levi (1980a: chs. 4–10) for an elaboration of details not discussed here.

7.2 Extended value structures

Let the set U of feasible options contain n members the ith of which is representable as choosing true proposition a_i $(i = 1, 2, \ldots, n)$. Assume further that the agent X knows at t that if he chooses a_i true, exactly one of the propositions $c_{i1}, c_{i2}, \ldots, c_{im_i}$ is true. Let o_{ij} assert that both a_i and c_{ij} are true; O_i is the set of propositions $o_{i1}, o_{i2}, \ldots, o_{im_i}$. From X's point of view, choosing that a_i is true is the same as choosing true that at least and at most one element of O_i is true.

Set O is the union of the O_i for all a_i in U. In situations where X endorses a value commitment which he cannot apply directly to the descriptions of the options given by the statements a_i, he may still find a set O of propositions having the character described above and such that he can apply his value commitments to the conditions characterized by these propositions.

The value commitments of agent X will induce an *extended value structure* $EV(O)$ representable by a nonempty, convex set of real-valued *extended value functions* (*ev*-functions) closed under positive affine transformations.

Sometimes the agent's value commitments induce an extended value structure on O where, for every i, O_i contains exactly one member. In that case, X knows that choosing a_i true is the same as choosing $o_i = a_i \& o_{i1}$ (which is the sole element of O_i) true. When this condition obtains, the agent faces a *decision problem under certainty*. In a decision problem under certainty, the extended value structure $EV(O)$ reduces to the value structure $V(U)$.

Not all decision problems are characterizable as decision problems under certainty. Recall the physician described in 7.1 facing the decision whether to abort a patient's baby. He is not in a position to apply his value commitments directly to the two options. For each option a_i, he can associate a set O_i of alternative possibly true descriptions of his option (given that it is chosen). He can, moreover, apply his value commitment to the elements of O so as to obtain a set of permissible ev-functions $EV(O)$ and, as a consequence, a set of permissible rankings of the elements of O. But the physician cannot obtain an evaluation of the elements of U from this because each O_i contains more than one element. This predicament instantiates problems of *decision making under uncertainty*.

7.3 Lexicography

In 5.2, we observed that an agent's value commitments can induce a hierarchy of value structures on the agent's set U of feasible options. This can happen because the agent regards the priority of certain desiderata to be so powerful as to nullify the force of other values except in cases where the dominating desiderata cannot be invoked to render a verdict among the feasible options.

This consideration applies *mutatis mutandis* to decision making under uncertainty. The value commitment first in the hierarchy induces a first-level extended value structure $EV_1(O)$ on O. This may be followed by a second-level extended value structure $EV_2(O)$, etc.

In decision making under uncertainty, however, the situation is more complicated than the story told in 5.2. There the second-level value structure was invoked to render verdicts among V_1-admissible options. Now we are no longer in a position to derive V_1-admissible options from the value structure $V_1(U)$ without first determining that value structure from the extended value structure $EV_1(O)$.

To obtain the set of V_1-admissible options, I suggest that we invoke another lexicographically ordered series of tests of admissibility each of which is related to the extended value structure $EV_1(O)$ in a different way. Only when these tests are exhausted do we obtain the set of V_1-admissible options and only then do we proceed to the second level and derive the set of V_2-admissible options from among the V_1-admissible options according to principles paralleling those operative on the first level. If necessary, this process is reiterated until the lexicographical hierarchy of extended value structures is exhausted.

In this chapter, we shall discuss the hierarchy of tests of admissibility relative to the extended value structure EV_i at level i. In illustrations, we shall focus on the first-level extended value structure. The controversial issues to be addressed may be examined by considering this level. Given the account of the subhierarchy of tests of admissibility at level i leading to a criterion of V_i-admissibility, the rest of the account of admissibility will proceed in accordance with the account given in 5.2.

7.4 Expected value

Suppose that Smith, like Jones, is interested in hiring a secretary. She has a choice of three candidates: Jim, Dave and Larry. Unlike Jones, Smith cares only about typing skills. The three applicants have taken the typing test, but the results have somehow been mixed up. Smith knows that the scores are either Jim 100, Dave 91 and Larry 90 (h_1) or Jim 90, Dave 91 and Larry 100 (h_2). Letting Smith's options be j, d and l, the extended value structure consists of all positive affine transformations of the ev-function characterized by the following table:

	h_1	h_2
j	100	90
d	91	91
l	90	100

Had Smith been certain that h_1 were true, she could have derived her value structure for the set of options $U = \{j,d,l\}$ from her extended value structure. Indeed, in that case the extended value structure would have consisted of all positive affine transformations of the values given in the first column of the table and this, in turn, would have been identical with the value structure for U.

The difference between that case and the one we are now considering concerns Smith's state of knowledge and ignorance. This suggests that the derivation of the value structure from the extended value structure requires an appeal to some feature of Smith's state of knowledge. Granted that Smith is neither certain that h_1 is true nor certain that h_2 is true, she still might assign h_1 a degree of belief or *credal probability* and do the same for h_2 as well. Let us suppose that these degrees of belief have definite numerical values. Given these degrees of belief, we might take the value of a feasible option to be a weighted average of the values imputed to the option when h_1 is true and when h_2 is true, where the weights are the probabilities assigned these hypotheses conditional on the option being chosen.

Thus, suppose that Smith judges it equally likely that h_1 is true as it is that h_2 is true given that she chooses x, where x is any one of the three options in U. The average value assigned to j will be 95, that to d will be 91 and that to l will be 95. (Of course, any positive affine transformation of these values will do as well.) Thus, we are able to derive a valuation of the elements of U which is unique up to a positive affine transformation that qualifies as a value structure for U.

The v-functions in the value structure are weighted averages of the values assigned the given options according to the extended value structure when these options are described by the possible o_{ij}'s.

If the hypotheses h_1 and h_2 had been assigned different credal probabilities p and $1 - p$ respectively, the calculation for the weighted averages would have proceeded in the same way. The value assigned to hiring Jim would be $100p + 90(1 - p) = 10p + 90$, that to hiring Dave 91 and that to hiring Larry $100(1 - p) + 90p = 100 - 10p$. The value structure would countenance as permissible all positive affine transformations of these values. (In the more general case where the probability of h_i given x is not the same for all x in U, the value assigned to j would be $10p_j + 90$, and that to l, $100 - 10p_1$.)

The general principle employed here presupposes that the agent Smith has a credal state expressible by a probability measure $Q(x/y)$ defined for hypotheses y consistent with the agent's body of knowledge and hypotheses x, where x and y are expressible in a suitable fragment of some regimented language. Here, $Q(h/e)$ represents the degree of belief or credal probability assigned h conditional on e relative to the agent's knowledge. The measure Q satisfies the requirements of the calculus of probabilities.[1]

Given such a credal state and given a decision problem, such as the predicament facing Smith, where the agent faces a set U of feasible options $a_1, a_2, \ldots, a_n$ and where a_i together with the agent's knowledge entails that at least and at most one o_{ij} is true, the credal state is represented by a probability function $Q(x/y)$ which defines for each a_i a function $Q(o_{ij}/a_i)$ which assigns a nonnnegative real value to each o_{ij}.

The *expected value* of a_i relative to a permissible ev-function in the extended value structure $EV(O)$ and relative also to the Q-function representing the credal state B is given by the following:

$$e(a_i) = \Sigma\, Q(o_{ij}/a_i)ev(o_{ij}) \tag{1}$$

When each permissible ev-function in the extended value structure $EV(O)$ is combined with a Q-function according to Eq. (1) to define a permissible expected value function $e(a_i)$ of the elements of U, the set $E(U)$ of expected value functions so constructed is called the *expected value structure*.

In the case of Smith as we have described it, the extended value structure is free of cardinal conflict. Because we are using only one Q-function in the calculations, the expected value structure is free of cardinal conflict as well. In this special case, there is a uniquely permissible ranking of the elements of U with respect to expected value which determines the set of options optimal with respect to expected value. These are the *E-optimal* options.[2]

It is tempting to equate the expected value structure $E(U)$ thus determined with the value structure $V(U)$ and the E-optimal options with the V-optimal options. The temptation should be resisted.

Suppose Smith assigns h_1 the credal probability 0.1. The expected value of hiring Jim is 91, which equals the expected value of hiring Dave. The expected value of hiring Larry is 99. Hiring Larry is obviously E-optimal and uniquely so. Under the circumstances, it should count as uniquely V-optimal and, hence, V-admissible.

Suppose, however, that Larry informs Smith that he has taken another position. Smith now has two options both of which have the same expected value of 10. Relative to this set of options, both are E-optimal. Should we say that both are V-optimal and, hence, V-admissible?

To adopt this terminological practice would be acceptable if we could take for granted that we cannot invoke any features of the extended value structure $EV(O)$ to decide between the options which are tied for E-optimality. In this view, if we are going to "break ties" we must invoke a second-level extended value structure and the second-level value structure determined by it. If it is at least open to the decision maker as a rational agent to invoke procedures for breaking ties which do not appeal to second-level value commitments and the (extended) value structures determined thereby, we should resist this approach.

Thus, granted that hiring Jim and hiring Dave bear the same expected value of 91, if Smith hired Jim, she might be hiring someone who scored 90 on the typing test, whereas if she hired Dave she would be secure in the knowledge that, no matter what, she would have hired a candidate who scored at least 91 on the test. Given Smith's commitment to hire the best secretary available and given that considerations of expected value fail to render a verdict, Smith would not be unreasonable in invoking considerations of security.

The type of reasoning involved here is analogous to that described in 5.2 and reintroduced in 7.3. Having taken into account the expected values of the feasible options relative to the extended value structure characterizing the aim of hiring a good typist, Jones is urged to evaluate those options which are admissible according to that test by appeal to another consideration.

There is, however, an important difference. When appealing to a hierarchy of value structures or extended value structures characterizing lexicographically ordered series of value commitments, we turn to the level $i + 1$ if we fail to render an utterly specific verdict at the ith level.

When we turn to the consideration of the "worst possible case" or security of each feasible option, the appraisal of worst possible cases or security levels remains relative to the same value commitment invoked to determine expected values. Thus, in determining security levels for hiring Jim and hiring Dave, Smith appeals to the extended value structure generated by her commitment to hiring a proficient typist. This is the same extended value structure as the one she used to evaluate her options with respect to expected value. Smith does not move up her hierarchy of value commitments and seek to break the tie with respect to expected value by appeal to stenographic prowess or status as a disadvantaged minority.

Perhaps, someone else might proceed differently than Smith and ignore considerations of security. I shall show later how this can be regarded as a degenerate case of invoking security considerations. If I am right about this, then we do not rule out, in advance, entertainable ways of assessing the admissibility of feasible options by refusing to equate E-optimality with V-optimality or V-admissibility in our example.

These considerations suggest that a sensible way to proceed is to regard the expected value structure $E(U)$ relative to extended value structure $EV(U)$ (and credal state B) as the first in a hierarchy of value structures concerned with the same level of value commitment and the extended value structure $EV(O)$ determined thereby. To mark this first-level value structure, we shall equate $E(U)$ with $VE(U)$ and equate E-admissibility (E-optimality) with VE-admissibility (VE-optimality).

As we shall see, we can think of considerations of security as providing an alternative to considerations of expected utility for deriving a value structure from an extended value structure. We can label that value structure $VS(U)$.

I shall elaborate shortly on how considerations of security are intended to operate and how many levels are to be considered in a subhierarchy of value structures related to the same-level extended value structure. Assuming that we have some account of this, we can then say that given a first-level extended value structure $EV_1(O)$ we can determine the VE_1-admissible options and then ascertain which options are VS_1-admissible (if considerations of security are the second level in the subhierarchy) and among these determine which pass additional tests relative to $EV_1(O)$. The V_1-admissible options will be those which survive all these tests of admissibility.[3] If there is more than one survivor, a similar subhierarchy of tests can be applied relative to $EV_2(O)$ to establish the V_2-admissible options, etc.

7.5 Credal indeterminacy

In 7.4, we assumed that Smith's extended value structure and credal state are free of conflict. In that case, the expected value structure is free of conflict and, as a consequence, the first-level value structure $VE(U)$ related to the agent's value commitments determining the first-level extended value structure is free of value conflict. If there is any role for considerations of security to play, it concerns breaking ties for optimality with respect to expected value.

This is a very special case. Yet it is the only kind strict Bayesians recognize as appropriate to rational agents. To be sure, strict Bayesians do not, as a rule, invoke principles for breaking ties for optimality as I have suggested. Any option which maximizes expected "utility" is admissible. And whether one should be obliged to consider security when there are ties in expected value is not a terribly gripping issue if, indeed, the only kind of predicament facing ideally rational agents is the sort in which both extended value structures and credal states are free of cardinal conflict.

One of the main themes of this book is that conflicts in value structures can be generated by conflicts among value commitments. According to this view, it is to be expected that value commitments can induce conflict in extended value structures even if the credal state is free of conflict. And this will be enough to generate conflict in the expected value structure – counter to strict Bayesian dogma. Strict Bayesians not only insist on the absence of conflict in the extended value structures of rational agents but, because they deny conflict in value structures and, hence, expected value structures as well, they deny conflict in credal states.

Consider the well-known proposals of F. P. Ramsey (1950) and B. de Finetti (1964) to represent degrees of belief (personal or credal probability) by betting rates which the agent would regard as just fair in evaluating gambles on the propositions whose certainty is in question. Ramsey explicitly acknowledged that he was assuming in advance that rational agents maximize expected value. But there is more to the Ramsey–de Finetti approach than invoking considerations of expected value.

Given some proposition g, an agent is invited to identify the least upper bound on the price he would be prepared to pay for a gamble whereby he receives S units of value if g is true and nothing if g is false. The value P^*, which is the threshold value such that the agent would refuse gambles at higher prices and accept gambles at lower prices, not only is assumed to exist but is supposed to be such that the agent ranks the gamble whereby he receives $S - P^*$ if g is true and $-P^*$ if g is false as equal to the option of refusing the gamble and neither gaining nor losing. Under these conditions, both the extended value structure and the expected value structure for the set of options consisting of gambles with stake S for all prices from $P = S$ to $P = 0$ and the option of refusing to gamble and neither gaining nor losing is free of conflict. Commitment to the criterion of expected value guarantees in this case that the credal state must be numerically definite and, indeed, assign g the credal probability $P*/S$ as Ramsey and de Finetti require.

Suppose the agent is offered a gamble whereby he receives $-S$ units of value if g is true (loses S units) and neither gains nor loses if g is false. He is asked to identify the smallest inducement $P**$ ($P**$ positive; $-P**$ is supposed to be a negative price) such that the agent would rank accepting the gamble with that inducement as equal in value to not gambling at all. According to the Ramsey–de Finetti view, $P**/S$ should equal P/S.

Finally and most importantly, Ramsey and de Finetti showed that under these conditions, persons who wish to have their betting practices secure against sure loses should avoid credal states where the credal function violates the requirements of the calculus of probabilities.[4]

It is tempting to conclude from all of this that rationality requires that one be committed to a numerically definite state of credal probability as well as to an extended value structure unique up to a positive affine transformation.[5] Such a conclusion is premature. It presupposes that value structures are free of conflict.

Thus, Ramsey and de Finetti assume that the agent ranks the gamble on g with positive stake S and price $P*$ together with neither gaining nor losing. But the price $P*$ such that the agent refuses to accept the gamble for greater prices and accepts it for lower prices need not be understood this way once one abandons the requirement that value structures be free of conflict. The reason that the agent refuses the gamble at prices higher greater than $P*$ might be that the option of accepting the gamble is not categorically comparable with the option of refusal relative to the expected value structure and the agent bases his decision on considerations of security which favor refusing the gamble. When this is the case, it is possible that $P**$ is not equal to $P*$. (This will be explained in more detail in 7.6.) Ramsey, de Finetti and their followers rule out this possibility from the start. Their arguments from considerations of prudential betting beg the question against views which seek to recognize the rationality of decision making under unresolved conflict.

Many critics of strict Bayesianism seek to undermine this doctrine by questioning the priority it gives to the injunction to maximize expected value in determining a value structure on the basis of a credal state and extended value structure. Such critics are often anxious to preserve the requirement that the value structure be free of at least ordinal conflict.

In my judgement, this approach is on the wrong track. When an agent's value commitments are sufficiently free of conflict to induce a conflict free extended value structure and a credal state representable by a single credal probability measure, the expected value principle is extremely attractive. I know of no way to prove that it ought to be endorsed which avoids begging some question that a sufficiently determined skeptic might wish to make. Still the arguments of Ramsey and de Finetti, refined as they have been by subsequent generations, seem to me quite compelling when there is no conflict in values or probability judgements.

A more compelling case may be made against strict Bayesian doctrine by considering how daunting it is to satisfy the requirements of applicability it imposes. The extended value structure must be free of *cardinal* conflict. The agent must be committed to numerically definite credal probability assignments. Neither condition is one which even ideally rational agents should be expected to satisfy on all occasions.

This line of opposition to strict Bayesian dogma should not be confused with another complaint. Even if agents are committed to numerically definite credal states and extended value structures free of cardinal conflict, they cannot live up to these commitments. Psychological inhibitions, emotional disturbances and failures of memory prevent an agent from recognizing those values and beliefs to which he is committed. Limitations of computational capacity prevent him from making the calculations required to determine the value structure derivable from his credal state and extended value structure once the situation has even a modicum of complexity.

Serious as these two problems are they do not seem to me to present strict Bayesianism with difficulties more serious than those facing any sophisticated rival view. No matter what principles one uses to evaluate options in a decision problem, it is to be expected that there will be some class of problems for which the theory proposed will find the task of identifying solutions computationally daunting. It does not seem to me, therefore, that objections to strict Bayesianism derived from reflections on the severe demands made upon our capacities in order to make decisions in conformity with its requirements ought to be decisive against it. We do not urge modification of logic (whether it is classical or intuitionistic) merely because the injunction to believe all logical truths or to be consistent cannot be satisfied to the letter by anyone. Nor can we expect relief from our emotional infirmities, memory failures and computational limitations through an alternative to strict Bayesian doctrine. The best we can hope for is assistance from the various technologies related to information processing, from mathematicians and from psychologists, neurophysiologists and other therapists who might contribute something to our capacities to store information and make computations.

These technologies are important because they offer hope that with their assistance we may live up to the commitments we have to extended value structures and credal states by enabling us to identify these commitments as precisely as is required to determine which options among those are admissible and which are not. To do this, it is important that we have some clear idea of those normative principles of coherence and consistency which constrain the way in which credal probability judgements, extended value structures, and value structures are to be constructed. If we differ on these normative principles or ideals, we shall, obviously enough, differ to some extent on how these technologies can help us live up to our commitments (Levi, 1980a: 28–30, 88).

This consideration accentuates what, in my judgement, is the soft underbelly of strict Bayesian doctrine. That approach requires that expected value structures and, hence, the value structures determined from them (the VE-structures) be free of cardinal conflict. Strict Bayesians represent in an extreme and relatively precise form a point of view which, as I have argued already, is shared by utilitarians, Kantians, and various types of moral relativists and skeptics. What is different about the Bayesians is that they focus on the question of uncertainty. Moral theorists tend to ignore this matter. In any case, the denial of the rationality of decision making under unresolved conflict has awkward implications for conceptions of credal probability judgement akin to those confronted by moral theory.

Recall that the need to recognize decision making under unresolved conflict as legitimate was grounded in the Deweyite view that we often do not know what we ought to do, all things considered, and that such ignorance is a proper occasion for inquiry, just as it is in science. Since we often must choose before coming to a satisfactory resoluton and since resolving conflict without warrant through inquiry is arbitrary, we should conclude that it is often reasonable to choose without being in the position to claim that what is chosen is for the best relative to a value structure free, at least, of ordinal conflict.

The picture painted by those who reject this view of the matter denies a role to moral inquiry. Either we can resolve moral dilemmas before the moment of choice by invoking higher order principles or, if not these, moral intuitions, or at the moment of choice we can resolve the conflict by our choice – i.e., without justification. A parallel dialectic is operative when we turn to a consideration of credal probability judgement.

Necessitarians (like R. Carnap and H. Jeffreys) seek to identify principles of inductive rationality or "logic" so powerful that any agent is constrained by these principles and the information available to him to make numerically definite credal probability judgements of just one sort.

Personalists (like B. de Finetti and L. J. Savage) doubt that principles of rationality so powerful as this can be obtained. Reason cannot confine an ideally rational agent to numerically definite credal probability judgements relative to the information available to him. There are many numerically definite credal states allowed by reason and the available information.

Intemperate personalists contend that a rational agent is free to select any numerically definite credal state relative to his knowledge which meets the very weak demands on rational credal probability judgement which may be sustained. But a rational agent is prohibited from endorsing a credal state recognizing more than one credal probability function as permissible. Numerical indeterminacy is forbidden.

Tempered personalists (A. Shimony is an example) are prepared to let contextual considerations other than the available knowledge constrain how probability judgements are to be made. But the extra constraints beyond the context-independent principles of probabilistic rationality which can be used are rarely powerful enough to single out a unique probability function as mandatory in the given context. Hence, tempered personalists, like intemperate personalists, insist that the agent, to be rational, should choose arbitrarily from the many functions which survive criticism one which is to serve as his uniquely permissible credal probability function.

The participants in this debate refuse to entertain as alternatives to this necessitarianism or personalism of the strict Bayesian variety a point of view according to which one should refuse to restrict oneself to numerically definite probability judgements when the grounds for moving to such a position do not warrant favoring one way of making such judgements rather than another.

Strict Bayesian necessitarians deny the existence of predicaments where there is no warrant for numerically definite probability judgements according to a specific function. Such views parallel moral theories which insist that there is a principled way of resolving every moral dilemma. Personalists admit, indeed insist, that such predicaments do obtain, but they also contend that to be rational one should be committed to a numerically definite credal state. In effect, to be rational one is obliged to choose one from a large menu of numerically definite probability functions to represent one's credal state without having any reason to do so and even though the choice can make a considerable difference as to how one should choose among feasible options. To be sure, personalist Bayesians urge people of good sense to think as hard as they can before fixing on credal probability judgements – presumably so as to be sure that they are thinking as coherently as is feasible and that the coherent view they come up with is as accurate a reflection of their true convictions as they can mus-

ter. But no matter how much rhetoric is employed to cover up the
fact, strict Bayesians are obliged to make a virtue out of a very de-
plorable necessity.

Necessitarians pursue the quixotic task of constructing principles of
insufficient reason with considerable mathematical ingenuity – an
ingenuity which is typically frustrated by inconsistency and, even when
it seems to have escaped the toils of inconsistency, is vulnerable to
the charge of arbitrariness it seeks to avoid.[6]

Personalists recognize the troubles necessitarians face. Still they insist that rational agents maximize expected utility where the expected value structure is free of cardinal conflict. At the moment of
choice, one is committed willy-nilly to numerically definite probability judgements, for if one is rational, one must choose for the best,
all things considered. Just as for Sartre, our choices both resolve and
manifest the resolution of our conflicts. For Sartre, the conflicts resolved are in our value commitments; for the strict Bayesian personalist, the conflicts may be in our credal states. We must have numerically definite credal probability judgements because we must choose
and our choices reveal our expectations.

Personalists often seek to soften the impact of the arbitrariness they
endorse as a hallmark of rationality by insisting that, given enough
evidence, strict Bayesians would modify their probability judgements, which would bring them into approximate agreement with
other agents who shared their evidence but not their initial probability judgements (see, e.g., Savage, 1967: 597).

Attention to the fine print of this argument makes it apparent that
this holds only if the decision maker's probability judgements satisfy
some rather strong requirements in addition to the weak conditions
of coherence which personalists require for rationality. Perhaps it is
a mark of good sense to observe these conditions under appropriate
circumstances, but strict Bayesians of the personalist variety have no
principled way to explain why this should be so.

The troubles with personalism are not removed by a reversion to
strict Bayesian necessitarianism. Personalists are right in claiming that
the context-independent constraints on credal probability judgement
are relatively weak "coherence" requirements. In addition to such weak
constraints, methods for fixing credal probability judgements relative to bodies of knowledge (confirmational commitments in the terminology of The Enterprise of Knowledge) depend not only on the
available evidence but on other aspects of the agent's "situation", such
as the problems he is facing, the research programs he embraces and
the like. To this extent, tempered personalists like Shimony seem to
be on the right track. But even such "contextualists" should recognize the difference between situations where the context fails to sin-

gle out a numerically definite probability function and situations where it does. In the former type of case, one is obligated and not merely permitted, to suspend judgement – i.e., to refuse to commit oneself to one method of framing probability judgements rather than another. Strict Bayesians of personalist persuasion, whether they are intemperate or tempered, refuse to countenance this possibility. One may be in doubt as to which of several probability functions represents one's strictly Bayesian credal state, but one cannot be in a credal state which recognizes several different probability functions to be permissible to use in determining ev-functions. One must be committed, whether one knows it or not, to a definite credal probability function even though neither inductive logic nor the relevant contextual features furnish any reason for adopting that function rather than another.

This implication of strict Bayesian personalism is sufficiently disturbing to afford a strong case for giving a hearing to alternatives which do not presuppose that rational agents must be so opinionated as to have numerically definite credal probability judgements when they make decisions. The suggestion that rational agents may make decisions even when their states of credal probability judgement suffer from cardinal and even ordinal conflict is intended to represent just such an alternative. When there is no warrant for favoring one credal distribution over another, neither distribution should be ruled out as impermissible for use in calculating expected values. In this sense, the agent should remain in suspense among the alternative distributions as well as all other distributions which represent potential resolutions of the conflict between these alternatives.

The approach I am advocating does not reject all ingredients of the strict Bayesian view. To the contrary, it prides itself on its readiness to acknowledge strict Bayesian doctrine as applicable in an important special class of cases where both the agent's extended value structure and his credal state are free of cardinal conflict.

The idea is to modify the strict Bayesian approach along the lines already suggested earlier in discussing cardinal and ordinal conflict in value structures. An extended value structure is conflicted if the set of ev-functions $EV(O)$ defined over O is not unique up to a positive affine transformation. Similarly, the credal state B suffers from conflict if more than one credal probability function $Q(x/y)$ is permissible in that credal state. (Just as the extended value structure is convex, so should the credal state be.)

Having allowed for conflict of both kinds, we may still be loyal to this much of Bayesian doctrine. Given each permissible ev-function and each permissible Q-function, an expected value function (e-function) is determined and is to count as permissible in $E(U)$. The set of all such e-functions constitute the expected value structure and, hence, the VE-structure. The set of E-admissible (VE-admissible) options can be identified and choice restricted to these. In effect, they are the options in U which are optimal according to some permissible e-function.

To follow this approach is to give priority to considerations of expected value just as strict Bayesians do. However, it acknowledges that considerations of expected utility often fail to render determinate verdicts due to the existence of conflicts in values and probabilistic belief – conflicts which strict Bayesians wrongly and, indeed, absurdly condemn as manifestations of irrationality.

7.6 Upper and lower betting quotients

Suppose $P*$ is such that an agent regards accepting a gamble on g whereby he receives $S - P$ if g is true and $-P$ if g is false (S positive) as uniquely V-admissible in a pairwise choice between the gamble and neither gaining nor losing provided that P is less than $P*$ and regards refusing the gamble as uniquely admissible if P is greater than $P*$. Let us then consider gambles on g with "stakes" $-S$ (where S is the same as before) and determine the value $P**$ such that the agent regards accepting a gamble on g whereby he receives $-S + P$ if g is true and P if g is false as uniquely admissible in a pairwise choice with the option of refusing the gamble provided that P is greater than $P**$ and regards refusing the gamble as uniquely admissible if P is less than $P*$. $P*/S$ will be called the *lower betting quotient* for g and $P**/S$ the *upper betting quotient*.

Strict Bayesian doctrine requires that $P*/S = P**/S$ and that the common value be the degree of credal probability for g. This common betting quotient is sometimes called the betting quotient or betting rate which the agent regards as fair. That such a betting quotient must exist according to strict Bayesian principles follows from the fact that the expected value of a gamble on g with stake S and price $P*$ should be equal to the expected value of refusing the gamble, so $r(S - P*) - (1 - r)P*$ (where r is the credal probability assigned g) should equal 0. Hence, $P*/S$ should equal r. By similar reasoning for gambles with negative stake $-S$ and price $-P**$ (inducement $P**$), $P**/S$ should also equal r. The crucial assumption here is that the agent has a numerically definite credal probability for g. Given that the extended value structure is adequately represented by the numerical payoffs specified and, hence, is free of conflict, the expected value structure is free of conflict and, hence, entitles us to reason in the manner just indicated.

Suppose, however, that more than one credal distribution over g

and $\sim g$ is permissible. For example, g might be the claim that the next ball drawn from a given urn will be black. It might be known that between 40 and 60% of balls in the urn are black and the next ball is to be drawn at random. Some agents might be prepared to regard every credal probability assignment to g between .4 and .6 as permissible. More generally, g may receive a lower credal probability of r^* and an upper credal probability r^{**}.

If the stakes S are positive, then gambles with prices less than $P' = Sr^*$ will be uniquely E-admissible (VE-admissible) and, hence, uniquely admissible. When the price is greater than $P'' = Sr^{**}$, refusing the gamble will be uniquely E-admissible. For prices from P' to P'' inclusive, both accepting and refusing the gamble will be E-admissible (VE-admissible) in pairwise choices.

If we took the position that the condition of E-admissibility – i.e., VE-admissibility – is necessary and sufficient for V-admissibility, then as long as we did not invoke secondary value commitments and extended value structures, we would have to conclude that both accepting and rejecting the gamble were not only V-admissible but admissible. As a consequence, we would be compelled to deny not only the existence of a fair betting quotient but the existence of upper and lower betting quotients as well. Observe that P' is not a lower betting quotient because it is not the case that for prices greater than P and positive stakes, refusing the gamble is uniquely admissible or even V-admissible – as long as VE-admissibility is equivalent to V-admissibility. Similar remarks apply to P''.

Many agents, however, supplement the criterion of E-admissibility by an appeal to other considerations such as security when considerations of expected utility fail to render a verdict. Indeed, when the price for a gamble on g with positive stake S is greater than P' and less than P'', refusing the gamble maximizes the security level among the two E-admissible options and, hence, is S-admissible among the E-admissible options. Those who favor security as a secondary criterion of admissibility relative to the given first-level extended value structure will then treat P' as a price P^* such that P^*/S becomes a lower betting quotient equal to r^* (and P'' as a price P^{**} such that P^{**}/S becomes an upper betting quotient equal to r^{**}).

Thus, it is sensible to suppose that an agent who regards considerations of expected value as ground-level tests of admissibility so that all admissible options must be E-admissible, and who, in addition, has upper and lower betting quotients for g, is committed to appealing to considerations of security when considerations of expected value no longer can arbitrate.

One important qualification should be made concerning this way of reasoning. Consider the following example. An agent is confronted with the urn described before. He knows that either 40% of the balls are black ($h_{.4}$) or 60% are black ($h_{.6}$), but he does not know which. A ball is to be selected at random. He is compelled to choose between the following two options:

A_1: If a black is drawn (g), the agent loses 5 units of value. If a black is not drawn ($\sim g$), he wins 5 units.

A_2: If $h_{.6}$ is true, the agent receives 2 units of value. Otherwise he loses 2 units of value.

Table 1 gives the payoffs:

Table 1

	$h_{.6}$ & g	$h_{.6}$ & $\sim g$	$h_{.4}$ & g	$h_{.4}$ & $\sim g$
A_1	-5	5	-5	5
A_2	2	2	-2	-2

Under the circumstances, it is sensible to require that $Q(g/h_{.6}) = Q(\sim g/h_{.4}) = 0.6$ and that $Q(g/h_{.4}) = Q(\sim g/h_{.6}) = 0.4$ for all permissible credal probability distributions in the agent's credal state.[7]

The credal state for $h_{.6}$ is not given. For illustrative purposes, let it permit all real values between 0.1 and 0.9. Armed with this information, we can compute expected values for the two options conditional on $h_{.6}$ and $h_{.4}$ respectively (table 2).

Table 2

	$h_{.6}$	$h_{.4}$
A_1	-1	1
A_2	2	-2

The expected value of A_1 for some permissible value $Q(h_{.6}) = x$ becomes $-x + (1 - x) = 1 - 2x$. The expected value of A_2 becomes $2x - 2(1 - x) = 4x - 2$. For values of x less than 0.5, A_1 bears higher expected value than A_2, and for values of x greater than 0.5, A_2 beats A_1. Given that values of x are permitted in both ranges, both options are E-admissible.

Suppose the agent turns to considerations of security to help render a verdict as to what he should do given that considerations of expected utility do not help. There are at least two ways in which this might be done, and they lead to different verdicts.

Think of the payoffs laid out in table 1 as distinct "consequences". The worst possible case for option A_1 yields payoff -5. The worst possible case for option A_2 yields payoff -2. It appears that A_2 should be chosen.

However, this same decision problem may be viewed in a different light. In evaluating E-admissible options with respect to security, the agent could focus on the consequences of choosing A_i when $h_{.6}$ is true and it is false. The values of these consequences are given in table 2. Relative to the representation given in table 2, the security level for option A_1 is better than that for A_2. Thus, considerations of security may be made to favor A_2 or to favor A_1 relative to the same extended value structure – depending on how one identifies consequences of options for the purpose of defining security levels or worst possible cases.

Appeal to security is at the core of the so-called minimax or maximin principle of rational choice. According to the version of minimax theory explored by A. Wald (1950: ch. 1), the set of options admissible in a given decision problem consists of all those *feasible* options which maximize security. This stands in contrast to the approach favored here where the injunction is to maximize security among all *E-admissible* options. In special cases (like the example under consideration) the verdicts rendered by the two approaches coincide. But when the E-admissible options are a proper subset of the admissible options, they need not do so. This difference between Wald's use of minimax and the approach favored here is a crucial one. But in the present context, the difference is not salient. What matters more is that Wald examined only one way of identifying security levels – illustrated in our example by the method of fixing security grounded on table 2.

The hypothesis $h_{.6}$ specifies that a ball be selected at random from an urn with 60 black balls and 40 white. As already emphasized, choosing A_1 when that experiment is performed may be viewed as yielding one of two possible outcomes (payoffs), as in table 1. Or the two possible outcomes may be grouped together and their disjunction viewed as expressing a single outcome, as in table 2. Since the hypothesis $h_{.6}$ stipulates a definite value for an objective or statistical probability (chance), the credal probabilities used to compute the expected value of A_1 conditional on $h_{.6}$ are grounded on the hypothetical assumption of a statistical or chance hypothesis – namely, $h_{.6}$. In cases like this, Wald and many others following him appeared to think that the expected value of A_1 conditional on $h_{.6}$ (or the expected loss conditional on $h_{.6}$ or the risk incurred by choosing A_1 when $h_{.6}$) can be calculated from the original extended value structure and objective probabilities and, hence, is qualified to be considered as a single payoff for the purpose of determining security levels. Reasoning in this way leads to the use of table 2 rather than table 1 for the fixing of security levels.

This approach to fixing security levels is the one generally understood by statisticians and decision theorists when speaking of minimax risk or maximin theories of decision making. We may wonder, however, why fixing security levels in this particular manner is a necessary condition for the rational use of security levels either in minimax theory or as a secondary principle when considerations of expected value fail to render a verdict.

In my judgement, an account of rational choice ought not to mandate a definite procedure for this purpose. Just as value commitments which determine the extended value structure are exogenous conditions controlling how the principles of choice determine which options are admissible, so too the selection of a procedure for fixing security levels is an expression of other value commitments. This does not mean that such selections are beyond critical review and control. That is no more the case when we review the choice of security levels than it is when we consider the adoption of an extended value structure. In both cases, the controversy concerns the choice of some kind of value commitment. This will entail the kind of inquiry Dewey envisaged as necessary for struggle of the second kind. There is no context-independent principle, I think, which mandates a way to fix security levels suitable for all occasions (see Levi, 1980a: 156–162).

If the adoption of a method for fixing security levels is similar to the adoption of a value commitment, provision is made for the possibility that an agent might fix security levels in a vacuous way – i.e., by grouping together all possible consequences of implementing some given option and taking the value assigned to that consequence as the security level for that option. When this approach is adopted, what may be called the security value structure $VS(U)$ for the options in U becomes identical with the expected value structure $VE(U)$ and the S-admissible options must coincide with the E-admissible options. Thus, an agent's failure to invoke any criterion over and above E-admissibility is a special case in which S-admissibility is invoked in a vacuous manner.

Those who think that E-admissibility ought to be necessary and sufficient for admissibility are best understood as proponents of certain kinds of values – i.e., certain kinds of attitudes towards security. But those who might want to appeal to nonvacuous tests of S-admissibility are also advocates of certain, rather different attitudes towards security. To insist on invoking principles of rational choice to mandate one point of view towards security is to make principles of rational or coherent decision making arbitrate concerning matters which ought properly to be left to more substantive inquiries into values.

This claim cuts two ways: It argues against those who favor as a matter of rational principle that security be fixed in the manner favored by Wald – i.e., by means of "risk" functions. It also argues against those who would insist that as a matter of rational principle E-admissibility be not only necessary but sufficient for V-admissibility.[8] Both positions confuse issues pertaining to the selection and modification of value commitments with questions of general principles of rational choice which are taken to hold independent of context and the particular values to which the agent is committed. For example, the approach to detecting upper and lower credal probabilities through determination of upper and lower betting quotients which was proposed by C. A. B. Smith[9] must be condemned as irrational by those who think E-admissibility is sufficient for admissibility.

It is one thing to insist that appeal to nondegenerate ways of fixing security levels is mandatory as a matter of rational principle. It is quite another to insist that it not be prohibited as a matter of rational principle. That is all my position amounts to.

To be sure, the position I am taking appears to presuppose a contrast between prescriptive principles of rationality and principles which characterize substantive value commitments. And I confess that I am not able to provide any precise demarcation between the two types of prescriptive principles. I regard principles of rationality as relatively fixed, as applicable to all agents no matter how widely their values otherwise vary and as regulating the coherence of their deliberations and valuations. To come to grips with the distinction more precisely requires construction of the norms or prescriptions which constitute principles of rationality. Although I favor supplementing considerations of expected value (E-admissibility) with appeals to security, it seems to me that we ought to recognize many ways in which such appeals might be made by intelligent people, including a refusal to make any such appeal. Consequently I have sought to formulate context independent principles of VS-admissibility in a manner which is neutral with respect to this issue recognizing many different ways of responding to considerations of security to be coherent.

Those who reject this view by insisting that E-admissibility is sufficient for admissibility are obligated to claim that the practices which Smith considers violate canons of rationality. By contending that it is irrational to adopt upper and lower quotients for propositions, they overextend themselves. Smith's conception of betting behavior is far from being incoherent.

This modest appeal to the betting behavior characterized by Smith offers support for the view that commitment to upper and lower betting quotients equal to the upper and lower credal probabilities is not irrational. In the same spirit, we may appeal to some other kinds of responses to predicaments of rational choice which must be ruled out as unacceptable by those who insist that E-admissibility is sufficient for rationality.

7.7 Ellsberg's problem

In an important and provocative paper, D. Ellsberg invited consideration of the following pair of decision problems (Ellsberg, 1951: 653–656):

You are told that an urn contains 30 red balls and 60 balls which are either black or yellow in some unspecified proportion. In problem A, you are offered two options, I and II, and in problem B, you are also offered two options, III and IV. It is important to understand that you are not being offered the two problems jointly so that you could regard the pair of problems as a single decision problem with four feasible options ⟨I,III⟩, ⟨I,IV⟩, ⟨II,III⟩ and ⟨II,IV⟩. Rather you are to consider how you would choose in two distinct hypothetical situations where there are only two options feasible apiece. The payoffs in the two-choice situations are given as follows:

Problem A

	30	60	
	Red	Black	Yellow
I	$100	$0	$0
II	$0	$100	$0

Problem B

	30	60	
	Red	Black	Yellow
III	$100	$0	$100
IV	$0	$100	$100

Notice that if a yellow is drawn, the payoff differs in problems A and B. Yet in both problems the payoffs are the same for yellow regardless of which option is chosen. Otherwise the payoffs in problems A and B are identical. Under these circumstances, it seems that if one weakly prefers I over II (II over I) in problem A, one should weakly prefer III over IV (IV over III) in problem B. This is the main import of the sure-thing principle formulated by L. J. Savage (1954: 22–23).

Ellsberg reported that many of those he asked about these problems were prepared to choose I over II and IV over III. Ellsberg did not say so, but it is clear that these respondents regarded I as uniquely admissible in problem A and IV as uniquely admissible in problem B. Ellsberg thought that this response revealed violation of the sure-thing principle. Those who think that Ellsberg is right are faced with two alternatives: One might insist that the choices reported by Ellsberg are well within the bounds of rationality and conclude that we ought to abandon the sure-thing principle as a constraint on rationality. However, the sure-thing principle may appear so compelling that it will seem preferable to regard the responses reported by Ellsberg as manifestations of confusion to be corrected by careful attention to rational principle.

In my judgement, the sure-thing principle ought to be retained as a principle of rationality, and at the same time, I think the acceptability of the responses reported by Ellsberg may also be recognized. What we should do is question the assumption that when someone declares a choice of I in problem A he or she is revealing a strict preference for I over II and that a choice of IV over III in problem B reveals a preference for IV over III. Thus, I am prepared to insist that one need not abandon the sure-thing principle in order to defend the rational virtue of the respondents to Ellsberg's problem. Counter to the received view, we have a third alternative to abandoning the sure-thing principle or denying the propriety of the dominant response to the Ellsberg problem.

Under the specifications of the two problems, the agent knows that the statistical probability or chance of the ball selected on a random draw being a red is $1/3$. Given this knowledge and the absence of other knowledge about the draw which would undermine the relevance of this statistical probability for determining the agent's degree of belief that the ball drawn on the specific occasion being contemplated is red, the agent is justified in assigning a credal probability of $1/3$ to the hypothesis that on the particular draw under consideration, the ball drawn is red. Thus, the agent's credal probability assignment that a red is drawn on the particular occasion he faces is grounded in knowledge of chance or statistical probability.

In contrast, the agent does not know the objective probability or chance of obtaining a black on a random selection except that the objective probability is representable by $x = i/90$, where i is an integer from 1 to 60. (The chance of a yellow is, of course, $2/3 - x$.)

Now the agent could entertainably assign a numerically definite credal probability to the hypothesis that on the particular draw which is the object of interest the ball selected is black. But he cannot justify that assignment by appealing to his knowledge of the chances of obtaining a black on a random selection – except insofar as he can claim, with justification, that this credal probability should be restricted to values between 0 and 2/3. Even so, strict Bayesians insist that the agent, to be rational, must be committed to a definite value of x, and how he chooses in both problems A and B depends on how he calculates expected value for the options A and B relative to that same value for x.

On the assumption that the agent facing problems A and B (at least hypothetically) cares only for money in these contexts and given, under this assumption, that there are only two distinct evaluations of the consequences of feasible options – to wit, the value of receiving $100 and the value of receiving $0 – we can represent the extended value structures of both problems by the set of all positive affine transformations of a v-function assigning $100 the value 1 and $0 the value 0. Using this v-function and assuming, as strict Bayesians do, that the agent is committed to a specific credal probability x that a black is drawn (in the specific random draw which is at the focus of the agent's attention), the expected value of each of the four options is given as follows: $ev(I) = 1/3$, $ev(II) = x$, $ev(III) = 1 - x$ and $ev(IV) = 2/3$.

Observe that $ev(III) = ev(I) + 2/3 - x$ and $ev(IV) = ev(II) - 2/3 - x$. Obviously I will be weakly preferred to II if and only if III is weakly preferred to IV, as the sure-thing principle requires. Clearly if I is uniquely E-admissible in problem A, then III must be uniquely E-admissible in problem B. Hence, for those strict Bayesians who think that E-admissibility is necessary and sufficient for admissibility, someone who regards I as uniquely admissible in problem A and IV as uniquely admissible in problem B is deviating from acceptable standards of rational deliberation.

Of course, for a strict Bayesian who assigns the hypothesis that black is selected the credal probability 1/3 (which equals the credal probability that red is selected and, hence, that a yellow is selected as well), both I and II are E-admissible in problem A and both III and IV are E-admissible in problem B. If the strict Bayesian who makes this judgement is prepared to invoke considerations of security to break ties, one can appeal to security in such a way as to make I uniquely S-admissible in problem A and IV uniquely S-admissible in problem B. I shall elaborate on the argument for this shortly.

Thus, even a strict Bayesian can identify a special case where the typical response to Ellsberg's problem is a reasonable one and where *there is no violation of the sure-thing principle*. The reason the sure-thing principle remains inviolate is that in the special case we have just noted options I and II are equal in expected value in problem A and III and IV are equal in expected utility in problem B. If the reference to weak preference in the formulation of the sure-thing principle concerns preference with respect to expected value, then the choices Ellsberg reports do not violate the sure-thing principle.

Of course, if preference is defined in terms of basic revealed preference (see 6.6) where revelation is relative to S-admissibility along the lines which yield the typical response to the Ellsberg problem, the sure-thing principle is violated. But no strict Bayesian should want to regard violation of the sure-thing principle in this sense as untenable. When there are ties in expected utility, some strict Bayesians may say that the agent is free to choose one way or the other – all options optimal with respect to expected value are admissible. Others may recognize the legitimacy of invoking considerations of security as additional values in a manner which simulates the behavior reported by Ellsberg. In neither case is a rational agent prohibited from choosing I in problem A and IV in problem B.

The trouble with this strict Bayesian treatment of the Ellsberg problem is that it requires that the value of the personal credal probability x be exactly $1/3$. But since the agent does not know the objective statistical probability or chance of obtaining a black in a random selection from the urn (because he does not know the proportion of black balls in the urn), the selection of this value for x will appear to many to be arbitrary. Only a slavish devotee of the principle of insufficient reason could think otherwise.

In any case, if we modify the Ellsberg problem by specifying that the number of reds in the urn is 32 whereas the number of blacks and yellows is 58, it still seems acceptable for an agent to regard I as uniquely admissible in problem A and IV in problem B. The strict Bayesian rationale would then require that the credal probability that a black is selected be equal to the credal probability that a red is selected, which equals $16/45$. But why, given his ignorance, would the agent regard the selection of a red more likely than the selection of a yellow?

Still, the strict Bayesian rationale for the typical response to Ellsberg which has just been rehearsed does contain an important insight. If both options are E-admissible in each of the problems and considerations of security legislate in favor of I in problem A and IV in problem B, there is no violation of the sure-thing principle with respect to preferences defined relative to expected value, and the typical response reported by Ellsberg is vindicated.

This possibility is available to us if we abandon strict Bayesianism and allow credal states to go indeterminate. In the Ellsberg problem, it is surely not unreasonable for an agent to refuse to assign a numerically definite credal probability to the hypothesis that the ball selected is black. In his ignorance concerning the composition of the urn, he might be prepared to recognize a range of values as permissible. To be sure, the range is restricted to the interval from o to 2/3 since the hypothesis that a red is drawn bears credal probability 1/3, but a reasonable agent could endorse any subinterval of that range and might fairly be expected to endorse a rather broad one. This would have the effect of rendering both I and II E-admissible in problem A and III and IV jointly E-admissible in problem B. Option I is not weakly preferred to II in problem A with respect to expected value. The expected value structure $E(U)$ does not induce a categorical preference relation between I and II – i.e., they are noncomparable with respect to this value structure. The same is true regarding III and IV in problem B. Hence, the sure-thing principle is vacuously satisfied when weak preference is with respect to expected value (which, please remember, is the respect which, strict Bayesians and I agree, is the one relative to which the sure thing principle ought to apply). There is then room for invoking considerations of security without violating the sure-thing principle.

The next thing to consider is whether security can be invoked to secure the response Ellsberg reports as the predominant one. Ellsberg argued that by invoking minimax principles one cannot rationalize the predominant responses in problems A and B. If one looks at the payoff matrixes given above, the security level is o for each of the options so that considerations of security cannot be the basis for deciding between I and II in A or III and IV in B (Ellsberg, 1951: 656).

If one identifies consequences of the feasible options in the two problems in the manner indicated in these matrices, it is true that when both options are E-admissible in both problems, both options are also S-admissible and, hence, admissible. However, there is another way of determining the security levels available. Indeed, it is the method routinely used by A. Wald and others who have deployed minimax criteria.

Recall that the agent does not know what the composition of the urn is. In fact, 61 compositions of the urn are seriously possible relative to what the decision maker knows. Let h_i be the hypothesis that i of the 90 balls in the urn are black where i can take values from o to 60. The chance x_i of obtaining a black given that h_i is true is equal to $i/90$. Hence, for the agent, the conditional credal probability of obtaining a black given the truth of h_i is equal to x_i. We may, therefore, compute for each of the options in each of the two problems its expected value conditional on h_i for each i from o to 60. In this way we identify 61 possible outcomes with each option rather than 3 and determine security levels relative to this method of characterizing possible outcomes. For each h_i, the expected values are 1/3 for I, $i/90$ for II, $1 - i/90$ for III and 2/3 for IV.

Rewriting the payoff matrix in this fashion makes no difference to the assessment of the options with respect to expected value. Because we have no basis for assigning a definite credal distribution to the h_i's on knowledge of chance, we may recognize many credal distributions over these hypotheses as permissible. This will lead to the verdict with respect to expected value described before: Both I and II are E-admissible in A, and III and IV are E-admissible in B.

What comes out differently is the way we assess security. The security level for option I is $1/3$ since this value is constant for all h_i. The security level for II is 0, for given h_0, the expected value of II is 0. The minimax (or maximin) solution for problem A is I according to this analysis. Turning now to problem B, the maximum security level is $1/3$ for III and $2/3$ for IV; IV is the maximin solution. Thus, if we fix security levels in the manner favored by Wald and most authors who have exploited minimax principles, I is to be recommended in problem A and IV in problem B.

When Ellsberg reported that many people he interrogated, including some sophisticated about issues in decision theory, responded by declaring for I in problem A and IV in problem B, he observed that many of these respondents were prepared to stick with their answers even after some consideration (Ellsberg, 1951: 655–656). This is understandable. There is no pressure to reconsider due to questions of coherence, consistency or, if one likes, rationality. In particular, there is no reason to do so on the grounds that the sure-thing principle has been violated.

Why did Ellsberg and many other serious authors think otherwise? The choices described appear to violate the sure-thing principle because the choices recommended by the respondents are taken to reveal their preferences in the sense relevant to applying the sure-thing principle. I have already shown that even strict Bayesians need not take that view, but as a matter of fact, it appears that they customarily do. So, in fact, have critics of the Bayesian approach like Ellsberg himself. Thus, it comes about that both sides of the debate about the merits of Bayesianism have endorsed the assumption that the value structure over the feasible options in a decision problem ought to be free, at the very least, from ordinal conflict. Once one takes this position, one is faced with the alternatives of dismissing the responses of agents to the Ellsberg problem as lapses from rationality and of modifying the sure-thing principle.

Both views seem untenable. It ought to be noncontroversial that the sure-thing principle applies when preference is with respect to expected value (i.e., is categorical preference relative to an expected value structure). At the same time, the typical responses to the Ellsberg problem, though not obligatory for all rational agents, are surely allowed as reasonable responses. I conclude, from this, that we ought to give up the requirement that credal states be free of cardinal conflict and expected value structures free of ordinal conflict. My argument does not amount to a demonstration. I have no such demonstration. But the possibility of deploying the approach to decision making I favor in making sense of responses to the Ellsberg problem supplements other considerations arguing in favor of abandoning strict Bayesianism and allowing for unresolved conflict.

Someone may object that the agent who chooses I in problem A is proceeding as if his degree of belief or credal probability that the ball selected is black is less than 1/3, whereas in choosing IV in problem B, he is proceeding as if his credal probability for black is greater than 1/3. Being guided by appeals to security leads to an inconsistency or, at least, inconstancy in credal probability judgement.

This outlook lurks behind the widely held view that minimax principles are expressions of an unwarranted pessimism or paranoia. More accurately, such an idea lurks behind the objection that minimax is a form of negative wishful thinking. Instead of adjusting degrees of belief or credal probability so as to give higher probability to better prospects, the minimaxer adjusts credal probabilities in favor of worse prospects. He keeps on the gloomy rather than the sunny side of life. From the point of view of a Bayesian, both the optimistic and pessimistic views are objectionable because they let wishes and value commitments determine credal probabilities of prospects.

Thus, because the security level of IV is greater than the security level of III in problem B, whereas the security level of I is greater than the security level of II in problem A, the degree of credence assigned the prospect of a black is less than 1/3 in problem A and greater than 1/3 in problem B. In shifting from problem A to problem B, the agent is shifting his credal probabilities due entirely to a difference in the payoff matrix.

This objection to the use of considerations of security does not apply to the position I have been advocating. In recognizing I as uniquely admissible in problem A, the agent is not acting as if the credal probability that black is selected is less than 1/3 – at least not necessarily. He could be acting as if his credal state for black being selected were indeterminate. Indeed, if we suppose that the agent does not alter his belief states without careful consideration, the fact that the agent recommends IV rather than III in problem B drives us to the conclusion that the agent's credal state is indeterminate. In both problem A and problem B, the agent chooses the option with the higher security among those options not ruled out by considerations of expected value. If two or more options are E-admissible, then either they bear the same expected value and invoking considerations of security does not imply that the option bearing higher security is better in expected value or the two options are noncomparable and appealing to security does not reveal the option bearing higher security to be better than the other option with respect to expected value. Appealing to considerations of security begins only when considerations of expected value cannot render a verdict. For that reason, it is a mistake to conclude that the appeal to minimax presupposes a hostile nature, a pessimistic or paranoid attitude or the like. The appeals to security are made precisely in those situations where the agent can no longer appeal to his beliefs to determine useful assessments of expected value. These appeals do not favor modification of the credal states involved – at least not by the use of minimax or maximin. Rather they seek advice when the agent's credal state is no longer useful in assessing expected value.

Care must be taken in interpreting the proposal for addressing the Ellsberg problem I am outlining. It is assumed here that the agent is offered the choice between options I and II in a context where he takes for granted that he is not being offered the choice between III and IV. In real life, no decision maker with a minimal amount of consciousness and memory can be placed in both contexts. The responses we have been considering are reactions to distinct hypothetical scenarios.

If the decision maker were offered both pairs of options simultaneously or in some temporal order and were to recognize before making any decision that this were the case, he should address both problems together. He would then be taken to have four options: Choose I and III, I and IV, II and III and II and IV. Each of the four options turns out to be E-admissible. When considerations of security are taken into account, only the choices of I and IV and II and III are admissible. Yet when the two problems are considered separately, one cannot regard B as uniquely admissible in the first problem and C as uniquely admissible in the second.

Ellsberg himself was prepared to acknowledge that a rational agent may not be in a position to rule out all but one subjective or credal probability distribution over the hypotheses that a red, black or a yellow is drawn (Ellsberg, 1951: 657–659). Unfortunately, even though he does distinguish between objective statistical probability or chance, on the one hand, and subjective credal probability, on the other, the distinction is blurred by Ellsberg's tendency to treat credal probability distributions as if they were hypotheses which were true or false so that one might intelligibly be uncertain as to their truth values.

Ellsberg manifests this tendency in the following manner. If probability distributions over the states "red is drawn", "black is drawn" and "yellow is drawn" are treated as possibly true hypotheses concerning the correct distribution, one can compute an expected value for each option conditional on each of these hypotheses. This conditional expected value corresponds to Wald's risk relative to that distribution.

Not only does Ellsberg consider "possible" distributions (his language) in this way; he is prepared to assign "relative weights" to the alternative probability distributions "reflecting the relative support given by his information, experience and intuition to these rival hypotheses" (Ellsberg, 1951: 659). Ellsberg is able accordingly to identify two distinct ways to evaluate the feasible options: (a) by taking a weighted average of the possible distributions and using that new distribution to calculate expected values for each of the options and (b) by identifying a security level for each option in terms of the simulated risk function he constructs relative to each possible distribution.

By computing a weighted average of the possible distributions, Ellsberg proceeds as if he were regarding the possible distributions as hypotheses as to the correct statistical or objective probability distribution and assigning a credal probability distribution to these hypotheses. Yet Ellsberg seems to deny that the possible distributions are anything more than "subjective" probability distributions.[10]

To compound this confusion, Ellsberg's method (b) for evaluating options becomes a version of minimax risk along the lines of Wald and, as Ellsberg recognizes, this principle yields I in problem A and IV in problem B. Within a few pages of having denied that the minimax criterion can account for these choices, Ellsberg (without apparent awareness of the confusion he is promoting) implies the exact opposite for a procedure equivalent to Wald's minimax risk – i.e., the version of minimax standardly deployed in the literature (Ellsberg, 1951: 662).

But even if we tolerate these difficulties, we are not yet out of the woods. When discussing method (a), Ellsberg presupposes that the agent will have a numerically definite system of weights usable for computing an average probability distribution – perhaps, a uniform distribution over the "possible" distributions. In effect, these weights represent a conflict-free credal state over the rival distributions construed as statistical hypotheses. As already noted, we may derive from this distribution over the possible distributions a distribution over the hypotheses as to which color ball will be drawn.[11]

Ellsberg draws back, however, from the implications of endorsing the "average" distribution as a uniquely permissible credal distribution over the hypotheses about the color of the ball selected. He realizes that the agent could reasonably be "unsure" about maximizing expected value according to that distribution. Instead of understanding this lack of confidence as an inclination to recognize several credal distributions as permissible for use in computing expected values, he construes it as attributing weight less than 1 to the expected value of an option computed relative to the average distribution and positive weight to the security level of the option as calculated using method (b). The weight attributed to the expected value increases with the level of confidence the agent has in using the average distribution to compute expected values (Ellsberg, 1951: 664).

In all fairness to Ellsberg, he does not insist on this method of weighting expected values and security levels in evaluating feasible options. This is a proposal. But if we have difficulty with the notion of uncertainty attached to a subjective probability distribution over the hypotheses as to which color ball is drawn, these difficulties are compounded when we consider higher order uncertainties over these uncertainties.

Perhaps, however, we should overlook these abstruse conceptual difficulties and focus on the ramifications of Ellsberg's proposals for decision making. Ellsberg's idea does yield an ordering of the feasible options in both decision problems and, hence, provides for a value structure free of ordinal conflict to be used in assessing admissibility. It does so, however, in a manner which admits the rationality of choosing I in problem A and IV in problem B. As a consequence, the sure-thing principle is violated.

Of course, Ellsberg obtains this result only when the ordering induced by method (b) outweighs the one induced by (a). The idea of employing the ordering generated by (b) has been advocated by P. Gärdenfors and N.-E. Sahlin (1982a: 374–377). According to their approach, the various "possible" probability distributions over hypotheses as to the color of the ball selected are assessed with respect to "reliability". Whether this reliability is a probability is left open. In any event, distributions which are sufficiently unreliable are eliminated, and the agent is to determine for each option the lowest expected value generated by an unrejected possible probability distribution. The admissible options are those which maximize this lowest expected value. The principle recommending that lower expected values be maximized is called "gamma minimax" by J. O. Berger, who credits H. Robbins with the first explicit formulation of this idea.[12] Whatever the origins, both Ellsberg's method (b) and the proposal advanced by Gärdenfors and Sahlin relative to a set of possible probability distributions from which unreliable distributions have been eliminated are species of this gamma minimax principle. Gamma minimax does recommend option I in problem A and option IV in problem B. It does so because it ranks I over II in A and IV over III in B. As a consequence, gamma minimax leads to violations of the sure-thing principle. In contrast, the approach I favor does not rank I over II or IV over III, yet option I is uniquely admissible in A and IV in B. The same recommendations for choice are made as sanctioned by gamma minimax, but the sure-thing principle is not violated. Thus, advocates of gammma minimax are prepared to deviate from the dictates of strict Bayesian decision theory, but they are unwilling to recognize the rationality of decision making under unresolved conflict.

H. Raiffa (1961: 691) reported that when he was confronted with the Ellsberg problem and responded to it without "pencil pushing", he chose I over II and IV over III. In his own words, "I was found wanting. I was inconsistent". Of course, Raiffa was committed in advance to the conditions of consistency entailed by strict Bayesian doctrine. Even so, he did offer an argument to support his abandonment of his initial unreflective responses as misguided.

Raiffa invited consideration of a decision problem where one can choose the "mixed option" of obtaining the payoff from I if a fair coin lands heads and the payoff from IV if the coin lands tails, and one also has the mixed option of receiving the payoff from II if the coin lands heads and the payoff from III if the coin lands tails. Raiffa pointed out that regardless of the color of the ball selected from the urn, the expected value of each mixed option (where the probabilities used to compute expected values are grounded in knowledge of objective statistical probabilities) is the same as that of the other mixed option. Raiffa concluded that the two mixed options are "objectively identical" and should be ranked together of equal value (Raiffa, 1961: 694). Gamma minimaxers should concede Raiffa's point because this "objective identity" guarantees that the lower expectations of the two mixtures must be the same.

However, Raiffa argued, the first mixed option should be chosen over the second according to Ellsberg because I is preferred to II and IV to III so that the first mixed option dominates the second. Raiffa thought this result was inconsistent, but advocates of gamma minimax would deny inconsistency. By their own principles they would be compelled to admit that there is no basis for choice between the two mixed options. Given any possible distribution, the expected values of the two mixtures are the same. Hence, the lower expectations must also be equal. So they would have to be prepared to say that sometimes one is justified in concluding that even though one mixture dominates the other, the dominating mixture is not strictly preferred to the dominated mixture.

They might try to defend the admissibility of dominated options in such cases by seeking to restrict the injunction against choosing a dominated option in certain ways. The dominating mixture domi-

nates in the sense that whether the coin lands heads or tails, the lottery selected from the dominating mixture (I or IV respectively) is
rated better than the corresponding lottery (II or III) selected from
the other mixture. The gamma minimaxer must concede that such a
relation of domination obtains, for the superior rating of the outcomes of tossing the coin according to the first mixed strategy derives from appealing to the gamma minimax principle. The gamma
minimaxer can point out, however, that the relation of dominance
obtains only if we characterize the "possible consequences" of the
mixed strategies in terms of the lotteries selected as the result of the
outcome of the toss of the coin. But if the possible consequences are
characterized as the expected benefits of the two mixed strategies
conditional on the color of the ball drawn, neither option dominates
the other. And if the possible consequences are characterized in terms
of the monetary rewards received after the coin is tossed and the ball
selected from the urn, neither option is dominated. It might be suggested that it is domination in this latter sense which ought to be
avoided.

Seidenfeld has shown that this defense of gamma minimax does
not work. Imagine a shell game with two shells, the left and the right.
According to option L, the agent wins $100 if there is a peanut un-
der the left shell and $10 if the peanut is under the right shell. Ac-
cording to R, the agent wins $100 if the peanut is under the right
shell and $10 if the peanut is under the left shell. A gamma mini-
maxer should pay no more than $10 for either gamble. Consider now
a 50–50 chance of receiving L or R. The gamma minimax value for
this gamble in utility is equal to the expected utility of a 50–50 gamble for $100 or $10, and this will have a dollar value greater than
$10. Let it be $25. Consider now a choice between the following pair
of lotteries: According to lottery 1, if a fair coin lands heads up, the
agent has a choice between L and $9, and if the coin lands tails up,
the choice is between R and $9. According to gamma minimax, both
L and R are preferred to $9. Lottery 1 is equivalent to a 50–50 chance
of receiving L or R, and this has a value of $25. According to lottery
2, if the coin lands heads up, the agent has a choice between L and
$11, and if the coin lands tails up, he has a choice between R and
$11. If lottery 2 is taken, the agent will choose the money regardless
of what happens according to gamma minimax. Hence, lottery 2 is
worth $11, which is less than the value of lottery 1. However, if the
coin lands heads up, the dollar value of 1 (according to gamma minimax) is $10. That of 2 is $11. The same holds if the coin lands tails
up. If dollar values are substituted for L and R in options 1 and 2,
one will come away with less money for following option 1 than one
will if one chooses 2.

These considerations argue very strongly, I believe, against the use of gamma minimax as a principle of choice and, hence, against its use in a rationalization of the violation of the sure-thing principle in the Ellsberg problem. This does not mean, however, that Raiffa's argument supports his own view that choosing I in problem A and IV in problem B violates standards of rationality. Raiffa, like Ellsberg, takes for granted that choosing I over II in problem A reveals a preference for I over II and choosing IV over III in problem B reveals a preference for IV over III. But if the agent's credal state is sufficiently indeterminate so that both options are E-admissible in both problems and considerations of security argue for I in problem A and IV in problem B, we cannot say that the mixture of I and IV dominates the mixture of II and III in the relevant sense. There is no violation of the recommendation to avoid choosing an option dominated by another in ranking the two mixtures as both admissible in a pairwise choice while regarding I as uniquely admissible in A and IV as uniquely admissible in B.

A similar conclusion obtains when we turn to the Seidenfeld example. According to the decision criteria I have proposed, L and $10 are admissible in a choice between the two. This does not mean that they are of equal value or utility. The same holds for a choice between R and $10. Indeed, both L and $11 are E-admissible in a pairwise choice, as are R and $11. Hence, in my view, option 2 does not dominate option 1. It is possible to recommend 1 without recommending a dominated option.[13]

Of course, to obtain these results, it is necessary to abandon the idea that value structures ought to be free of ordinal conflict. Ellsberg, Raiffa, Gärdenfors and Sahlin are loath to do this. If the sole reason for giving up that requirement were in order to address the Ellsberg problem in a way which saved the rationality of the typical respondents while retaining the injunction to avoid choosing mixtures dominated by other mixtures, one might, perhaps, sympathize with their reluctance. But once we recognize that conflicts in value due to tension among value commitments and due to indeterminacy in credal probability judgements cannot always be resolved by the moment of choice without dogmatic arbitrariness, our reluctance may be overcome. The approach to the Ellsberg problem which then becomes available may appear as a welcome bonus. As we shall see, other dividends can be reaped as well.

7.8 The Allais problem

Ellsberg's problem has been diagnosed as deriving from an unresolved conflict in assessments of expected value which derive, in turn, from unresolved conflict or indeterminacy in the agent's credal state. In his long-standing and sustained effort to undermine the injunction to maximize expected utility, M. Allais advanced counterinstances to the sure-thing principle which do not appear to stem from such credal indeterminacy (Allais, 1952, 1953).

You are told that a given urn contains 10 red balls, 89 black balls and 1 yellow ball. In problem C, you are offered options V and VI. In problem D, you are offered options VII and VIII. The monetary payoffs for these options are given below:

Problem C

	10 Red	89 Black	1 Yellow
V	$1,000,000	$1,000,000	$1,000,000
VI	$5,000,000	$1,000,000	$0

Problem D

	10 Red	89 Black	1 Yellow
VII	$1,000,000	$0	$1,000,000
VIII	$5,000,000	$0	$0

Unlike the Ellsberg scenario, in these cases the proportions of balls in the urn are fully specified. On the assumption that the ball to be selected is chosen at random, the objective probabilities or chances are given, and knowledge of these chances ground the adoption of subjective probabilities equal to them. If there is unresolved conflict in the expected value structure, it should not be due to unresolved conflict in the credal state.

Even so, Allais reports (and his report has been widely corroborated)[14] that many agents (including sophisticated ones) choose option V over option VI in problem C and VIII over VII in problem D. But since the problems are identical, except for the case in which a black is drawn, where the payoff is the same for each option in each of the problems though different for the two problems, the sure-thing principle insists that if V is preferred to VI in problem C, VII should be preferred to VIII in problem D. Hence, if choice reveals preference (as Allais appears to assume), we have a violation of the sure-thing principle.

Allais takes for granted as part of his own theory of rational choice that rational agents do weakly order their options according to their preferences or values.[15] Moreover, those who report the choice of V over VI regard the former as uniquely admissible and similarly regard VIII as uniquely admissible in problem D. Hence, either the sure-thing principle is being violated or in both problems both options bear equal expected value and the tie in expected value is broken by some other consideration such as security.

Presumably the agents are not expressing indifference between V and VI or between VII and VIII. To see this, suppose that the payoff of $0 is increased to $1 in both problems. Then if V had initially been ranked together with VI in problem C, presumably the modified VI would be ranked over the modified V. And since VII is hypothesized to be equal in value to VIII, the modified VIII would be ranked over the modified VII. Yet it is doubtful that those who initially chose V over VI would shift and choose VI over V. Perhaps, however, someone should check this experimentally.

The assumption that rational agents ought to resolve conflict in their values by the moment of choice and that choice reveals at least weak preference is just as questionable in the case of the Allais problem as it is in the case of the Ellsberg problem. And this suggests a way to analyze the typical responses to the Allais problem as not exhibiting a violation of the sure-thing principle or other "independence" assumptions.

Unlike the conflict in the expected value structure generated in the Ellsberg problem, the conflict to be found in the expected value structure in the Allais problem is traceable to conflict in the extended value structure and not the credal state.

Since the time of D. Bernoulli, it has been widely maintained by economists that in typical contexts, the "marginal utility" or value of money is not, in general, linear in the amount of money gained. Thus, even if the extended value structure is such that $5 million is categorically strictly preferred to $1 million, which is preferred to $0, the difference between the value of $1 million and 0 may be greater than the difference between the value of $5 million and $1 million – even though the differences in monetary gains are the reverse of this. Bernoulli argued for the use of the logarithm of the monetary gain as the appropriate index of value – although he was quite clear that this is a psychological matter and that the principle of diminishing marginal utility in this form or any other is not applicable in all contexts.[16]

Once it is recognized that there is no form grounded in either psychological or normative principles which mandates that the utility of money increase in one way rather than another even in those cases where the marginal utility of money is decreasing, it becomes entertainable that many agents have extended value structures for problems of the sort under consideration which regard the difference between $0 and $1 million as involving a greater increment in value or utility than the difference between $1 and $5 million but are in conflict as to the value of the ratio of these differences.

Thus, the extended value structure may contain permissible *ev*-functions for which this ratio is greater than 10/1 and others for which it is less. In that case, the expected value structure would suffer from both cardinal and ordinal conflict even though the extended value structure exhibited cardinal conflict without ordinal conflict. More to the point, both options would be E-admissible in both problems C and D, and neither option would be weakly preferred to the other.

This description does not appear to be too far-fetched. How many individuals who agreed that an extra $1 million would represent a far greater increment in value to them than an extra $4 million to the first million would then be prepared to say exactly what the ratio of the first increment in value was to the second?

Assuming then that considerations of expected value fail to render a verdict, can considerations of security do so? In decision problem C, the security level of option V is superior to that of option VI when security is determined by the payoffs relative to the hypotheses as to the color of the ball selected. In problem D, however, both options share a security level of 0. Even so, there is an important respect in which they differ. Consider the "second-worst" outcome of option VII. It pays $1 million. The second-worst outcome of option VIII pays $5 million. Thus, by reiterating the appeal to security, it is possible to identify option VIII as uniquely admissible. This kind of reasoning is typical of so-called lexicographical maximin principles which recommend invoking secondary levels when primary security levels fail to render a verdict and tertiary security levels when secondary levels fail, etc.[17]

In 7.6, I argued that the application of criteria of S-admissibility depends on aspects of the agent's value commitments additional to those which constrain the value structures and extended value structures. These new aspects constrain how security levels are chosen. In extending appeals to security lexicographically, the determination of secondary, tertiary, etc., security levels are a function of value commitments. For example, in option VIII, some agents might regard the consequence of receiving $0 for drawing a black as distinct from receiving $0 for drawing a yellow. In that case, the secondary security level of that option would be $0, as would the primary security level. Since the secondary security level of option VII is $1 million, VII would be uniquely admissible – in contrast to the result of our previous analysis.

Thus, the account I am proposing does not mandate the choice of V over VI and VIII over VII except when the agent's value commitments determine his security levels in a certain manner. This series of choices is not incoherent, however, and is, above all, consistent with the sure-thing principle. Indeed, given that V is not weakly preferred to VI with respect to expected value and VIII is not weakly preferred to VII in this respect, the satisfaction of the sure-thing principle is vacuous.

In recent years, there have been several attempts besides those of Allais himself to formulate descriptive accounts of decision making under risk which can accommodate the type of responses found to prevail in Allais-type predicaments.[18] These approaches tend to have in common with Allais' own position the requirement that an agent's value structure be understood to be free of ordinal conflict even though, as far as I can see, they marshal no experimental evidence for the assumption (which is relevant given the focus of authors like Kahneman and Tversky, MacCrimmon and Larsson and Machina on the descriptive adequacy of their proposals).

I do not put forth my proposals with the objective of seeking descriptive adequacy. These proposals are frankly prescriptive. Still, there is an advantage in being able to recognize the responses of *prima facie* sophisticated agents as reasonable without straining our interpretations of their responses. If one interprets the respondents to the Allais problem (as well as to other problems of a similar character discussed in the experimental literature) along the lines I have indicated, it does appear that the evidence for violation of the sure-thing principle evaporates.[19]

Some of these approaches boast that although they entail violation of the sure-thing principle and other independence postulates, they avoid violation of requirements of stochastic dominance.[20] That they succeed, however, is doubtful, thanks to considerations drawn to my attention by T. Seidenfeld.[21]

Not only does the proposal I favor recognize the good sense of respondents giving the prevailing response to the Allais problem (as do the proposals of Allais, Kahneman and Tversky, Machina, Chew, et al.), it does so while exempting them from violations of the sure-thing principle, stochastic dominance and independence principles – which these other proposals fail to do. In addition, this proposal invokes the same general principles of choice in addressing the Allais problem as it does in addressing the Ellsberg problem. None of the authors I have cited appear to have an approach to the Ellsberg problem.

Allais, like Ellsberg, is interested in both normative and descriptive aspects of risky decision making. He objects, quite rightly, to the tendency of many orthodox Bayesians to rule out aberrant choices to which he drew attention as irrational. I sympathize with his plea for greater toleration, but in my judgement, his concern is mislocated. It is not loyalty to the sure-thing principle which ought to be questioned. To the contrary, sure-thing reasoning is quite compelling and ought to be retained – as Seidenfeld's reflections on the ramifications of abandoning it indicate. However, there is good philosophical reason for rejecting the requirement that rational agents have value structures free of ordinal conflict.

The Ellsberg problem illustrates very nicely how conflict in the credal state can generate conflict in the value structure. The Allais phenomenon illustrates how conflict in the extended value structure can do the same thing. And both phenomena illustrate how considerations of security may be invoked in risky decision making when considerations of expected value fail us.

In contrast to other proposals, mine provides a unified approach to both Ellsberg-type problems and Allais-type problems. This ought to count in favor of acknowledging the rational acceptability of forming decisions while one's value structure suffers from ordinal conflict – at least when the conflict can be resolved before choice only in an arbitrary manner.[22]

7.9 Consistency of choice

In 6.6–6.8, choice functions were constructed in terms of lexicographical V-admissibility, and it was shown how they violate properties α, β, and γ. In this chapter, we have considered a lexicographically ordered series of criteria of admissibility concerned with conflicts generated by indeterminacy in credal probability judgements. It is easy to see that choice functions generated by a criterion of VE-admissibility will violate properties β and γ when the agent's credal state is conflicted even though the extended value structure is free of all conflict. When considerations of security are then invoked through successive applications of VS-admissibility, it is to be expected that the emergent criterion of V-admissibility will violate property α for precisely the same formal reasons that were discussed in 6.6–6.8.

The phenomenon is easily illustrated. Consider an urn with 100 balls in it. Hypothesis h_1 asserts that 90 of the balls are black and the remainder white; h_2 asserts that 10 of the balls are black and the rest white. The agent is told that either h_1 or h_2 is true and that a ball is to be selected at random from the urn. He is offered the following options:

	Black	White
G_1	55	−45
G_2	−46	55
R	0	0

Assuming that the agent adopts a credal state assigning h_1 as permissible all values from .1 to .9, both G_1 and G_2 are E-admissible (VE-admissible) in a three way choice. However, in a pairwise choice between G_1 and R (G_2 and R) both G_1 (G_2) and R are E-admissible. Clearly both properties β and γ are violated. If considerations of security are invoked, G_1 becomes uniquely VS-admissible in the three-way choice, but R is uniquely VS-admissible and, hence, V-admissible in the two-way choice between G_1 and R (G_2 and R). A violation of property α results.

In spite of the advantages, therefore, authors devoted to conformity with properties α, β and γ because they are bedrock conditions of "choice consistency" will reject the account of admissible options I have developed, grounded as it is in the recognition that value structures may suffer from ordinal conflict. Such a reaction is, of course, not restricted to strict Bayesians but is expressed by critics of Bayesianism (Gärdenfors and Sahlin, 1982a). Gärdenfors and Sahlin advance a view according to which the agent should identify the smallest expected value computed by a probability which has passed a test based on an assessment of reliability and choose the feasible option for which that minimum expected value is the largest. The value structure so generated is free of ordinal conflict. It can be used to address the more elementary versions of Ellsberg's problem. Because it is free of ordinal conflict, properties α, β, and γ are all satisfied. Unfortunately for the proposal, however, the option recommended need not be an E-admissible option. Thus, in the three way choice just discussed, R would be recommended − even though R is not E-admissible. This predicament is closely related to the objectionable consequence of the use of the Gärdenfors and Sahlin ideas pointed out by Seidenfeld and discussed in 7.7. A. Wald (1950: 68) sought to bypass this problem by restricting attention to "convex" sets of options. This requirement is satisfied if the agent considers himself to have at his disposal all "mixtures" of the feasible options G_1, G_2 and R. In that case, the agent not only has the three options just cited as feasible in the three-way choice but, among many other options, the mixed strategy where G_1 is chosen with statistical probability .5 and G_2 with statistical probability .5. Moreover, this option will be VE-admissible (E-admissible), as are G_1 and G_2 but not R. We may now turn to considerations of security to narrow down the set of admissible options.

Among the many ways of fixing security levels mentioned in 7.6, the method favored by Wald was cited as frequently used. One determines the expected values of a given feasible option conditional on the truth of states of nature specifying statistical probabilities of various payoffs being made. Utilizing these expected values (or risks), one identifies a security level. If this approach to determining security levels is used, the mixed option not only will be E-admissible but will bear higher security than either G_1 or G_2.[23] Hence, neither G_1 nor G_2 is admissible in this extension of the original three-way choice. As before, R will be favored in the two-way choice between G_1 (G_2) and R even if all mixtures are included as feasible options. But as long as all sets of feasible options are "convex" in the sense that they include all mixtures of feasible options in the set as feasible, violations of properties α, β and γ will be avoided.

The obvious objection to this way of avoiding violations of α, β and γ is that there will, in general, be no guarantee that the set of feasible options will include all mixtures of feasible options and, in this way, be convex. And to impose convexity of the set of feasible options as a normative requirement of rationality on the set of feasible options is surely an unwarranted extension of the domain of prescriptive norms. We cannot legislate the domain of feasible options. But even if the set of feasible options is convex, we are not entitled to assert that security levels ought to be fixed in the way recommended by Wald.

These considerations suggest that if one admits that rational agents may make decisions without fully resolving conflicts in their value structures owing to conflict in their credal states, one should be prepared to admit the legitimacy of choice functions failing to satisfy property α. The alternatives are either to allow as admissible options policies which are not E-admissible (Bayes solutions) and face thereby the sorts of unpleasant consequences confronting the Gärdenfors–Sahlin proposal or to restrict one's attention ostrich-like to decision problems where the feasible options include all mixtures of "pure" options and security levels are fixed after the fashion of Wald.

Furthermore, we have already seen that when conflicts arise because of tension among rival value commitments, pressure to violate property α can be generated even without invoking considerations of uncertainty. The Gärdenfors–Sahlin theory does not avoid such violations of α. If these deviations from orthodoxy are acceptable, why should they be avoided in decision making under uncertainty?

Of course, I cannot demonstrate that abandoning property α is sometimes legitimate. My argument, if it shows anything at all, points to the conclusion that the merits of property α stand or fall with the cogency of allowing rational agents to make decisions without resolving conflicts in their value structures.

7.10 Conclusion

I have sought to show that conflicts in value structures are not always generated by conflicts among value commitments. Indeterminacy in credal probability judgement is another important and legitimate source. At the same time, I have sought to show that the criteria for admissibility to be deployed when we face such indeterminacy exhibit the same general kind of structure involving the use of lexicographically ordered hierarchies of value structures which I maintain are operative when considerations of uncertainty are not salient.

To illustrate the power of the mode of analysis proposed here, decision problems of the type discussed by Ellsberg and Allais were examined. It was shown that this approach offers a third alternative to the two main views of these problems. According to one of these views, the responses often elicited from experimental subjects are mistakes. We should insist on a normative decision theory which requires that value structures be free of at least ordinal conflict and which obeys the independence postulate and sure-thing principle. The second view also mandates the irrationality of ordinal conflict but abandons the sure-thing principle while seeking to retain weakened injunctions against choosing dominated options. The proposal I favor agrees with the first approach in retaining the sure-thing principle but rejects the requirement it shares with the critics of the sure-thing principle – to wit, that value structures be free of ordinal conflict. Thus, it stands opposed to the first, relatively "orthodox" view, yet it preserves the important insights of the orthodox view concerning the sure-thing principle and dominance. Moreover, it does so in a systematic manner which covers both Allais- and Ellsberg-type problems. What must be given up is the assumption that the value structures of rational agents should be free of conflict. To my way of thinking, the systematic and general way in which this third approach addresses the Allais and Ellsberg problems as well as other phenomena of so-called preference reversal affords us another powerful argument for the sometime rationality of decision making under unresolved conflict.

Another context in which value conflict arises in an interesting way is group or social decision making. The following chapters are concerned with this matter.

8

Conflict and social agency

8.1 What is an agent?

I have been arguing that decision making under unresolved conflict not only is coherent but, on some occasions, may be the rationally sensible response. Some may be prepared to concede the point when it comes to institutions or social groups. These are not, so it may be claimed, agents properly speaking and, hence, should not be expected to meet the standards of rationality personal agents should satisfy. Before turning to the role of unresolved conflict in social choice theory, we shall devote some attention to this question.

Formal analogies between criteria for rational decision making by individuals and rational group or social decision making have been evident to some authors ever since Plato exploited analogies between the organization of the soul and the state in *The Republic* while expounding his conception of justice. Nonetheless, there is a widespread reluctance to acknowledge the existence of groups and institutions as agents. This leads to some bizarre juxtapositions.

Thus, neoclassical economists are not noted for their sympathy with notions of group mind. Yet in expounding the theory of consumer demand, they often allow families to qualify as consumers. Ideally, at least, such consumers are taken to be maximizers of their preferences or valuations subject to budgetary constraints. Given the indifference maps representing the consumer's preferences and given the budgetary constraints, demand curves are derived. Such analysis applies to any consumer, including families and firms, and is not restricted to persons. Families make choices from accessible commodity bundles given budgetary constraints. They are taken to be preference maximizers like individual consumers and to have preferences representable by indifference maps. No distinction is drawn between individual and group decision making.

Not only do corporations qualify under the law to be persons; but corporations and other business firms are taken in both positive and normative theory to make decisions relative to information available to them and to be liable to criticism depending on whether the decisions are intelligent given their aims.

Thomas Hobbes, the high priest of I. Hacking's "heyday of ideas", spoke of the endowments and actions of the "sovereign" in a manner neutral with respect to the status of the sovereign as a person, parliament or citizenry. His individualism did not prevent him from discussing group agency.

The best-known contemporary effort to apply canons of rational choice to social entities is that of K. Arrow. According to Arrow, appropriate social groups are representable as seeking to maximize the welfares of their citizens. Arrow's concern and the interest of the participants in the debate which followed his justly celebrated *Social Choice and Individual Values* focused chiefly on the relations which do or should obtain between the valuations made by individual citizens, whose interests are to be promoted by society as represented by rankings of the "social states" (or social options), and the social evaluation or preference ranking as represented by another ordering of the same social states. Arrow thought his approach might apply to such social institutions as markets in which producers and consumers exchange goods, leading to social states in which goods are allocated to individuals in certain ways and committees where decisions are made according to some voting mechanism.

J. M. Buchanan takes exception to Arrow's approach:

Voting and the market, as decision making mechanisms, have evolved from, and are based upon an acceptance of the philosophy of individualism which presumes no social entity. (Buchanan, 1964: 117)

Buchanan complains because he thinks that Arrow is committed to the existence of such social entities. He bases his charge on Arrow's insistence that decision-making mechanisms such as committee voting and the market are appropriately assessed with respect to their rationality, and their rationality is judged by reference to whether they maximize social preference where such preference induces a weak ordering over the feasible states. Because Arrow flouts individualism in this way, his approach is deeply flawed from the start.

One could resist Buchanan's objection by rejecting individualism. One might insist that social groups are sometimes agents in the sense that they make choices to promote given ends and that their evaluations of options and the choices they make can be assessed for rationality. The following passage reveals, however, that Buchanan does not believe that Arrow can reject individualism and remain true to his other commitments:

Rationality or irrationality as an attribute of the social group implies the imputation to that group of an organic existence apart from that of its individual components. If the social group is so considered, questions may be raised relative to the wisdom or unwisdom of this organic being. But does not the very attempt to examine such rationality in terms of individual values introduce logical inconsistency at the outset? Can the rationality of the social organism be evaluated in accordance with any value ordering other than its own?

The whole problem seems best considered as one of the "either–or" variety. We may adopt the philosophical bases of individualism in which the individual is the only entity possessing ends or values. In this case, no question of social or collective rationality may be raised. A social value scale as such simply does not exist. Alternatively, we may adopt some variant of the organic philosophical assumptions in which the collectivity is an independent entity possessing its own value ordering. It is legitimate to test the rationality or irrationality of this entity only against this value ordering. (Buchanan, 1964: 116)

According to Buchanan, there is nothing incoherent or inconsistent in attributing "organic existence" or agency to a social group such as a corporation. Buchanan's own metaphysical predilections favor individualism. He does not acknowledge institutional agents – especially in the case of groups participating in market exchange or committee voting. But his criticism of Arrow is not directed primarily to the issue of the organic existence of social groups. His charge is that Arrow's project suffers from incoherence because "the very attempt" to examine the rationality of group decision making "in terms of individual values" introduces "logical inconsistency" at the very start.

According to Buchanan, there is nothing incoherent in attributing social preference rankings of social states to social groups. That is quite consonant with the view of social groups as having "organic existence" apart from their members. The "logical inconsistency" emerges when Arrow seeks to represent social preference as a function of the social preferences of persons for the same states. Since Arrow must do this if he is to relate his analysis to markets or committees who make decisions by voting, Arrow can apply his theory to these cases only at the cost of "logical inconsistency".

Buchanan's critique of Arrow raises two distinct issues:

1. Should we attribute rationality to social groups?

2. When we do attribute rationality to social groups, may we consistently allow social preference to be a function of individual preference?

Recall that even students of market economies attribute beliefs, desires, goals, values and choices to families, firms and, of course, goverment agencies (which are bureaus rather than bureaucrats) as well as to persons. No doubt the mechanisms whereby the decisions made by social agents are to be explained typically involve reference to the behaviors of and, indeed, sometimes the decisions of individual and other social agents. Perhaps, group choices are redescribable as complex processes involving no choices other than those of persons. Even if this is true, it need not detract from the reality of such group choices any more than the redescribability of individual choices as complex neurophysiological processes detracts from the reality of individual choices. Nor should redescribability and explainability suffice to preclude the propriety of subjecting social choice to canons of rationality any more than it should preclude the propriety of subjecting individual choice to the very same canons.

When examining the beliefs, goals, choices and other propositional attitudes of social groups, we need not be concerned at all with the underlying mechanisms any more than we need worry about the underlying mechanisms when examining the propositional attitudes of humans or, for that matter, automata. Perhaps, differences in the "hardware" should make a difference in the view we take of principles of rational preference, belief, valuation and choice. But unless a decisive case is advanced that this should be so, it seems sensible to seek an account of rational choice, belief, preference and valuation which is indifferent as to whether the agent is human, automaton, animal, angelic or social.

Speaking of groups as agents may offend some ontological sensibilities. But anyone prepared to attribute beliefs, values and choices to groups as well as to individual humans and to think that such values, beliefs and choices ought to be regulatable by the same principles of rationality as are applicable to human agents recognizes such social entities as agents in the only sense that matters here.

Arrow appears reluctant to embrace the organic existence of institutional and social agents. In response to the critiques of Buchanan and I. M. D. Little, he contends that he was concerned with rules for arriving at social decisions which "may be agreed upon for reasons of convenience and necessity without its outcomes being treated as evaluations by anyone in particular" (Arrow, 1963: 106). Arrow cites with approval a comment from Karl Popper (1959: 55): "Not a few doctrines which are metaphysical, and thus certainly philosophical, can be interpreted as hypostatizations of methodological rules."

Nonetheless, according to his account of social choice, groups do choose from among feasible social states in an environment and, if rational, do so in a manner which is optimal relative to a social preference that weakly orders the social states. Arrow seems to think that in social choice we have choice without a choosing subject and preference without a preferring subject just as, for Popper, in science we have knowledge without a knowing subject.

C. R. Plott (1973: 107–108) points out that it is "operationally" difficult to distinguish efforts motivated according to Arrow's view from efforts motivated according to points of view which treat society as an organic entity. Plott's operationalistic rhetoric is irrelevant to the sound core of his observation. Any system, whether it is animal, vegetable or mineral, whether it is automaton, human or a group of automata or humans, can qualify as an agent for the purpose of discussing rational choice (which is the context in which Plott discusses Arrow's views), provided that choices, beliefs, preferences, values and goals are ascribable to the system and provided that it is appropriate to urge conformity to norms of rational preference, belief and choice. Saying this does not imply that all social groups act as agents or that those which do do so all the time. However, we cannot claim more for animals, automata or even human beings.

I have said that an agent is an entity which has propositional attitudes legitimately subject to criticism by appeal to norms of rationality. I do not have any independently specifiable criteria for determining such propriety, but we do not need any to appreciate the hard core of Plott's insight. Those who invoke objections to group minds as the basis for refusing to attribute agency to social groups should refrain from talk of social preference and social choice in any sense in which such preference and choice are subject to critical scrutiny by norms of rationality. Arrow and those who follow him cannot have their cake and eat it. Retreating to the third world is no more acceptable in discussions of social choice than it is in discussions of the growth of knowledge.[1]

This brings us to the second issue raised by Buchanan's objection – to wit, whether the preferences of institutional agents can consistently be allowed to be a function of the preferences of the citizens, subjects or clients of these institutions.

Some social institutions undoubtedly seek to promote their own selfish interests just as individuals do. Social agents, like human agents, can be self-directed or, if other directed, can be directed towards other social agents. Even so, on some occasions, human beings can seek to promote the interests and welfares of other human agents. So too, social institutions can seek to promote the interests of human agents who are related to the institutions in question as citizens, clients or patients. If there is no logical inconsistency in the one case, there should be none in the other.

Thus, it is not incoherent to regard a society which allocates commodity bundles through a market mechanism as an agent. The market mechanism in operation provides a procedure whereby the society makes certain kinds of social choices. We may ask two questions about the way such choices are made: Do the choices maximize some social preference? If the answer is affirmative, are the social preferences dependent on the interests of the participants in the market?

Arrow's impossibility theorem presupposes that affirmative answers may be given to both questions but then asserts that the dependency of social preference on the preferences of citizens cannot jointly satisfy several important conditions.

Perhaps, as Buchanan suggests, there is nothing disturbing about this result as it applies to the use by society of markets as choice mechanisms for the distribution of commodities to consumers. In any case, if there is trouble, it arises for any social agency seeking to maximize social preferences aimed at promoting individual welfares and not just for those social agencies which seek such ends through the use of market mechanisms.

Moreover, to declare that Arrow's result misses the mark because taking social groups to be maximizers of social preferences determined by individual values is incoherent is no way to neutralize the impact of Arrow's theorem. Buchanan to the contrary notwithstanding, nothing in logic prevents our taking social groups to be agents who seek to maximize just such social preferences. Blanket refusal to attribute agency of this kind to social groups is conceptual stonewalling which places roadblocks in the path of inquiry.

Insisting that social institutions should sometimes be recognized to be agents does not entail insensitivity to the differences between persons and social institutions – especially the morally relevant differences. Neither an unborn human fetus nor someone in coma is an agent subject to critical control according to canons of rational choice. Yet they are clearly objects of moral concern, and some apparently are prepared to insist that they be treated with the same moral respect as is accorded other human beings. We need not enter into the controversies which rage as to the propriety of this attitude. For us, it is enough that it is logically coherent to accord moral respect to individuals who are not agents. Conversely, attributing agency to animals, automata and social institutions does not entail granting such agents the same moral concern and respect we grant human agents.

Agency is undoubtedly a morally relevant trait, but it is one among many. We should not be deterred from scrutinizing the decisions and aims of insitutions with the aid of canons of rationality because of moral scruples any more than we should be prevented from doing so by metaphysical dogma.

8.2 Benevolence and conflict

Even if we may dismiss the objections of Buchanan, there is another objection to Arrow's approach of fundamental importance. According to Arrow, social groups are representable as maximizers of social values. The institutional agent is presented with a choice among social states belonging to some subset S of a domain U of entertainable social policies or states. According to Arrow, society has a uniquely permissible value ranking of the elements of U. The social value structure is free at least of ordinal conflict.

For Arrow, such freedom from ordinal conflict is a condition of rationality. Social agents ought, like personal agents, to resolve conflicts in valuation before choice to an extent sufficient to impose a weak ordering on feasible options. Thus, the decision maker, whether person or insitution, can be expected to maximize value.

I have already registered my misgivings concerning the notion that rational agents are obliged to resolve conflicts in value before to choice in cases where the agents are persons. Skepticism concerning the obligatory resolution of conflict should apply with as much force to cases where the agent is a social institution.[2]

Objection to the Arrovian demand that social agents maximize preferences represented by weak orderings of social states should not be confused with objections like Buchanan's which are grounded in preconceptions concerning when one can and cannot attribute agency to social institutions. According to the position I have taken, social and personal agents are subject to the same standards of rational valuation and decision making. There is no dispute with Arrow on this point. According to Arrow, however, rationality dictates that the decision maker, whether person or institution, should be free of at least ordinal conflict at the moment of choice. Just as I have insisted on the rationality of decision making under unresolved conflict for personal agents on some occasions, so too I hold that social decision making under unresolved conflict is sometimes rationally acceptable.

The issue is not whether preferences, values or goals do or do not come into conflict. Nor is it whether it is rational for an agent to suffer conflict in his, her or its values. That value conflict occurs and confronts even rational agents is widely acknowledged. What is questionable is whether rational agents should have resolved all conflicts when fixing on a decision so that they can claim that the option chosen is for the best, all things considered. The dominant view is that rationality prohibits decision making under unresolved conflict. I reject that view.

Ironically, Arrow's impossibility theorem itself offers a compelling case for concluding that social agents may retain their rationality while making decisions under unresolved conflict, just as personal agents do. One of the intended applications of Arrow's results is to contexts where political, economic and social agents, including not only public and governmental institutions but commercial concerns, private clubs and family groupings, take as their objective to benefit members of a certain group (the "clients", "club members" or "citizens"). However, the concern to benefit one of the clients may conflict with promoting the benefits of another. A conflict is present in the value commitments of the social agency. Arrow's social welfare functions are intended to be representations of rules which specify how a value structure free of ordinal conflict can be derived to resolve the conflict among the different rankings of social states representing the orderings of these states with respect to the benefits accruing to different citizens or clients.

However, Arrow insists that social welfare functions avoid resolving such conflicts in favor of promoting the benefits of one single client or citizen. No client can be a "dictator". At the same time, as we shall see in the next chapter, his proscription against appealing to interpersonal comparisons of benefits precludes adopting any other ranking consonant with the conditions on potential resolutions imposed in chapter 5. The net effect of these conditions is to rule out any potential resolution of the conflict among the welfares of different citizens from representing social preference.[3]

Arrow obtains a contradiction by insisting that the value structure adopted by the social agent be free of ordinal conflict anyhow. Such contradiction can be avoided if this assumption is abandoned. Arrow's result suggests that institutional agents can rationally make decisions without resolving conflicts, just as rational personal agents can.

To be sure, the Arrovian impossibility result remains troublesome even when we abandon the requirement that the social value structure be free of ordinal conflict. Recall that we are considering cases where institutional agents have value commitments to promote benefits for each one of a group of citizens or clients. We can avoid inconsistency by giving up insistence that society resolve conflicts among its commitments to its different clients by the moment of choice. But we cannot afford to remain complacent with the conclusion that such conflicts can never in principle be resolved by the moment of choice. In effect, by ruling out dictatorial social welfare functions and the relevance of interpersonal comparisons of benefits, Arrow drives us to this uncomfortable conclusion.

Thus, we need to explore in a systematic way the possibilities for resolving conflicts among value commitments marked by a concern for the benefits accruing to each citizen or client in a given group. Chapter 9 will address this question. We shall, of course, not only consider what needs to be done to resolve such conflicts fully but explore various conditions of partially unresolved conflict. Not only will Arrow's result be considered but the proposed view of value commitments marked by a concern for the benefits accruing to each citizen will be designed to recognize as special cases various forms of utilitarianism where interpersonal comparisons of increments in benefits are taken to be relevant and Rawlsian criteria for distributions of benefits where levels of benefits are considered. In other special cases, society may be justified in adopting a dictatorial rule or, at least, in restricting resolutions of conflicts to resolutions of conflicts among commitments to promoting the benefits of members of some oligarchy.

Nonetheless, society may often lack a warrant for making interpersonal comparisons or for favoring the values of some privileged group of citizens. In such cases, society should be prohibited from adopting any ranking of social states as a uniquely permissible basis for maximization. The account in chapter 9 provides for this as well.

Thus, Buchanan is right at least to this extent. Social agents should not always be thought to be preference maximizing. But counter to Buchanan, the trouble with Arrow's insistence that social choice maximize preference according to some social preference ranking is not that social institutions fail to qualify as agents whose choices are subject to critical assessment according to the same canons of rational valuation and choice applicable to persons. Social groups ought often to be treated as agents. So frequently should persons. We should devise our approach to rational choice with this in mind.[4] But just as personal agents may terminate deliberation and make decisions without having resolved the moral, political, economic, aesthetic or cognitive conflicts relevant to their predicaments, so too social agents committed to promoting the welfares of their clients or citizens might justifiably make decisions without settling on a way to balance the competing interests of these clients.

9

Distributing benefits

9.1 Benevolence for each and benevolence for all

Many agents, agencies and institutions are committed to furnishing benefits to members of some group who are the "clients" served by the agency, its "club members" or its "citizens". Such agents include public and governmental institutions, commercial concerns, private clubs and family groupings as well as persons. The benefits being promoted may be of diverse kinds. Some clubs provide opportunities for recreation of various sorts. Other institutions provide educational opportunities, insurance, travel opportunities and the like. The institutions promoting the benefits (whatever they might be) may be regarded as endorsing certain value commitments which impose constraints on the value structures they use to evaluate feasible options in various kinds of decision problems.

Utilitarians urge that all value commitments be constrained by the requirement that utility accruing to all human beings (or, at least, all human beings in some more restricted class) be promoted. Utilitarians have differed among themselves concerning the precise character of the benefit they seek to confer on their clients under the guise of utility, happiness or well-being. We need not address that matter now. Still, utilitarian value commitments are themselves but a species of a more general category of value commitments marked by benevolence.

Some value commitments marked by benevolence are marked by benevolence for *each* client, citizen or member of the club. Others are marked by benevolence for *all* clients, citizens or members of the club. Some are marked by both benevolence for each and benevolence for all. This contrast must now be explained.

Sometimes an agent (or institution) is concerned to promote the welfare or other goods of members of some group I in the sense that when faced with a choice among feasible options belonging to some set U, he is committed to evaluating the elements of U with respect to the extent to which it benefits each and every member of I taken individually. That is to say, the agent's value structure for U is obtained by considering a series of value structures $V_1(U), V_2(U), \ldots, V_n(U)$, where $V_i(U)$ is the value structure generated by the commitment to promote the benefit in question for the ith individual in I. The value structure for the agent is some subset $V(U)$ of the convex hull of the n value structures, one for each of the n individuals in I.

According to this conception, the benevolent agent sees himself as committed to promoting the benefit of each and every member of I taken separately. We may say that the agent endorses n distinct value commitments, each of them marked by benevolence for some specific individual i in I. Alternatively, we may say that the agent endorses a value committment marked by benevolence for each i in I.

When this concern does not yield a unanimous ordering of the elements of U, the agent faces a conflict in value commitments. He is committed to promote the benefit of individual i and also of individual j, but it is not feasible for him to do both. The agent faces a moral struggle of the second kind. He should move to a position of suspense among the several value commitments and, if feasible, undertake to identify a potential resolution of the conflict. If successful to the extent of removing all cardinal conflict, the agent will be able to represent the conflict-free value structure as the set of positive affine transformations of a value function which is a weighted average of some n-tuple of value functions over U, one for each i in I, and where the weights are nonnegative values assigned to each i in I which sum to 1.

The basis for this result is presented in chapter 5, especially in 5.4. Three conditions L_1–L_3 were taken to be reasonable requirements to impose on potential resolutions of conflict. Utilizing an argument of Blackwell and Girshick, the propriety of the weighted average principle was established. This principle is intended to apply to all contexts of value conflict and not merely to conflicts in valuations of options due to endorsement of value commitments marked by benevolence to different clients. It is just as apt when one is considering the predicament of Jones, the office manager, as it is when one is writing a will so as to benefit each of one's children to the greatest extent feasible.

Sometimes efforts to resolve conflicts among commitments marked by benevolence to different individuals may appeal to a value commitment marked by benevolence to all. According to such a value commitment, the feasible options in U are evaluated on the basis of a comparison of the benefits accruing to each individual in I from each of these options. For this reason, the agent's value commitment imposes constraints directly on valuations of the domain consisting of elements of the Cartesian product $U \times I$ rather than on the elements of U. I shall call such a set of valuation functions a *benefit comparison structure* $BC(U \times I)$, and its elements are permissible benefit comparison functions of the type $bc(x,i)$. As always, the set of such functions is required to be convex and closed under positive affine transformation. Otherwise, it is constrained by the specific features of the value commitment marked by benevolence to all. In particular, that value commitment will need to specify some procedure for deriving a value structure for U from the benefit comparison structure.

The difference between an n-tuple of value commitments marked by benevolence towards the specific individuals in I and a value commitment marked by benevolence towards all the individuals in I mimics the difference between decision making under certainty and decision making under uncertainty at least to this extent. In decision making under certainty, conflict in the value structure derives exclusively from conflict in the value commitments applied to the particular set of feasible options. This is precisely what happens in the case where we consider n distinct value commitments each marked by benevolence towards a different member of I. Each of these value commitments applies directly to the set U of feasible options. Conflict arises solely from differences in the benefits accruing to the different members of I according to feasible option (social state) x in U.

In decision making under uncertainty, we begin with an extended value structure defined over all "consequences" in O. These commitments apply to elements of O as constraints on the extended value structure. Given the extended value structure $EV(O)$, one seeks to derive a value structure $V(U)$ for the elements of U from that extended value structure and other features of the situation.

Value commitments marked by benevolence for all also proceed indirectly. Instead of applying immediately to elements of U, they constrain the evaluation of the elements of the Cartesian product $U \times I$ – i.e., they constrain the benefit comparison structure $BC(U \times I)$ defined for elements of $U \times I$. A value structure for U is derived from the benefit comparison structure and other features of the situation.

As in the case of decision making under uncertainty, several methods of derivation may be employed which are themselves arranged in a hierarchy so that a lexicographically ordered sequence of tests of admissibility may be deployed. Thus, a value commitment marked by benevolence for all defines a value structure for U by first imposing constraints on the way benefits accruing to each member of I are compared with one another (i.e., by determining a benefit comparison structure) and then employing some principle to derive the value structure from these comparisons.

In cases where the agent endorses a value commitment marked by benevolence for each of n individuals in I and finds the commitment to each i in I at odds with the commitment to some other j in I, an effort might be made to resolve the conflict. Value commitments marked by benevolence for all members of I can sometimes be used for this purpose.

Not every commitment to promote the benefits for all members of I can be deployed to resolve conflicts among n commitments to promote the benefits of each member of I separately. Certain conditions must be met:

(i) The benefit comparison structure $BC(U \times I)$ must reproduce the value structures $V_i(U)$ for each i in the sense that every permissible bc-function in the benefit comparison structure must be identical with a permissible function in $V_i(U)$ when i is held constant, and conversely each permissible v_i-function in $V_i(U)$ must be the restriction of some permissible bc-function in the benefit comparison structure. This requirement ensures that the notion of personal or individual benefit remains the same for the commitment to promote i's benefit and for the commitment to promote the overall benefit.

(ii) There must be a *concern structure* $L(I)$ over the domain of individuals I. This concern structure is a convex set of real-valued nonnegative functions $l(i)$ defined over the elements of I such that $\Sigma\, l(i) = 1$.

(iii) The value structure $V(U)$ is obtained from the benefit comparison structure $BC(U \times I)$ and the concern structure $L(I)$ by means of the *average benefit principle*. Here $v(x)$ is a permissible v-function if and only if there is a permissible bc-function and permissible l-function such that $v(x) = \Sigma\, l(i)bc(x,i)$, where the sum is over the i's in I.

When a value commitment marked by a concern for overall benefit satisfies these conditions, the value structure that emerges must be a convex subset of the convex set of v-functions representing the conflict among the n distinct commitments to promote individual benefits. In the extreme case where the two sets coincide, the commitment to overall benefit fails to resolve the conflict at all; but in other cases where conditions (i)–(iii) are satisfied, some partial or complete resolution of conflict may be available.

It must be emphasized that individuals and institutions may endorse value commitments marked by a concern for overall benefits which satisfy none or only some of the requirements (i)–(iii). The overall benefits evaluated in the benefit comparison structure may not reflect the personal benefits involved in the n personal benefit structures. Even if they do, there may be no commitment to derive a value structure from the benefit comparison structure via the average benefit principle with the aid of a concern structure. One might derive value structures from benefit comparison functions in accordance with principles formally like the difference principle invoked by J. Rawls. However, if the value commitment is going to be used to resolve the conflict in the value structure of the agent held in suspense or unresolved conflict among the n separate commitments to promote the benefits of each member of I separately, the appeal to the average benefit principle is required.

To be sure, one could question this claim by reopening the question as to what constitutes a potential resolution of conflicts among distinct ways of evaluating feasible options. I, however, shall continue to endorse the weighted average principle of 5.4 and for the reasons already advanced there. What I am concerned to emphasize now is that the weighted average principle as a condition characterizing the representation of potential resolutions of conflicting ways of evaluation does not entail the average benefit principle. The argument appealing to the theorem of Blackwell and Girshick used in 5.4 to explain the weighted average does not carry the same force when adapted to the problem of deriving a value structure from a benefit comparison structure. It may seem plausible, perhaps, that assumptions L_1 and L_2 should apply *mutatis mutandis* to our current problem, but there is no obvious reason to insist that an agent concerned to promote overall benefit must construe overall benefit in a manner which requires satisfaction of L_3. Only if one is invoking an appeal to overall benefit so as to reduce conflict among rival commitments to promote individual benefits does it seem possible to obtain a compelling argument.

Utilitarianism is, if it is focused on anything, focused on promoting overall benefit where benefits are understood in terms of utility or well-being in one of the many senses of that idea. Moreover, utilitarians typically claim that their doctrine is capable of resolving all conflicts in value. Any value conflicts we may face must derive solely from ignorance, which may, according to the account being given here, derive from the sort of credal indeterminacy described in the previous chapter. Hence, one way of defending the use of some method of averaging to obtain a utilitarian value structure is that utilitarianism must yield value structures which are convex subsets of the convex set of v-functions characterizing permissible assessments of the personal welfares of each of the members of I. One can, of course, object to the use of the average benefit principle. But one must then abandon the goal of deploying one's commitment to promote overall benefits understood as utility or welfare to reduce the conflict in one's commitments to promote the personal welfares of the members of I. If a value commitment marked by benevolence for all is to be used to resolve conflicts generated by a value commitment marked by benevolence for each member of I, it must obey the average benefit principle.

Of course, utilitarianism is not the only value commitment marked by benevolence for all which might resolve conflicts among commitments marked by benevolence for each. Utilitarians insist on a concern structure according to which exactly one distribution of concern is permissible – to wit, the egalitarian distribution assigning equal concern to each element of I. Value commitments marked by benevolence for all which observe the average benefit principle need not be egalitarian in this sense. Such value commitments are not utilitarian. Yet they can yield potential resolutions of conflicts among value commitments marked by benevolence for each. Furthermore, as already noted, there are conceptions of benefit which differ from the range of conceptions favored by utilitarians.

It is currently fashionable to complain of the insensitivity of utilitarianism to the problem of the fairness of the distribution of benefits to the members of I. Alternative methods, like the Rawlsian proposal, are alleged to be superior in this respect. *Prima facie* the charge of insensitivity to the fairness of the distribution of benefits should apply to any value commitment marked by benevolence for all which invokes the average benefit principle. Thus, we have a tension between the average benefit principle, which is useful in resolving conflicts among value commitments marked by benevolence for each member of I, and principles, like the difference principle, which advertise themselves as sensitive to fairness in the distribution of benefits.

In my judgement, this way of looking at matters expresses at best a half-truth. A commitment to the average benefit principle as a means of deriving value structures from benefit comparison structures may be adopted consistent with extreme sensitivity to questions of equitable distribution. To this extent, the currently standard outlook on the matter is simply in error. At the same time, it is true that the average benefit principle may be used in a way exhibiting sensitivity to equitable distribution only if its usefulness as a means of resolving conflicts among commitments marked by benevolence for each is reduced. Thus, although the average benefit principle is not in conflict with the demand for sensitivity to equity in distribution, its use to resolve conflicts is.

In general, the average benefit principle is effective in resolving conflicts among commitments marked by benevolence for each only insofar as conflict can be resolved in the benefit comparison structure and the concern structure. When these conditions fail, there is greater scope for invoking secondary criteria for evaluating the options. In particular, analogues of maximin and leximin criteria used as secondary in decision making under uncertainty can be invoked as secondary to the average benefit principle.

The discussion of these matters in this chapter is conducted on a relatively abstract level. In particular, it ignores issues pertaining to the peculiarities of some specific value commitments marked by benevolence for all which claim to be in a position to resolve conflicts among value commitments marked by benevolence for each. In chapter 10, we shall ask whether utilitarian value commitments can sustain their claim to provide criteria for resolving conflicts among commitments marked by benevolence for each individual in I. I shall argue that they cannot. Ironically, this result suggests that utilitarianism is rather more sensitive to questions of fair distribution than it is currently fashionable to allow, but it is rather less successful as a system of principles for resolving value conflicts than it is advertised to be.

Before reviewing these aspects of utilitarianism, however, the ideas just sketched concerning the use of the average benefit principle in value commitments marked by benevolence for all must be explained in somewhat greater detail.

9.2 Benefit comparison structures

A person or institution addressing the problem of distributing benefits to citizens, clients or members of a club or family with the intention of promoting the overall benefits accruing to the group needs to evaluate and compare the benefits received by the various members of I from each of the feasible options in U. Such assessments are to be represented here by means of benefit comparison structures.

Strictly speaking, the comparisons of the benefits accruing to the members of I ought to be according to hypotheses concerning the outcomes of the feasible options in the set O so that the benefit comparison structure ought to be defined over the Cartesian product $O \times I$ rather than $U \times I$.

This point becomes salient when we focus on questions pertaining to uncertainty in decision making. Two points perhaps should be considered which were not examined in chapter 7. One question concerns whether the benefit comparison structure over $O \times I$ ought first to be reduced to a benefit comparison structure over $U \times I$ through computations of expected value and then reduced to a value structure over U or whether the benefit comparison structure over $O \times I$ ought first to be reduced to an extended value structure over O by appeal to the average benefit principle (or whatever alternative principle of reduction such as maximin or leximin one is using) and then reduced to a value structure over U by considerations of expected value. Equivalent results are obtained if the average benefit principle is employed and the same probability distributions (e.g., those permissible according to the policy maker's credal state) are used to compute all expected values.

The second problem concerns the issue of whether one should use the individual client's credal state or the policy maker's credal state to compute expected values. I suspect that there is no fixed answer to this question appropriate to all occasions and that we shall have to tolerate the availability of diverse value commitments marked by a concern for the benefits of all, some of which respect the clients' opinions and others of which do not. Recognition of the point is, to be sure, an embarrassment for utilitarians and others who regard commitment to overall benevolence as a means of resolving conflict because it points to one source of conflict among commitments which utilitarian principles appear impotent to resolve. It is not the only source.

For the rest, the issues which arise concerning decision making under uncertainty remain basically as examined in chapter 7. There is little point in rehearsing such issues here. For this reason, the benefit comparison structure will be taken as defined over $U \times I$. (Hence, for the purpose of this discussion, the feasible options in U correspond to what are often called "social states" in the social choice literature.)

Our concern is to explore various ways of deriving value structures over U from comparison of the benefits accruing to person i in state x with the benefits accruing to j in state y. Such comparisons are presumably made on behalf of an agent committed to allocating benefits to members of I according to a value commitment marked by benevolence for all members of I.

The assessments may be *grounded* in truth-value-bearing assumptions concerning the amount of money, happiness or power accruing to the various members of I in the various social states, but the comparisons themselves are evaluations of the condition of i in state x as compared with j in state y. To illustrate in what is undoubtedly a simplistic way, the social agent may be involved in distributing money to the clients in I. Obviously one can compare the amounts of money received by i in state x and j in state y in a numerically definite way. It does not follow that the social agent will evaluate $\langle i,x \rangle$ and $\langle j,y \rangle$ by means of a numerically definite benefit comparison function (unique up to a positive affine transformation) which is itself a positive affine transformation of the amounts of money received by the i and j in the respective states x and y. His evaluations of the two pairs in $U \times I$ will be partially constrained by information about money held but will not be uniquely determined thereby. A procedure for deriving the evaluation from the information about the money held will have to be given. The procedure used need not itself invoke appeal to any other truth-value-bearing information aside from information about the money held. Still, we cannot say that the resulting evaluations of the pairs in $U \times I$ are equivalent to truth-value-bearing propositions, although they may presuppose some such.

The distinction being pressed becomes more apparent if the benefits being promoted are multifaceted. The social agency may be providing clothes and shelter and may be able quite well to compare social policies or states with respect to allocations of clothes to the clients in I and with respect to allocations of shelter. But the evaluations of the elements of U might conflict. The social agency might hit upon a resolution of the conflict. That resolution could be represented by a v-function which is a weighted average of v-functions for clothes and for shelter. The resulting benefit comparison structure will no doubt be grounded in truth-value-bearing information about clothes allocations and shelter allocations. But this information does not uniquely determine the comparative evaluations of the pairs $\langle x,i \rangle$ and $\langle y,j \rangle$ without supplementation by principles of evaluation which are not themselves easily reducible to truth-value-bearing assumptions.

Given a benefit comparison structure $BC(U \times I)$ determined by a value commitment marked by benevolence for all, it is possible to derive n distinct *personal benefit structures* $B_i(U)$ – one for each i in I. For fixed i, such a structure is the set of permissible benefit comparison functions in $BC(U \times I)$ restricted to the given i.

If the value commitment marked by benevolence for all is intended *inter alia* to resolve conflicts among n value commitments each marked by benevolence for a specific member of I, each of the personal benefit structures should coincide with a value structure $V_i(U)$ representing the commitment marked by benevolence for individual i. The stipulation that $B_i(U) = V_i(U)$ is, of course, condition (i) of 9.1.

According to some value commitments marked by benevolence for all, $B_i(U)$ should represent the decision maker's estimate of the value structure adopted by person i for the elements of U. That is to say, personal benefit structures should be grounded in society's estimate of the desires, values or preferences of the citizens. Such a view is characteristic of what I shall call "preference utilitarianism" (but not only of that view).

"Classical utilitarianism" (Rawls, 1971: 22–27) presupposes that as a matter of fact there is an objective magnitude $h(x,i)$ which is the amount of happiness or well-being accruing to i in state x. Typically, as in Sidgwick (1907: 413, also 123–125), such happiness is taken to be the net of pleasure over pain. But we might entertain other ideas of happiness or well-being understood as an objective magnitude in alternative views of classical utilitarianism. Given such a magnitude, classical utilitarianism stipulates that $BC(U \times I)$ consist of all and only positive affine transformations of $h(x,i)$.

Commitments marked by benevolence might determine the benefit comparison structure and the personal benefit structures by grounding them in other "objective" features of the states. One might, for example, appeal to some index of Rawlsian "primary goods". Or one might emphasize neither the holding of goods nor utility but what Sen has called "functioning" and further what Sen calls "basic capabilities" to function.[1] One might seek to constrain benefit comparison structures by appealing to considerations of any one of these kinds. Or one might develop some function of several of these types of considerations and generate benefit comparison structures by appeal to such functions. Finally, one might take the convex hull of the benefit comparison functions recognized as permissible in benefit comparison structures constructed in any of these ways. All of the benefit comparison structures so constructed (and others which are obtained by appeal to appropriately specified benefits) qualify as expressions of value commitments marked by benevolence for all. The two types of utilitarian commitment mentioned above are but two species of a much larger genus. When, for some i, $B_i(U)$ is free of ordinal conflict (i.e., unique up to a positive monotonic transformation), i's personal benefit structure may be said to be *ordinally measurable*. If the personal benefit structure is free of cardinal conflict (i.e., unique up to a positive affine transformation), it is *cardinally measurable*.

All kinds of measurability assumptions (including ordinal and cardinal measurability, but not only these) may be represented with the aid of benefit comparison structures. The most frequently discussed assumptions take for granted that personal benefit structures are ordinally measurable or are cardinally measurable.

Many different benefit comparison structures may share the same measurability assumptions. That is to say, where n is the number of individuals in I, all of these benefit comparison structures may define the same n-tuple of personal benefit structures. Benefit comparison structures which agree in their measurability assumptions, but which otherwise differ, differ with respect to the way *interpersonal comparisons of benefits* are made.

Given a system of shared measurability assumptions, there are different types of interpersonal comparisons which have been salient in contemporary discussions.[2] To characterize them, it will be convenient to identify two distinguished benefit comparison structures sharing specific measurability assumptions: $BC^*(U \times I)$ consists of all bc-functions in the Cartesian product of all of the personal benefit structures $B_i(U)$. In addition, we may identify a set $BC^{**}(U \times I)$ of bc-functions (a) whose restrictions to the individual i generate the functions in $B_i(U)$ and (b) is such that no other set satisfying (a) is a convex subset of it closed under positive affine transformation. BC^{**} is a minimal set compatible with the given personal benefit structures. There may be several such minimal sets. There is only one maximal set BC^*.

Noncomparability (NC) is assumed by a benefit comparison structure $BC(U \times I)$ if and only if $BC(U \times I)$ is identical with BC^*.

Level comparability (LC) is assumed by a benefit comparison structure $BC(U \times I)$ if and only if this benefit comparison structure contains all and only positive monotone transformations in BC^* of benefit comparison functions in some minimal benefit comparison structure BC^{**}.

Unit comparability (UC) is assumed by a benefit comparison structure $BC(U \times I)$ if and only if the benefit comparison structure contains all and only those benefit comparison functions in BC^* which are obtainable by the transformation $bc'(x,i) = b_i + abc(x,i)$ for some $a \rangle$ o (held constant for all i) and some b_i from benefit comparison functions in some minimal benefit comparison structure BC^{**}.

Full comparability (FC) is assumed by a benefit comparison structure $BC(U \times I)$ if and only if the benefit comparison structure contains all and only those bc-functions in BC^* which are obtainable by the transformation $bc'(x,i) = b + abc(x,i)$ for some b and some positive a (where both a and b are the same for all i) from some permissible bc-function in a minimal benefit comparison structure BC^{**}.

In addition to these four types of assumptions of interpersonal comparability, three types of partial comparability have been discussed. *Partial full comparability* (PFC) is assumed by a benefit comparison structure which is a proper subset of BC^* but which contains a benefit comparison structure satisfying FC as a proper subset. *Partial level comparability* (PLC) [*Partial Unit Comparability* (PUC)] is assumed by a benefit comparison structure contained as a proper subset of BC^* but containing as a proper subset a benefit comparison structure satisfying LC(UC).

Given the two-dimensional taxonomy we have identified where one dimension characterizes measurability assumptions and the other comparability assumptions, it is now possible to identify important combinations of the two types of assumption embodied in a benefit comparison structure.

Consider first those benefit comparison structures which assume cardinal measurability – i.e., where the personal benefit structures are all free of cardinal conflict. The largest set of benefit comparison functions satisfying a given cardinality assumption of this type is, of course, obtained by taking the Cartesian product of all the personal benefit structures involved – i.e., by constructing BC^*. This set may also be characterized by considering some minimal benefit comparison structure BC^{**} satisfying the measurability assumption (this structure will consist of all positive affine transformations of some bc-function in BC^*) and constructing the set of variable unit-variable origin piecemeal positive affine transformations of that function and counting these among the permissible benefit comparison functions.[3] The resulting benefit comparison structure assumes *cardinal noncomparability* (CNC).

Cardinal full comparability (CFC) is assumed when there is a minimal benefit comparison structure BC^{**} free of cardinal conflict such that all and only positive affine transformations of functions in this minimal set are permissible (i.e., the minimal structure is the operative benefit comparison structure).

Cardinal level comparability (CLC) is assumed when there is a minimal benefit comparison structure BC^{**} (free of cardinal conflict) such that the operative benefit comparison structure consists of all positive monotonic transformations of elements of BC^{**} which are also in BC^*.

Cardinal unit comparability (CUC) is assumed by a benefit comparison structure when there is a minimal benefit comparison structure BC^{**} such that all and only constant unit-variable origin piecemeal positive affine transformations of bc-functions in this minimal structure which are also in BC^* are permissible.[4]

Cardinal partial full comparability (CPFC), cardinal partial level comparability (CPLC) and cardinal partial unit comparability (CPUC) are definable along lines already given for types of partial comparability.

If the benefit comparison functions are extended to include all mixtures of elements of $U \times I$, CLC must coincide with CFC over the extended domain. So must CPLC and CPFC. Hence, whenever CLC is satisfied by the benefit comparison structure defined over $U \times I$ but CFC is not, contemplation of a sufficient number of mixtures of elements of $U \times I$ should reveal a breakdown of level comparability as well. For this reason, I shall follow the general practice of ignoring CLC and CPLC.

When all personal benefit structures satisfy ordinal measurability in the sense given before, full comparability and level comparability assumptions become equivalent. So do assumptions of unit comparability and noncomparability. Hence, setting aside ordinal partial level comparability (OPLC) – which is the sole distinctive sort of partial comparability surviving – there are two types of benefit comparison structures to consider under the assumption of ordinal measurability:

1. *Ordinal level comparability* (OLC) is assumed by a benefit comparison structure if and only if there is a minimal benefit comparison structure BC^{**} (which, given the assumption of ordinal measurability of each personal benefit structure, must consist of all and only positive monotonic or order-preserving transformations of some particular bc-function) such that the operative benefit comparison structure is identical with BC^{**}.

2. *Ordinal non-comparability* (ONC) is assumed by a benefit comparison structure if and only if there is a minimal benefit comparison structure BC^{**} (unique up to positive monotonic transformation as

before) such that the operative benefit comparison structure consists of all and only piecemeal positive monotonic transformations of *bc*-functions in that minimal structure.[5]

Many other types of "measurability–comparability" assumptions may be represented using benefit comparison structures. In particular, we might address situations where personal benefit structures suffer from ordinal as well as cardinal conflict or situations where different personal benefit structures satisfy different measurability assumptions. The fact that the literature tends to ignore these possibilities is itself an indication of the widespread tendency to ignore conflict in the appraisal of personal benefit or to deny it.

9.3 The average benefit principle

If a value commitment marked by concern for all is to resolve the conflicts which arise when an agent is concerned with promoting benefits for each of *n* distinct individuals in *I*, not only should condition (i) of 9.1 be satisfied but conditions (ii) and (iii) should be met as well.

This claim is buttressed by the arguments for using the weighted average principle introduced in 5.4 as a characterization of potential resolutions among conflicting ways of evaluating a given set of feasible options. In my judgement, the considerations adduced in 5.4 are quite compelling. As already conceded, however, those who reject them will not be contradicting themselves, and I do not know how to construct an argument for the weighted average principle which a sufficiently determined skeptic cannot charge with begging some question he or she is willing to dispute.

Nonetheless, in order to avoid misunderstanding, it may still be worth repeating that the endorsement of the weighted average principle as a characterization of potential resolutions among conflicting ways of evaluation does not entail or mandate endorsement of the average benefit principle. Hence, someone committed to promoting some benefit for all (in some appropriate sense) need not adopt it. There is nothing in what I have said which mandates the rejection of principles like maximin or leximin as means of deriving value structures from benefit comparison structures.[6]

What is true, however, is that if one wishes to invoke a commitment to overall benefit to resolve conflicts among commitments to promoting the benefits of each individual in *I* separately, the average benefit principle must be used to derive a value structure from a benefit comparison structure. One need not have this ambition when seeking to promote an overall benefit. And, indeed, it seems fair to say that moralists who follow variations of the utilitarian tradition are more concerned to find a compromise among rival claims for given benefits than are those who focus on equality in distribution and embrace a dictatorship of the disadvantaged. For the latter it is the justness of the distribution which counts, and it is only in this sense that these moralists are interested in overall benefits.

To be sure, advocates of the average benefit principle are themselves confronted with two tasks: (a) to show that they can, indeed, succeed in resolving conflicts among commitments to promote the benefits of each and (b) to show that the allegations that they are insensitive to the equity of distributions are mistaken.

In my view, advocates of the average benefit principle cannot succeed in both of these efforts. They can establish the sensitivity of their views to questions of distributive justice (counter to their critics) but only at a considerable cost. They must abandon their ambitions to provide an ultimate basis for resolving conflicts among commitments to promote the benefits of each member of I and *a fortiori* to resolve other types of conflicts among value commitments. But insofar as they do abandon these pretensions, they undermine the force of arguments which appeal to the Blackwell–Girshick result or the Fleming–Harsanyi reasoning on behalf of the average benefit principle. My own view is that utilitarians and others who invoke an average benefit principle in characterizing a commitment to promoting benefits for all ought to abandon their reductionist pretensions and admit that their commitments are themselves confronted with conflicts in values they are impotent to resolve by the moment of choice. Hence, counter to prevailing wisdom, I maintain that advocates of the average benefit principle are quite capable of sensitivity to questions of distribution. But whether or not I am right about this, I do mean to insist that advocates of the average benefit principle are faced with a dilemma: either mute ambitions to resolve conflicts in values and to that extent give up one kind of argument for the average benefit principle or abandon efforts to establish sensitivity to questions of distribution.[7]

Use of the average benefit principle presupposes the availability of a concern structure $L(I)$. Such a concern structure is required to be a nonempty, convex set of l-functions [written in the form $l(i)$], each of which is a permissible *distribution of concern*.

A concern structure is *dictator permitting* if there is a permissible distribution of concern which assigns 0 concern to every member of I except one who is the dictator according to that distribution. A concern structure is *oligarchy permitting* if there is a permissible distribution of concern assigning all weight to some proper subset of I containing at least two members. A concern structure can be *dictator forbidding* and also *oligarchy forbidding*.

Concern structures may also be classified with respect to the character of the conflict in the concern structure. They may be maximally conflicted, as when all possible distributions of concern are permissible at one extreme, or free of cardinal conflict, as when exactly one distribution of concern is permissible.

Maximally conflicted concern structures recognize all concern distributions which assign 0 to one or more members of I. Hence, they are both dictator and oligarchy permitting. However, we may construct the open set of concern distributions obtained by deleting all concern distributions assigning 0 concern to one or more members of I from the maximally conflicted set. I shall call this concern structure *maximally conflicted dictator and oligarchy forbidding* even though in the strict sense it is not maximally conflicted. This concern structure differs from the maximally conflicted concern structure properly speaking through the deletion of all boundary points. There are other concern structures which differ from the maximally conflicted concern structure by the deletion of some boundary points but not others. Some of these may be dictator forbidding but not oligarchy forbidding whereas others may be oligarchy forbidding but not dictator forbidding. They may also be regarded as maximally conflicted in an extended sense. For the most part, they will not be of great interest.

Aside from the concern structures just identified, there are those which are conflicted but not maximally conflicted in any of the senses just indicated (e.g., a concern structure may be free of ordinal conflict but not cardinal conflict).

Concern structures may also be classified with respect to whether or not they are *symmetrical*. A concern structure is symmetrical if and only if all distributions of concern derivable from permissible distributions by permuting members of I are also permissible. The only symmetrical concern structure free of cardinal conflict is the *egalitarian* structure, according to which each member of I receives equal concern. (This same concern structure is also the sole concern structure which is both symmetrical and free of ordinal conflict.) There are, however, other symmetrical concern structures. The maximally conflicted concern structure in the strict sense is one example. So is the maximally conflicted dictator- and oligarchy-forbidding concern structure. And there are innumerable other concern structures exhibiting conflict of intermediate intensity which also qualify as symmetrical.

Thus, one cannot advance an argument in favor of the egalitarian distribution of concern which appeals to the desirability of using a symmetrical concern structure. One must, in addition, make the case that the concern structure is free of at least ordinal conflict.

From the point of view of someone whose ambition it is to devise a value commitment which can resolve conflicts among the value commitments promoting the benefits of each member of I taken individually, it is automatically desirable to embrace a conflict-free concern structure. If, in addition, symmetry is demanded, the egalitarian distribution becomes uniquely permissible.

Of course, embracing a uniform distribution of concern over the elements of I is not sufficient to guarantee avoidance of value conflict in the value structure derived from the benefit comparison structure via the average benefit principle. The benefit comparison structure must itself be sufficiently free of conflict. In particular, it must either assume CFC or CUC to guarantee freedom from cardinal conflict in the value structure.

Thus, if a value commitment marked by benevolence for all claims a capacity to resolve conflicts which arise from conflicts among commitments marked by benevolence for each, it must meet some very demanding requirements; and it does not take too much reflection to realize how difficult it should be to sustain such claims. Before exploring this point in greater detail, however, we shall pay some attention to principles for deriving value structures from benefit comparison structures which violate the average benefit principle but which are more sensitive to questions about the distribution of benefits.

9.4 Benefit level dictatorship

According to the average benefit principle, a dictator is a member of I who receives all the available concern represented by the l-value of 1, leaving no concern for other members of I. No matter what benefit comparison function is used to derive a permissible value function and no matter what option or social state in U is considered, only the benefits of that member of I are taken into account. Given a benefit comparison function bc and a social state x in U, there are at most n distinct values which the benefit comparison function assigns to the n members of I. Hence, for integral values of k from 1 to n, we may adopt a rule that the benefits accruing to those members of I whose benefits in x are the kth smallest level (the kth highest level) shall represent the value of option x derived from the given permissible bc-function. These individuals form a *bottom-up* (*top-down*) *kth benefit level oligarchy* if there are several individuals in the category or *dictatorship* if there is but one for the specific benefit comparison function and social state.

To characterize formally the kind of rule which determines kth-level dictatorship or oligarchy, first define the following functionals:

$\text{min}b(k,bc,x) =$ the kth smallest distinct bc-value accruing to a member of I in state x if there are k such distinct values. Otherwise, $\text{min}b(k,bc,x)$ $= \text{min}b(k-1,bc,x)$.

$\text{max}b(k,bc,x)$ = the kth largest distinct bc-value accruing to a member of I in state x if there are k such distinct values. Otherwise, $\text{max}b(k,bc,x)$ = $\text{max}b(k-1,bc,x)$.

$\text{MINB}(k,bc,U)$ = the set of all positive affine transformations of $\text{min}b(k,bc,x)$, where k and bc are fixed and x ranges over U.

$\text{MINB}(k,BC,U)$ = the set of functions $\text{MINB}(k,bc,U)$ for all permissible bc-functions in BC and fixed k. Since BC is convex, this set will be convex and closed under positive affine transformations.

$\text{MAXB}(k,bc,U)$ and $\text{MAXB}(k,BC,U)$ are defined in a corresponding manner.

Given a benefit comparison structure BC and a set of feasible options U, a bottom-up (top-down) kth benefit level oligarchy (or dictatorship) determines a value structure $\text{MINB}(k,BC,U)$ [$\text{MAXB}(k,BC,U)$].

The best-known rule for deriving a value structure from a benefit comparison structure of the type under consideration is a bottom-up first-level dictatorship or oligarchy. When applied to the problem of distributing so-called primary goods, it is known as the Rawlsian difference principle or maximin principle.

9.5 Admissibility

Given a concern structure, the average benefit principle yields a rule for deriving a value structure over U from a benefit comparison structure over $U \times I$. Relative to that value structure, we may define a set of V-admissible options in the usual manner. I shall call the value structure obtained in this manner the ABL(I)-structure $ABL(I)(U)$ and the set of admissible options the ABL(I)-admissible options.

In a similar manner, we can use a bottom-up (top-down) kth level dictatorship or oligarchy rule to determine a value structure $\text{MINB}_k(U)$ [$\text{MAXB}_k(U)$] and relative to that structure define the set of MINB_k-(MAXB_k-)admissible options.

Value structures derived from benefit comparison structures often suffer from cardinal and even ordinal conflict and, even when they do not, several options may tie for optimality. All the principles considered here allow for several options to be admissible. When the agent's primary value commitment fails in this way to render a verdict, it is entirely appropriate to invoke a secondary value commitment to fill the void if the secondary commitment fails to invoke a third and so on until all resources are exhausted.

In this chapter, the focus is on cases where the agent aims to promote the overall benefits of the citizens in I. Hence, the value commitments eligible for use in hierarchy should be restricted to those which use only information available in the benefit comparison structure to derive value structures. That is to say, the value commitments should be representable by functional relations between benefit comparison structures and value structures.

One familiar way of organizing a hierarchy of value commitments meeting these requirements is by starting with bottom-up first-level dictatorship (the maximin or difference principle). The set of $MINB_1$-admissible options is identified. Then the set of $MINB_2$-admissible options among the $MINB_1$-admissible options is determined. These are the $MINB_1-MINB_2$-admissible options. The $MINB_1-MINB_2-MINB_3$-admissible options can be defined analogously and the process reiterated until further reduction of the set of admissible options is no longer possible. The set of options surviving this sequence of tests of admissibility is called the *leximinb-admissible options*.

When the benefit comparison structure is free of cardinal conflict, $MINB(k,BC,U)$ is also free of cardinal conflict for every k. In this special case, the set of leximinb-admissible options may be identified with options which are optimal according to a lexicographical ordering of the elements of U in which all options are ordered according to first-level bottom-up dictatorship, ties are broken according to second-level bottom-up dictatorship and so on. When U is finite, the ordering could be represented by a real-valued v-function but not in a useful way; and when U is embedded in a continuum of states, the ordering cannot, in general, be represented by a real-valued v-function at all. Hence, I have avoided recognizing lexicographical orderings as permissible according to a value structure and preferred instead to think in terms of hierarchies of value structures and lexicographically ordered tests of admissibility instead. The difference does not loom very large as long as the benefit comparison structures satisfy either CFC or OLC, for in both of these cases, there is the possibility of seeing leximinb-admissible options as optimal according to a lexicographical ordering. This breaks down for other types of benefit comparison structures, and then the approach I am adopting appears to be a sensible way to generalize. Setting this important difference to one side, we may regard the criterion of leximinb-admissibility as a descendant of the lexicographical maximin or leximin principle introduced into social choice literature by Sen.[8]

Obviously other lexicographically ordered sequences of value structures and associated tests for admissibility can be envisaged. We cannot review all of them here. There is, however, one other important hierarchy to be considered.

Suppose that the primary value commitment in the hierarchy is characterized by the average benefit principle relative to a given concern structure $L(I)$. In that case, the first test for admissibility is ABL(I)-admissibility. The secondary value commitment is bottom-up first level dictatorship, so that the second test for admissibility selects the $MINB_1$-admissible options from among the ABL(I)-admissible options. These are the ABL(I)–$MINB_1$-admissible options. We can then reiterate using second-level bottom-up dictatorship, third-level bottom-up dictatorship and so on. The options which survive a hierarchy of tests of this sort are *abl(i)lex-admissible*.

Like the criterion of ABL(I)-admissibility, this procedure is grounded in the priority of the average benefit principle and, as a consequence, may be deployed in cases where value commitments marked by benevolence for all are being used to resolve conflicts among commitments marked by benevolence for each. But abl(i)lex-admissibility also displays some sensitivity to questions of the equality or the justness of the distribution of benefits which, so it is claimed, use of the average benefit principle lacks. Furthermore, use of this criterion of admissibility is not a novel proposal within the utilitarian tradition, which historically at any rate is the major expression of value commitments marked by benevolence for all. H. Sidgwick endorsed the idea of breaking ties in total happiness as determined by the average benefit principle when equal concern is assigned to all members of I. Although he did not state his principle with great precision, he was clearly interested in furnishing as equal a distribution of happiness among the elements of I as is feasible when breaking ties (Sidgwick, 1907: 416–417). And indeed, it seems that he was proposing to use some form of leximin to break ties generated by the average benefit principle. This is clearly a special case of abl(i)lex-admissibility. Sidgwick (1907: 416) acknowledged that "if all the consequences of actions were capable of being estimated and summed up with mathematical precision, we should never find the excess of pleasure over pain exactly equal in the case of two competing alternatives of conduct". But he then proceeded to suggest that he would take questions of distribution into account even in those cases where there was no "cognisable" difference in total utility. Sidgwick's formulations are by no means clear, but his remarks are clearly sympathetic not only to the tie-breaking function of considerations of distribution but to the more useful and important role of such considerations in contexts where maximization of total benefits cannot render a verdict.[9]

The critical question to be faced then is whether the criterion of abl(i)lex-admissibility displays sufficient sensitivity to the question of equal distribution to defuse criticism of the average benefit principle on this score. If it does, then since it also accommodates the demand to find compromise among the claims of commitments marked by benevolence to each member of I taken seperately, we may have found a means of undermining one of the most popular complaints leveled against utilitarianism in particular and advocates of the use of the average benefit principle in general.

9.6 Fair distribution

To assess the adequacy of the criterion of abl(i)lex-admissibility with respect to questions about the fairness of the distribution of benefits, we shall use as comparative benchmarks the criteria of ABL(I)-admissibility and leximinb-admissibility. As might be expected, abl(i)lex-admissibility will display more sensitivity to such equity than ABL(I)-admissibility and less than leximinb-admissibility. The critical issue will be whether it represents a sufficiently appropriate balance between the demands to find a resolution of the conflict arising from value commitments focused on promoting the benefits of each member of I and the demand that the distribution of benefits be fair.

There are two dimensions along which such comparisons may be made: (a) with respect to measurability and comparability assumptions embedded in the benefit comparison structure and (b) with respect to the type of concern structure.

When the personal value structures of the members of I [which, by hypothesis, we are equating with the personal benefit structures $B_i(U)$] themselves suffer from cardinal or ordinal conflict, the hope of obtaining value structures representing a commitment to benevolence for all which are free of at least ordinal conflict must be abandoned. This does not mean that the use of the average benefit principle cannot reduce some of the conflict among the interests of members of I, but it cannot reduce the conflict within the value structure of any given citizen in I. To focus on the most promising cases, therefore, we shall attend for the time being to contexts in which all the personal benefit structures of the members of I are either free of cardinal conflict or are all free of ordinal conflict. That is to say, personal benefit will be assumed to be either cardinally measurable or ordinally measurable. Keep in mind that when we do not make these assumptions, not only will the opportunities for resolving conflict in the value structure representing a concern for overall benevolence be limited but concern with fairness of the distribution of benefits will also be frustrated.

When we assumed previously that all personal benefits are cardinally measurable, we singled out the following types of benefit comparison structures: those assuming full comparability of benefits (CFC), those assuming unit comparability (CUC) and those assuming noncomparability (CNC). In addition, there are forms of partial comparability which I will not discuss and also cases of level comparability which, as I argued in 9.2, are of limited interest.

When personal benefits are ordinally measurable, we singled out for discussion (excluding cases of partial comparability) ordinal level comparability (OLC) and ordinal noncomparability (ONC).

When the concern structure $L(I)$ is free of all conflict so that exactly one l-function is recognized as permissible, the average benefit principle yields a conflict-free value structure when CFC is assumed. Moreover, the value structure represents a potential resolution of the conflicts among commitments to benevolence for each member of I. The criterion of ABL(I)-admissibility will recommend choosing an option which is optimal according to that potential resolution regardless of how uniform the distribution of benefits is. The criterion of abl(i)lex-admissibility will also recommend choosing an option which is optimal according to that potential resolution. But when there are two or more such options, it will recommend choosing one which favors equality of distribution of benefits. The criterion of leximinb-admissibility deploys a hierarchy of value structures each of which is free of cardinal conflict. But none of them, especially the first, represents in general the resolution of a conflict among commitments to benevolence for each member of I separately. In contrast, it will favor that option or those options among the feasible items in U which promote equality in the distribution of benefits where abl(i)lex-admissibility promotes equality only among the ABL(I)-admissible options. This, of course, is the case where Sidgwick allowed considerations of equality of distribution to break ties. As Sidgwick himself conceded, such occasions may be rare; and if these were the only contexts where advocates of giving top priority to the use of the average benefit principle could claim sensitivity to questions of equality of distribution, one might justly argue that they are not sensitive enough. Even so, at least in that context, advocates of the average benefit principle supplemented by appeal to leximin in a secondary manner do display sensitivity to equality of distribution of benefits. Moreover, they can do so while favoring resolutions of conflicts of the claims of individual citizens in I to have their interests promoted. Advocates of the criterion of leximinb-admissibility may place more emphasis on equality, but they give up the pretense of seeking to promote the interests of each.

Under the conditions of unit comparability (CUC), the criterion of abl(i)lex-admissibility reduces to ABL(I)-admissibility and displays no sensitivity to questions of equality of benefits received. But under these conditions, leximinb-admissibility cannot do so either. Indeed, the latter is utterly useless for the purpose of ruling out any options (other than those which are "Pareto dominated" by other options in the sense that these other options are unanimously strictly preferred to them). And it fails to resolve any conflicts among the competing interests of the members of I. Here it should seem obvious to anyone who is concerned to resolve such conflicts and also to take fairness of distribution into account that the use of the average benefit principle is superior.

When we turn to OLC, the appeal to the average benefit principle fails to reduce conflict in the value structure. Indeed, only Pareto-dominated options are ruled out as not ABL(I)-admissible. Hence, the abl(i)leximin-admissible options coincide with the leximinb-admissible options.

Consider then the cases of noncomparability, whether cardinal or ordinal. The ABL(I)-admissible options consist of all options except those which are Pareto dominated, and these in turn coincide with the leximinb-admissible options and also with the abl(i)leximin-admissible options. Thus, anyone who seeks a value commitment marked by benevolence for all which will resolve conflicts among commitments marked by benevolence for each and who also cares about fair distribution of benefits should be in a position to say the following in cases where the concern structure is free of cardinal conflict:

1. The criteria of ABL(I)-admissibility, leximinb-admissibility and abl(i)leximin-admissibility are on a par when CNC or ONC obtains.

2. Leximinb-admissibility and abl(i)leximin-admissibility are on a par with respect to the question of fair distribution when OLC obtains and [and, in this respect, both are better than ABL(I)-admissibility]. In addition, they are no worse than ABL(I)-admissibility with regard to the resolution of conflicts among commitments marked by benevolence for each.

3. When CUC obtains, ABL(I)-admissibility and abl(i)leximin-admissibility are on a par with respect to the question of resolving conflicts (and they are both better than leximinb-admissibility in this respect). Furthermore, they are no worse than leximinb-admissibility with regard to the question of fair distribution.

Thus, if we consider these cases alone, it seems fairly clear that someone who seeks commitment marked by benevolence for all capable of resolving conflicts among commitments marked by benevolence for each and is also capable of sensitivity to fairness of distributions should favor abl(i)leximin-admissibility over ABL(I)-admissibility and leximinb-admissibility.

Controversy might arise when we consider CFC. It ought to be granted that abl(i)leximin-admissibility ranks as well as ABL(I)-admissibility with respect to the question of resolving conflicts in this case and clearly is better than leximinb-admissibility in this respect. It is better than ABL(I)-admissibility with respect to the question of fairness of distributions. However, it does not give the same emphasis to fairness that leximinb-admissibility does in this case. If someone complains that abl(i)leximin-admissibility is not sensitive enough to the question of fairness and that, therefore, we should endorse leximinb-admissibility rather than it, the superiority of abl(i)leximin-admissibility with respect to the question of resolving conflicts in the context of CFC and also CUC is being forgotten.

There is another point to consider. Both Rawls and Sen (see note 9) take up Sidgwick's advocacy of a criterion which appears to be abl(i)leximin-admissibility or something like it for contexts where CFC obtains [so that the supplementation of ABL(I)-admissibility by considerations of equity is for the breaking of ties in maximum utility, welfare or benefit]. They observe that occasions where there will be ties are likely to be rare so that under conditions CFC, opportunities to display sensitivity to questions of fairness of distributions will be rare as well.

That is quite so (as Sidgwick himself seems to concede), but there are other occasions where such opportunities can arise. We have noted that abl(i)leximin-admissibility accommodates fairness just as well as leximinb-admissibility when OLC obtains. Furthermore, under CPFC, we can often obtain sensitivity to fairness while also accommodating the question of resolving conflicts. Moreover, as we shall see, under CFC, there are opportunities for abl(i)leximin-admissibility to display sensitivity to distributional considerations when the concern structure goes conflicted.

But suppose we concede that scope for applying abl(i)leximin is extremely limited when CFC obtains. Rare cases are either to be ignored or to be taken seriously. If they are to be ignored (as Rawls and Sen seem to suggest), one cannot mount an objection against abl(i)leximin because it is not sufficiently sensitive to questions of fairness in these rare cases.

I do not mean to suggest that the considerations just noted will convince someone of the merits of abl(i)leximin-admissibility whose commitments are given over to questions of the fairness of distributions to the disregard of everything else. But for those who acknowledge the desirability of resolving conflicts among commitments marked by benevolence for each through an appeal to a commitment marked by benevolence for all, these considerations ought, it seems, to be quite compelling.

Thus far, however, we have addressed only those cases where the concern structure is free of cardinal conflict. And it must be admitted that the scope of the criterion of abl(i)leximin-admissibility is limited as long as this assumption is made. Even so, when cardinal conflict is absent, abl(i)leximin comprehends the use of ABL(I)-admissibility when CUC obtains as one special case and leximinb-admissibility when OLC obtains as another.

When the concern structure is conflicted, the sensitivity of abl(i)leximin to fairness becomes more signifigant. This is apparent in the case of CFC. When the concern structure is maximally indeterminate [and whether or not it is dictator permitting (oligarchy permitting)], the abl(i)leximin-admissible options coincide with the leximinb-admissible options. Of course, in this case, the appeal to the average benefit principle to resolve conflicts among commitments marked by benevolence for different members of I is of little use. But one can consider concern structures characterized by convex sets of l-functions displaying less than maximal conflict while remaining sufficiently conflicted to display sensitivity to questions of fair distribution.

Suppose, for example, that there are 2 members in I and the set $L(I)$ consists of all the weighted averages of the two l-functions, one of which assigns person 1 concern .9 and person 2 concern .1 and the other of which does the opposite. Let the agent face two options A and B for which the benefit comparison function assigns the values $bc(A,1) = bc(A,2) = 0$, $bc(B,1) = b > 0$ and $bc(B,2) = a < 0$. If $-b/a > 9$, B is uniquely ABL(I)-admissible and, hence, uniquely abl(i)leximin admissible. If $-b/a < 1/9$, A is uniquely ABL(I)-admissible and, hence, uniquely abl(i)leximin-admissible. If $1/9 < -b/a < 9$, both options are ABL(I)-admissible but A is uniquely abl(i)leximin-admissible. Option A is uniquely leximinb-admissible in any event.

Thus, the criterion of abl(i)leximin-admissibility does not always favor A, which yields the equal distribution of benefits. Although option B favors person 1 over person 2 and renders 2 worse off than he or she would have been under option A, if the improvement of 1's position over the egalitarian position is sufficiently great as compared with 2's loss from the egalitarian position, option B will be recommended because no matter what permissible system of concern values is employed, B will yield greater average benefit than A. If the benefits accruing to 1 are not sufficiently great or the sacrifices incurred by 2 are too great, however, A will be recommended, not because it is regarded as promoting overall better benefits than B but because there is no basis for reaching a decision on the basis of average benefit. Considerations of equity are to be invoked.

In this example, the benefit comparison structure is free of all conflict and assumes cardinal measurability and full comparability – just as the utilitarians do. Furthermore, just as the uniform distribution of concern favored by the utilitarians exhibits symmetry, so does the maximally conflicted concern structure which yields an equivalence between abl(i)leximin- and leximinb-admissibility and the partially conflicted concern structure I have considered here. In effect, the criterion of abl(i)leximin-admissibility displays sensitivity to equality of distribution to the extent that it is applied relative to a conflicted concern structure.

Recall, however, that the raison d'être for insisting on the use of the average benefit principle is the undertaking to use a commitment marked by benevolence for all to resolve conflicts among commitments marked by benevolence for each. This is done best by utilizing a conflict-free concern structure, although when this is done, sensitivity to questions of fair distribution is reduced to a marginal case when options tie for the weighted average benefit. To increase sensitivity, conflict must be injected into the concern structure. But this reduces to some degree (depending on how much conflict lurks in the concern structure) the efficacy of the abl(i)leximin criterion of admissibility in mediating conflicts among commitments to promote rival personal interests.

Thus, it is not quite right to claim that advocates of the average benefit principle must perforce be insensitive to questions about the equality of distributions of benefits. And it is also not quite right to suggest that there is no rationale for invoking the average benefit principle. What is true is that the conditions where use of the average benefit principle is compatible with sensitivity to questions about fair distribution tend to be such that the average benefit principle will be relatively unsuccessful in resolving conflicts among commitments marked by benevolence for each. Hence, the rationale for using the average benefit principle will to this extent be undermined. Advocates of the use of the average benefit principle will have either to abandon pretensions to sensitivity to questions of fairness in distribution or to revise their arguments in favor of the average benefit principle.

Neither alternative can be palatable to writers in the utilitarian tradition, who tend to insist that utilitarian criteria can be invoked to resolve all conflicts in value, who advocate a conflict-free concern structure recognizing only a uniform distribution of concern to be admissible and who, nonetheless, want to claim that questions of fair distribution are handled adequately within the utilitarian framework.

Still, from the vantage point of a pluralist inquiry-oriented approach to value conflict of the sort I have been advocating, one may retain considerable respect for value commitments marked by benevolence for all which rely on the average benefit principle – especially when that principle is combined with leximin principles to yield the abl(i)leximin criterion of admissibility. Such commitments cannot pretend to resolve all conflicts in value which arise – not even those among commitments marked by benevolence for each. But they can sometimes do so, and they do not always display the sensitivity to equity which leximin criteria show. Still, the tempered sensitivity they do exhibit may often seem more acceptable than the ruthless egalitarianism of those who advocate leximin. In the example of the choice between equal distribution A and unequal distribution B, it will seem absurd always to choose the equal distribution. An excessive discrepancy between the benefits accruing to the disadvantaged under the unequal distribution and under the equal distribution may be offensive. But if one group acquires a great benefit as compared with the benefit under equal distribution and the other sacrifices only negligibly, favoring equality may be seen as an expression of *ressentiment*.

When the criterion of abl(I)leximin-admissibility is employed, how the tension between fairness and benefit maximization is handled depends on the indeterminacy in the concern structure. But there is another aspect of the matter captured by this criterion and by no other which merits attention.

Let us suppose that we face three options and that the "individuals" 1 and 2 described before are regarded now as two classes of individuals. In addition to the options A and B there is a third option C, which the benefit comparison function assigns to group 1 the benefit a and to 2 the benefit b. Let us suppose that $b = 2$ and $a = -1$. Thus, B and C are two inegalitarian policies, one favoring group 1 and the other favoring group 2. However, the group which is deprived does not lose very much as compared with what it would receive from egalitarian option A, whereas the advantaged group does receive a substantial increase in its benefits compared with that benchmark.

The ratio $-b/a = 2$ and, hence, in a pairwise choice between A and B both options would be ABL(I)-admissible but only A would be abl(i)leximin-admissible. However, in a three-way choice, A is not ABL(I)-admissible. Only B and C are, so that the agent is constrained to choose between these. Thus, the predicament has formal trappings like the predicaments described in 6.6–6.8 and 7.9, where property α is violated.

More to the point, the violation of α conforms with a presystematic tendency on our part to object to favoring an unequal distribution over an equal one in a pairwise choice but to be more tolerant of such inequality (under restricted circumstances) when among the feasible alternatives are options which yield the advantages to the competing groups of citizens in a symmetrical manner. Indeed, if we have the option of tossing a fair coin and deciding between B and C, the propriety of pursuing that mixed option rather than the egalitarian policy A should seem even more compelling. All of this can be rationalized with the aid of abl(i)leximin-admissibility but not by either ABL(I)-admissibility alone or leximinb-admissibility alone – provided that we see sufficient conflict in the concern structure.

Of course, this argument does not show that reason commands assent to the use of abl(i)leximin-admissibility. No pure practical reason can adjudicate between the merits of abl(i)leximin-admissibility and its rivals. The resolution of conflicts concerning value commitments in which these different standards of admissibility are embedded is, according to the Deweyite approach I favor, a matter for inquiry. Exploration of the structure of diverse value commitments marked by benevolence for all is surely a useful preliminary to any such inquiry even though it cannot settle all debatable issues. That is all that I have sought to do in this chapter.

10

Utilitarianism and conflict

10.1 The sources of conflict

In the previous chapter, I argued that the average benefit principle can be made sensitive to questions of fair distribution if it is embedded in a criterion of abl(i)lex-admissibility. Thus, a currently fashionable complaint leveled against utilitarian and other types of value commitments marked by benevolence for all can be defused to a considerable degree. At the same time, this sensitivity is manifested only in cases of unresolved conflict. When utilitarians boast that their principles can form the basis for resolving conflicts in values, they are claiming that their value commitments are free of such conflict and to this extent cannot manifest the sensitivity to equity which abl(i)lex-admissibility allows.

Perhaps, however, utilitarians should not exhibit the regard for fair distribution their critics insist they should. Their strength resides in their boast that their principles enable us to resolve conflicts in values by appeal to antecedently available general criteria. Can they make good their boast? In this chapter, I shall point to three sources of conflict where, it seems to me, utilitarians should find themselves in considerable difficulty.

10.2 Concern and conflict

Utilitarians agree that each member of *I* ought to be an object of equal concern. This agreement transcends differences in the understanding of utility which divide classical from preference utilitarians or rule utilitarians from act utilitarians. Still, utilitarians often differ concerning the specification of the set *I* of objects of concern. Perhaps most utilitarians may feel comfortable in dismissing the parochialism which gives greater weight to attending to the welfare of one's family than to the welfare of one's city and to one's city rather than to one's nation or to the world community – although I, for one, find no justification for such complacency. But there are some self-styled utilitarians who insist that the set of objects of concern ought to include animals as well as humans (although it is not always clear whether they mean to say that the welfare of a cow ought to be given the same weight as the welfare of a human being). Once one becomes so catholic in one's concern, it is unclear why corporations, intelligent automata and other agents should not be included in I.

These questions may provoke diverse responses within the community of utilitarians. My concern is not to arbitrate among them but to emphasize that utilitarian principles provide little guidance as to how to settle them.

It may be insisted that the issues to which I am directing attention concern the determination of the domain I of objects of concern but not the utilitarian requirement that, given the domain I, the allocation of concern ought to be uniform. But suppose it is unsettled whether the domain I should be I_1 or I_2. The position implied by the commitment to I_1 is equivalent to saying that uniform concern distribution is to be applied to the elements of I_1 and o concern assigned to elements of I_2 which are not in I_1. The same holds *mutatis mutandis* for the position which takes I_2 as the domain of objects of concern. If the agent is in doubt as to which of the domains to use, then while he is in conflict, he is committed to acknowledging all of the members of the union of I_1 and I_2 and construing the two views he is debating as assigning nonuniform distributions of concern of different sorts over this enlarged domain. (These distributions are oligarchy permitting.) Potential resolutions of the conflict will be various distributions of concern which are weighted averages of these distributions, and only one of these distributions will be uniform.

Thus, it seems to me that conflicts over the domain of objects of concern reduce to conflicts over distributions of concern, and the two issues may be treated together. In any event, utilitarianism lacks the resources to settle such controversies.

Of course, if the value commitments marked by benevolence for all are not utilitarian in either the classical or the preference utilitarian sense but seek to promote other benefits, the demand that concern distributions over I be uniform becomes even less obvious. Different types of benefits might call for different types of distributions of concern. But the possibility of conflict is, if anything, more apparent.

10.3 Average versus total utility

A context in which conflict over concern distributions may arise is one in which agents seeking to promote utility face options which alter the total number of individuals in I. Thus, one policy might eventuate in the existence of individuals in domain I_1, whereas a second policy might eventuate in individuals in domain I_2. The two sets typically overlap but are not coincident. Which, if either, of these sets ought to

constitute the objects of concern to which the average benefit principle is to apply? One might focus on I_1, I_2, their intersection or their
union.

Consider the point of view that the union of I_1 and I_2 ought to be
the domain of the objects of concern. The obvious problems with this
approach are defining a benefit comparison function which assigns
benefits to individuals in I_2 but not I_1 in the social state x_1 representing
the first social policy where these individuals do not exist and likewise
assigning benefits to members of I_1 who are not in I_2 in the state x_2
where they do not exist. For classical utilitarians, the answer would
appear to be straightforward. In social state x where individual i does
not exist, $h(x,i) = 0$; i receives 0 net pleasure over pain. Hence, each
individual should be assigned the same bc-value in any state x in which
it does not exist as any other individual is assigned in a state in which
it does not exist.

Preference utilitarianism faces more difficulties in answering the
question. According to preference utilitarianism, given a feasible set
of options U, every permissible benefit comparison function over U
$\times I$ must be in agreement with some permissible value function in the
value structure of person i in I for all pairs $\langle x,i \rangle$ in $U \times I$ for which i
is the second term.

This formulation presupposes that i's value structure is defined for
all feasible options in U. However, if i is sure that he or she does not
exist in state x_2 corresponding to policy 2, the implementation of policy 2 is not a serious possibility as far as i is concerned. (To avoid
misunderstanding, it should be clear that if i exists before the choice
among options in U is made and ceases to exist according to some of
them, i is said to exist, for i has a value structure at the moment of
choice. I am considering cases where i does not exist at the moment
of choice, and the issue is whether or not to bring i into existence.)

In situations where an agent is sure that a certain state will not obtain or a certain option will not be chosen, that option or state is not
in the set U. Of course, one can extend the value structure by hypothetical extension to a larger domain and embed the original value
structure over U in that extended value structure.

To be sure, i might consider how someone might value these options in a knowledge state where it is not settled as to whether option
1 or option 2 is implemented. But the value structure relative to such
a knowledge state cannot, even hypothetically, be said to be i's. To
make the required valuations, i needs to pretend to be someone other
than i, for in the counterfactually hypothesized state of knowledge, it
is unsettled as to whether i will or will not exist. Of course, i is going
through the exercise of hypothesizing but cannot engage in the ex-

ercise and claim the valuations of policies 1 and 2 are i's in the sense required to warrant plugging them into the preference utilitarian benefit comparison structure.

This suggests that in a choice between policies 1 and 2, the personal benefit structure for individual i in I_1 but not in I_2 cannot be constrained by i's value structure for these options simply because there is no relevant value structure to invoke. Hence, insofar as preference utilitarians rely on the value structures of the members of I to determine personal benefit structures, they are bereft of their resource for this purpose.

This does not mean that preference utilitarians are forbidden to extend i's personal benefit structure to cover policies 1 and 2. It does mean, however, that preference utilitarians need to supplement the preference utilitarian constraint on benefit comparison structures which requires that personal benefits agree with the value structures of the individuals whose benefits are being promoted. Hence, it is open to us to introduce a principle similar to the one which holds for classical utilitarianism to this extent. We can stipulate that for every permissible bc-function in the benefit comparison structure, $bc(x,i) = bc(y,j)$ for every i and every j and every x in which i does not exist and every y in which j does not exist. (i and j may be the same or different). This still leaves open whether policy 1 is ranked over policy 2 according to i's value structure. Classical utilitarians can offer an answer depending upon whether the hedonic value (net of pleasure over pain) accruing to i from policy 1 is positive or negative, but preference utilitarians need to invoke considerations additional to their preference utilitarianism. If preference utilitarians follow the practice I have just described, they can agree with classical utilitarians that in states in which i does not exist, the benefit assigned to i is standardized in a manner which is the same for all persons.

With this understood, if we follow the practice of taking as the domain of concern the union of the sets I_1 and I_2, it will follow that evaluating policies 1 and 2 using total utility or using average utility (where the weights are equal) will yield equivalent results. The same is true if the intersection of these two sets is the domain of concern or if it is I_1 alone or I_2 alone. There is no difference between maximizing average utility and maximizing total utility. This is so both for classical utilitarianism and for preference utilitarianism when the latter is supplemented in the manner I have indicated. The idea that there is a distinction between maximizing average and maximizing total utility is a confusion pure and simple.

In all fairness, when Sidgwick (1907: 415) and Rawls (1971: 184) misleadingly contrast maximizing average and maximizing total utility, they do intend to make a serious distinction – to wit, between taking the union of I_1 and I_2 as the domain of the concern structure and taking the domain of the concern structure to be a variable one. In evaluating policy 1, the set of objects of concern is I_1, and in evaluating policy 2, the set of objects of concern is I_2. Of course, to use a variable concern structure to generate a value structure is not to derive a value structure from a benefit comparison structure via a version of the average benefit principle. Even if we can somehow think of a single benefit comparison structure by supposing it defined over the union of the two domains of concern, we do not use the same method of averaging when evaluating 1 and evaluating 2 for the purpose of deriving a single permissible value function in the value structure. Both Sidgwick and Rawls are right, therefore, in supposing that this use of a variable domain of concern (misleadingly called maximizing average utility) does not belong within the dominant utilitarian tradition, which is based on the use of a version of the average benefit principle.[1]

Nonetheless, utilitarians might find themselves in genuine conflict with respect to whether only the present generation is to figure in the domain of objects of concern or whether future generations are, and if they are whether they are to be assigned as much concern as individuals in the present generation. Even though average utilitarianism as understood by Rawls is incompatible with the average benefit principle and *a fortiori* with the average benefit principle relative to a uniform distribution of concern, questions about population control and the welfare of future generations are of genuine concern; and one can entertain addressing them by invoking value commitments marked by benevolence for all which invoke the average benefit principle.

To illustrate by appeal to a simplistic scenario, suppose that I_1 is a proper subset of I_2. The difference between options 1 and 2 is that the former yields a smaller total future population than option 2. The average benefit of the members of I_1 when 1 is adopted could be greater than the average benefit of the members of I_1 when 2 is adopted. The average benefit of members of I_2 when 1 is adopted could, nonetheless, be smaller than when 2 is adopted. Taking I_1 (which is the intersection of the two sets) as the domain of concern entails that policy 1 maximizes total (and average) utility for the domain of concern. If one takes I_2 (which is the union of the two sets) as the domain of concern, policy 2 maximizes total (and average) utility. To see this keep in mind that the average utility for policy 1 is taken over I_2 and not over I_1.

Observe that the issue here does not concern maximizing totals versus maximizing averages. That is a bogus issue. It concerns, instead, whether I_1 or I_2 should be the focus of concern.

Of course, the conflicts as to which domain of concern to adopt may be more complex than suggested by the simplified case I have described here, although I do not think the scheme is any more simple than those used by Rawls and Sidgwick to distinguish between average and total utilitarianism. But seeing such conflicts as reflections of differences over the domain of concern opens the way for recognizing that potential resolutions of such conflicts may be represented by nonuniform distributions of concern over sufficiently encompassing domains. And once this much is acknowledged, the possibility that conflict over the concern structure may go unresolved becomes a possibility meriting serious exploration.

10.4 Classical utilitarianism

We have seen that the criterion of abl(i)leximin-admissibility displays sensitivity to fairness in the distribution of benefits while respecting the average benefit principle in cases where the benefit comparison structure assumes CFC and the concern structure exhibits some moderate conflict. If conflict in the concern structure disappears, the sensitivity to fairness becomes negligible, whereas if the conflict becomes maximal, considerations of fairness reduce the efficiency of the average benefit principle as a means of resolving conflicts among rival interests.

As we have also seen, when CFC is not assumed, these observations must be modified. Under CUC there is no room for sensitivity to fairness while under OLC there is no sensitivity to the average benefit principle. And under CNC = ONC, there is no sensitivity to either maximizing average (= total) benefits or equality of benefits. These results do not undermine the abl(i)leximin principle as compared with the principle of leximinb-admissibility or ABL(I)-admissibility. The appeal to abl(i)leximin-admissibility is no worse and sometimes better than the appeal to ABL(I)-admissibility and to lexminb-admissibility. What it does show is that an appeal to value commitments marked by benevolence for all cannot be invoked to resolve conflicts among commitments marked by benevolence for each (not to speak of other value conflicts) unless the benefit comparison structures make some rather strong assumptions about the measurability of personal benefits and the interpersonal comparability of such preferences. Of course, what kinds of assumptions of measurability and comparability are warranted will depend on the kinds of benefits being promoted, and, indeed, conflict concerning the benefits to be sought can itself generate difficulties in both dimensions.

A comprehensive survey of these matters cannot be undertaken here. However, it may be useful in the context of this discussion to consider how some fairly familiar issues related to measurability and comparability of utilitarian benefits, whether understood according to classical utilitarian or preference utilitarian principles, should be approached within the analytical framework being developed here. We shall consider classical utilitarianism first.

Classical utilitarianism posits a measure of hedonic value $h(x,i)$ defined over $U \times I$ and then adopts as a requirement that all and only permissible bc-functions in the benefit comparison structure $BC(U \times I)$ be positive affine transformations of $h(x,i)$. To the extent that the presupposition is correct and the requirement is met, the benefit comparison structure will satisfy CFC and our discussion of the use of the abl(i)leximin-admissibility criterion (which appears to be favored by that archclassical utilitarian Sidgwick) applies.

There is, of course, one important qualification to be made. The agent committed to promoting overall utility may not know the precise values of the h-function. He might regard several different h-functions as possibly correct representations of hedonic value over $U \times I$. If his credal state were itself free of cardinal conflict, he could determine an *expected hedonic value* function $\hbar(x,i)$, which gives the expected hedonic value (net of pleasure over pain) accruing to i in state x, and adopt as his benefit comparison structure the set of all positive affine transformations of $\hbar$.

Keep in mind, however, that the agent's credal state itself will not be free of conflict. Hence, there will, in general, be an infinity of $\hbar$-functions forming a convex set, and these will determine a benefit comparison structure which could in many cases be quite severely conflicted so that not only will CFC fail to be satisfied but so will OLC and CUC.

Thus, classical utilitarianism does not avoid conflict in the benefit comparison structure but reduces the conflict to conflict in the credal state pertaining to the unknown but true measure of hedonic value. This conflict, however, cannot be eliminated by appeal to the principles of classical utilitarianism itself.

It may, perhaps, be thought that there is some advantage to obtaining such a reduction. Conflicts in the benefit comparison structure are allegedly attributable to human ignorance, which can be remedied by scientific inquiry. There is no denying the desirability of inquiry to mitigate ignorance. But it is not necessary that the ignorance concern which rival hypothises about some unknown condition (in this case the unknown true representation of the hedonic function) is true. Indeed, in our case, the conflict does not arise because of ignorance concerning the correct h-function but because there are many permissible probability functions in the credal state, none of which has a truth value, and, hence, many permissible h-functions, none of which has a truth value. I think that sometimes we might be in a position to settle controversies concerning how to reduce the set of permissible probability functions even though the ignorance thereby mitigated is not concerning "the truth of the matter". Invoking the existence of an unknown but true hedonic function is not sufficient to preclude conflict, nor is it necessary in order to guarantee the removal of conflict through inquiry.

In any case, even the existence of a measure of hedonic value is a debatable question. Moreover, assuming that such a measure exists, it is quite doubtful that the members of I desire to maximize their hedonic benefits. This last doubt need not deter a classical utilitarian from persisting in trying to give the members of I what is good for them even though they do not want it. But the matter becomes quite problematic for anyone who thinks that what the citizens want is a relevant factor to be taken into account even if it need not always be decisive. And classical utilitarianism purports to offer us a criterion for resolving conflicts among rival valuations. No doubt classical utilitarianism can consistently pretend to offer us a principled way of addressing conflicts between hedonic value (i.e., expected hedonic value) and the agent's desires. One should always ignore the agent's desires in those cases. For those who find this prescription unsatisfactory, the pretensions of classical utilitarianism to be a principled approach to the resolution of conflict will appear doubtful. And since, given credal indeterminacy, it cannot even formally succeed in this task, we should, perhaps, consider preference utilitarianism.

10.5 Preference utilitarianism

One of the main attractions of preference utilitarianism is that it does not constrain benefit comparison structures by appeal to some allegedly available objective magnitude where it remains an open question as to whether citizens are or are not seeking to maximize that magnitude. Instead, preference utilitarians constrain personal benefit structures by appeal to the personal value structures of the citizens involved. To this extent, preference utilitarians need not recognize conflicts between promoting the sort of personal benefits they assign to citizens and the citizens' own valuations of the same social states. One source of objections to classical utilitarianism is removed.

But another problem returns to haunt preference utilitarians. The preference utilitarian constraint imposes conditions on intrapersonal comparisons but imposes no additional constraints on interpersonal comparisons. To say this does not imply that hypotheses comparing i's evaluations with j's for the same or different states are cognitively meaningless. The trouble is rather that there are many distinct construals of such interpersonal comparisons – all of them compatible with the same preference utilitarian conception of interpersonal comparisons of welfare. We have an abundance of riches. The problem is to decide among them. To my knowledge, there is no preference utilitarian answer to this question. Insofar as there are many potential solutions, there are many opportunities for unresolved conflict of a sort which preference utilitarian principles cannot resolve.

Suppose we are considering a set of feasible social policies or states U in which are found two elements x and y such that every i in I strictly favors x over y. No matter what the benefit comparison structure may otherwise be like, the fact that each personal benefit structure must agree with the corresponding value structure according to the preference utilitarian constraint means that the value structure representing a preference utilitarian commitment must strictly categorically prefer x over y.[2]

Suppose in addition that the personal value structures of the members of I are all free of cardinal conflict so that preference utilitarianism assures us that the measurability assumption of cardinality is satisfied. To obtain full comparability and, hence, CFC it is sufficient that the following two conditions be met: (i) for each i and j, the benefit attributed to i in state x equals the benefit attributed to j in x. (ii) For each i and j, the benefit attributed to i in state y equals the benefit attributed to j in state y.

But there are other ways to obtain CFC. For example, one might preserve (ii) and stipulate the common benefit to be o and specify a value $a(i)$ for each i in I which may be different for each I in violation of (i). This specification need not be arbitrary. Perhaps there is some objective feature of state x which impinges on the members of I differently (such as personal income) and which can be used to determine the value of $a(i)$. Indeed, there may be many such objective criteria. Of course, instead of modifying (i), we might modify (ii) or both and obtain ways to satisfy CFC.

The point to be emphasized here is that no matter how well founded such comparisons might be according to some value commitment or other, preference utilitarianism is compatible with all of them as long as the preference utilitarian constraint that personal benefit structures agree with personal value structures is satisfied.

It may be thought that the way I have characterized interpersonal comparisons implies that insofar as they represent objective features of the relations between the conditions of members of I in different states in U, they are the same conception of benefit. Every assumption in the family of assumptions about interpersonal benefits is compatible with the same system of personal value structures. Each of them generates a different benefit comparison structure, but no relevant feature of the decision problem is altered. The different benefit comparison structures relate to one another as representations of distance in terms of miles and in terms of kilometers.

This objection presupposes that the only features of the decision problem which the preference utilitarian can take into account in making interpersonal comparisons are characterized by the value structures of the members of I. I suppose one might insist on considering a type of value commitment according to which the only relevant determinant of the benefit comparison structure is the preference utilitarian constraint and that all benefit comparison structures satisfying this constraint are equivalent in the sense that meters and feet are equivalent. But this latter claim is incompatible with the average utilitarian principle when the concern structure is free of conflict or indeed is anything less than maximally conflicted. Under these circumstances the set of ABL(I)-admissible and also the set of abl(i)leximin-admissible options differs for benefit comparison structures the objection alleges to be equivalent. Although I myself have argued that concern structures may often legitimately suffer from conflict, we should not rule out the standard utilitarian position that each individual in I receives equal concern as somehow incompatible with preference utilitarianism.

Preference utilitarianism, as I understand it, insists that in determining personal benefit structures for members of I, only the personal preferences or values of the members of I be taken into account. This leaves the preference utilitarian entirely free to invoke such considerations as real income, social status, and political power in determining the appropriate interpersonal comparisons for the states x and y. One might, for example, group all members of I into k categories characterizing income level, stipulate that members of I in the same category receive the same benefit from x (and from y) and introduce some formula for determining the relations between benefits accruing to persons in different categories in states x and y. One might contemplate alterations in the number of categories to obtain a genuinely different index utilizing different information concerning income distribution. Or one might begin with an index of real income, social status and political power. Even a factor such as geographic location could be brought in. Each one of the suggestions thus so casually thrown out will introduce a genuinely distinct conception of interpersonal comparability of benefit, and each will, nonetheless, be compatible with preference utilitarianism.

One might consider grounding interpersonal comparisons in estimates of hedonic value. To take this view does not imply that all citizens seek the net of pleasure over pain but only that insofar as i and j agree that x is strictly better than y, the hedonic value accruing to i in state x and the hedonic value accruing to j in state x determine whether $bc(x,i)$ is greater than, equal to or less than $bc(x,j)$ and similarly for y. The index of hedonic value need not determine the entire benefit comparison structure but may be invoked in special ways. I am not at all concerned to explore these many possibilities here. My point is that preference utilitarians have no dearth of ways to supplement the preference utilitarian constraint. If there is a problem of interpersonal comparison, it is to be found in this abundance.

Recall that both preference utilitarians and classical utilitarians boast of the capacity to settle value conflicts by invoking their principles. But preference utilitarianism does not specify which of the many ways to ground interpersonal comparisons of benefit is to be selected. Hence, preference utilitarianism cannot resolve conflicts in value which might arise when two such objective notions of interpersonal benefit are proposed as the bases to be adopted in determining the benefit comparison structure. The difficulty is not that the selection of a supplementary criterion itself expresses a value judgement. That goes without saying. The problem is that preference utilitarianism cannot arbitrate between values generated by entertaining two such supplementary criteria.

The fact that preference utilitarianism entails no constraints on interpersonal comparisons of welfare was appreciated by L. Robbins a long time ago and became the basis of his effort to banish welfare economics from the precincts of positive economic study (Robbins, 1962: ch. 6). Welfare economics is allegedly concerned with exploring the extent to which institutions for distributing goods do or do not promote the "general welfare", where "welfare" is often understood to be benefits as determined according to either classical or preference utilitarian criteria. In particular, attention has been focused on the extent to which perfectly competitive markets exemplify the thesis of the "invisible hand" according to which participants in such markets behave in a manner calculated to promote their personal welfares whereas the net effect of their exertions is to promote the "general welfare".

One does not need to advocate benevolence for all where the benefits are welfare so understood in order to investigate this question. To be sure, some conception of personal welfare must be employed in the analysis. Moreover, it should be a conception according to which it is at least approximately correct to claim that participants in a perfectly competitive market seek to maximize their personal welfares. This requirement is difficult to meet if one uses a measure of the net of pleasure over pain as the index of personal welfare. It is trivial, however, to assert that insofar as their value structures are free of ordinal conflict, individual agents seek or should seek to maximize their own welfares. Whether or not one directly defines personal welfare according to preference utilitarian requirements, the conception of personal welfare used should conform to the dictates of the preference utilitarian constraint on benefit comparison structures. The welfare economist who observes this requirement need not adopt a preference utilitarian value commitment or, for that matter, any other type of value commitment marked by benevolence for all.

The problem of measuring personal utility or welfare remains acute even if one is prepared to rest content with ordinal measurement. For better or for worse, economists have convinced themselves that consumers and producers are, at least on average, free of ordinal conflict in their personal value structures so that, to a good approximation, aggregate market behavior simulates what would result were individuals to promote their own welfares, where welfare is understood according to preference utilitarian conceptions (Little, 1957: ch. 3, especially 48–50). They need some such assumption in order to use their theoretical resources for purposes of description, explanation and prediction quite independently of their ethical interests.

According to the position I have taken here, it is doubtful that consumers or other agents ought to be free of unresolved conflict at the moment of choice as frequently as economists say they actually are. I do not wish to speculate, however, as to how wide the gap is between what ought to be the case and what is.

Robbins observed that when we seek to explain the operation of the perfectly competitive market or to make predictions about economic behavior, the supplementary constraints on preference utilitarian conceptions of welfare needed to obtain strong assumptions about interpersonal comparison are not needed.

To be sure, with the aid of the supplementary constraints a sense may be given to claims that a particular economic policy does or does not promote economic welfare. But that does not enhance the explanatory or predictive power over the old range of phenomena. Nor does it do so over some new range of phenomena. Rather it singles out a new range of phenomena for study. More to the point, we can alter the verdict concerning the efficiency of the economic system in promoting general welfare by revising the way the preference utilitarian conception of welfare is supplemented without in any way revising any other assumption of positive economics.

L. Robbins (1962: 138–140) goes beyond what is warranted by this entirely sound observation when he denies that interpersonal comparisons of welfare are testable. As Little (1957: 52–60) and Sen (1970a: 92) have argued, we are quite capable of making assertions concerning whether i is better off than j in state x and offering evidence supporting such claims. Sen points out that there are many different ways in which preference utilitarian conceptions of welfare may be supplemented to furnish testable interpersonal comparisons of welfare or utility (Sen, 1982: 265–270).

But the issue of testability is irrelevant to Robbins' main thesis. Robbins (1964: 141) contends that conceptions of interpersonal comparability are "interesting" as "ethical" postulates even though they contribute nothing to positive economic science. In contrast, the preference utilitarian conception of intrapersonal comparisons of welfare is a significant constituent of familiar microeconomic theories. If this claim is right (as I think it is), it holds even if the diverse conceptions of interpersonal comparability considered are testable.[3]

Thus, Robbins ought not to be saddled with the claim actually endorsed by A. Bergson (1966: 20) to the effect that interpersonal comparisons of welfare are value judgements without cognitive content. Robbins' claim is weaker and more plausible – to wit, that interpersonal comparisons of welfare are "interesting" only when made within a framework of ethical postulates.

At the heart of Robbins' thesis is the observation that preference utilitarian conceptions of welfare do not entail any particular conception of interpersonal comparability. Robbins used this observation to reach a conclusion about the relation between positive and welfare economics. I have used the same assumption to reach a different conclusion about the pretensions of preference utilitarianism as an arbiter of conflicts in values. Because there are many different ways to supplement preference utilitarian constraints on benefit comparison structures consistently, preference utilitarians can differ with one another as to how one should make interpersonal comparisons of welfare or value. And a single preference utilitarian can be in conflict concerning the choice of a supplementary principle. What emerges is a conflict in value which preference utilitarian principles cannot resolve.

The situation is still worse than this. Even if preference utilitarian principles cannot resolve all conflicts in values, at least they should be able to resolve conflicts among value commitments marked by benevolence for each by appeal to a commitment marked by benevolence for all (where the benefits are preference utilitarian welfare). To do this requires, however, some degree of interpersonal comparability, and this requires appeal to supplementary principles which may be subject to controversy. But preference utilitarian principles cannot be invoked to settle such disputes. As a consequence they cannot be said to arbitrate conflicts among commitments marked by benevolence for each member of I.

K. J. Arrow (1963: 110, 112) asserts that interpersonal comparisons cannot serve even as ethical postulates because they cannot be checked by observation. Unless such comparisons address observationally discernible differences, they cannot be signifigant according to Arrow. Hence, he insists, they cannot furnish content for any norms.

But even though the various methods described above for supplementing preference utilitarian constraints are fairly crude, they do allow for making interpersonal comparisons in a manner which can be decided just as easily by observation as intrapersonal comparisons are. I am not denying that there is a problem about interpersonal comparison of utility or welfare for preference utilitarians. But the problem does not concern the meaningfulness of such comparisons or their testability. To the contrary, there are too many meaningful ways preference utilitarians can consistently supplement their principles for the purpose of making interpersonal comparisons of welfare. However, the principles of preference utilitarian doctrine provide no guidance as to how to choose among these supplementary principles. Preference utilitarianism can furnish no guidance to someone caught in conflict among diverse principles for making interpersonal comparisons.

10.6 Conclusion

My aim in this chapter has not been to furnish an exhaustive critique of various forms of utilitarianism. The remarks made about classical and preference utilitarianism have focused on issues of relevance to the assessment of any value commitment marked by benevolence for all members of some group I insofar as such a value commitment is endorsed, at least in part, as a means of resolving conflicts among value commitments marked by benevolence for each member of I. I have argued that if a value commitment marked by benevolence for all is to perform this conflict-resolving function, the value structure derived from a benefit comparison structure should be obtained by means of the average benefit principle.

In chapter 9, the charge that the use of the average benefit principle ignores the fairness of the distributions was rebutted. It was suggested that the test of ABL(I)-admissibility based on the value structure derived via the average benefit principle may be supplemented by a form of lexicographical maximin principle. When the measurability–comparability assumptions implied by a benefit comparison structure support CFC, the sensitivity to fairness increases with the extent of conflict in the concern structure relative to which the average benefit principle is applied. Thus, the use of the criterion of abl(i)leximin-admissibility tends to be successful at resolving conflicts among value commitments marked by benevolence for each but to suppress fairness of the distribution when the concern structure is conflict free. Use of this criterion tends to emphasize fairness while proving inadequate as a means of resolving conflict among commitments marked by benevolence for each when the concern structure itself suffers from conflict.

In this chapter, I argued that conflicts in the concern structure can arise within a utilitarian framework owing to disputes about the domain I of objects of concern and that these conflicts cannot be resolved satisfactorily by appeal to utilitarian principles. In order for a value commitment marked by benevolence for all to resolve conflicts among value commitments marked by benevolence for each, it is necessary that some fairly strong assumptions of interpersonal comparability be made.

I have discussed two versions of utilitarianism, labeled classical and preference utilitarianism, which confront the question of interpersonal comparability differently. The former presupposes the existence of some measure of benefit (the net of pleasure over pain accruing to individual i in state x). There are, of course, technical questions of measurability confronting the appeal to such measures, and some may doubt whether there is such a magnitude. But that is not crucial here, for my concern is not with classical utilitarianism per se. There may be other value commitments marked by benevolence for all which invoke an appeal to some other magnitude (e.g., some index of primary goods, capabilities, etc.) whose intelligibility and measurability may or may not be so problematic. And the troubles facing classical utilitarians face those who endorse these other views as well – to wit, that the clients whose benefits are to be promoted may not want to maximize their holdings of these benefits. To point this out is not to suggest an inconsistency in classical utilitarianism or any other value commitment marked by benevolence for all for which this observation is correct. But at least in those cases when the clients or citizenry offer considerable resistance to the efforts of those who would be benevolent, many would find it difficult not to acknowledge the presence of a conflict in values calling for moral inquiry or struggle of the second kind.

Two features of this conflict are worth noting:

1. It is a conflict arising from two value commitments marked by benevolence for all, one of which satisfies the preference utilitarian constraint that personal benefit structures be identical with individual value structures. Neither value commitment marked by benevolence for all can be used, therefore, to resolve the conflict without begging the question.

2. The value commitment marked by benevolence for all satisfying the preference utilitarian constraint cannot be invoked to resolve

conflicts in value commitments marked by benevolence for each (which also satisfy the preference utilitarian constraint) unless appeal is made to supplementary principles not at all entailed by the preference utilitarian constraint to make interpersonal comparisons.

These considerations suggest, I think, that value commitments marked by benevolence for all are not fundamental value commitments which may be used to resolve all conflicts arising among value commitments and, indeed, are impotent to handle all conflicts arising among value commitments marked by benevolence for each.

Nonetheless, it does seem entertainable that persons and institutions do become committed to benevolence for all individuals in some group or other for some range of decision problems or other and, indeed, may become committed to several value commitments of this type which come into conflict. The scheme I have developed here offers an analytical framework for exploring such value commitments and the various sorts of conflict which may arise within such a value commitment, among them and between them and other commitments not marked by benevolence for all.

Ultimately, of course, it will prove desirable to offer an account of how inquiries concerned with resolving erstwhile unresolved conflicts of these kinds ought to be conducted – at least insofar as one can discern certain general features of all such inquiries regardless of the contexts from which they emerge. But in this volume, I have not addressed that problem. I have been defending the claim that it is sometimes rational to make decisions without having settled all relevant conflicts in value. Writers in the utilitarian tradition have tended to deny this and to buttress their denial by offering a ready-made system of principles for resolving conflicts. In this chapter, I have sought to show that utilitarian versions of such projects seem doomed to failure. What appears to be true of utilitarianism seems likely to hold for other types of value commitment marked by benevolence for all.

11

Social choice theory

11.1 Social benefit functionals

The account of value commitments marked by benevolence for all is related to the literature on social choice theory deriving from K. J. Arrow as elaborated along the lines pioneered by A. K. Sen. In this chapter, my aim is to explain in somewhat greater detail the relation between the technical apparatus I am using and the framework developed by Sen and those who have followed the paths he has explored. The discussion recapitulates many of the points emphasized in the previous two chapters but does so in a manner which relates them to the literature emanating from Arrow and Sen.

A *social benefit functional* (SBFL) is a functional relation between benefit comparison functions (defined over $U \times I$) and value structures (defined over U). An SBFL takes as arguments benefit comparison *functions* and not benefit comparison *structures*, although the values of these functionals are value structures and not value functions. However, given an SBFL defined for all benefit comparison functions, it will be possible to determine a value structure from an arbitrary benefit comparison structure, provided that two conditions are satisfied. The first is as follows:

CFC invariance: Let $F[bc(x,i)]$ be an SBFL and $bc' = abc + b$ for positive a and real b;

$$F[bc'(x,i)] = F[bc(x,i)].$$

The rationale for this condition is that two benefit comparison functions which are positive affine transformations of one another are equivalent in all respects considered relevant in the representation of benefit comparison structures. When this condition is satisfied, a benefit comparison structure free of cardinal conflict uniquely determines a value structure according to a given SBFL regardless of the permissible benefit function used to derive the value structure. The value structure may or may not suffer from cardinal or even ordinal conflict, but it is the same regardless of which benefit comparison function is permissible in the conflict-free benefit comparison structure employed in making the calculation. The SBFL is assumed to be invariant – i.e., to yield the same value structure – for all bc-functions which are permissible in a benefit comparison structure satisfying CFC.

The CFC-invariance condition determines the way an SBFL generates a value structure from a benefit comparison structure free of cardinal conflict. The second condition to be considered concerns the way in which value structures are to be derived from benefit comparison structures which suffer from cardinal conflict:

Convexity: Let F be any SBFL and let $bc = wbc_1 + (1 - w)bc_2$ for $0 \leq w \leq 1$; $F(bc)$ is the set of v-functions defined over U which are of the form $wv_1 + (1 - w)v_2$ for permissible v_1- and v_2-functions in $F(bc_2)$ and $F(bc_2)$ respectively.

Given an SBFL satisfying these two requirements, any benefit comparison structure determines a set of v-functions which is the set of v-functions in at least one of the value structures determined relative to at least one permissible bc-function. This set is closed under positive affine transformation thanks to CFC-invariance and convex thanks to convexity. In the subsequent discussion, I shall suppose that SBFL's satisfy CFC-invariance and convexity. Value commitments marked by benevolence for all are characterized by some procedure for deriving value structures from benefit comparison structures and, hence, are characterizable by SBFL's satisfying CFC-invariance and convexity.

Other types of value commitment not marked by benevolence for all are also characterized by SBFL's satisfying CFC-invariance and convexity, and we shall subsequently identify conditions which will distinguish those SBFL's which do represent value commitments marked by benevolence for all from those SBFL's which do not. In any case, we can use SBFL's as a device for studying and characterizing value commitments marked by benevolence for all instead of proceeding as I did in chapter 9 without utilizing SBFL's at all in any explicit manner. Bringing SBFL's in explicitly allows us to compare the ideas discussed in chapter 9 with the approaches to social choice theory developed by Arrow and subsequently extended by Sen.

Subject to some qualifications to be explained shortly, an SBFL is a generalization of Sen's notion of a *social welfare functional* (SWFL) (1970a: definition 8*2), which in turn is a generalization of Arrow's (1963: ch. 3) notion of a *social welfare function* (SWF).

An SWFL is a functional relation between benefit comparison functions (over $U \times I$) and weak orderings of the elements of U. If we restrict ourselves to weak orderings which are representable by real-valued v-functions defined over U, an SWF or SWFL is indeed an SBFL of a special kind – namely, one where the value structure is the set of all v-functions which define a specific weak ordering of U. Sen himself does not require that the weak orderings be representable by real-valued v-functions and, hence, does not rule out the possibility that the orderings are lexicographical ones such as an ordering according to a lexicographical maximin procedure. Hence, strictly speaking there are some SWFL's which are not SBFL's. However, we can, I think, modify Sen's characterization of SWFL's so as to exclude such orderings without any substantial distortion of his theory. We can think of lexicographical maximin in terms of a hierarchy of SWFL's each of which is an SBFL in my sense without distorting the criteria for determining the set of admissible options.

With this qualification understood, therefore, SWFL's may be treated as SBFL's of a special type. As Sen (1970a: 129) points out, Arrovian SWF's are characterizable by SWFL's "in which only individual ordering properties are used". That is to say, they are SBFL's which are SWFL's satisfying, in addition, the following condition:

ONC-invariance: If bc' is a positive monotonic transformation of bc,

$$F(bc') = F(bc).$$

The concept of an SBFL is more general than that of an SWFL in two respects: The value of an SBFL can be a value structure free of cardinal conflict. This is not true of SWFL's. It is true that Sen and others[1] who have used SWFL's as an analytical tool have often defined SWFL's (in effect) as the ordinalization of a functional relation between bc-functions over $U \times I$ and real-valued v-functions over U – i.e., where the value of the SWFL is the set of positive monotonic transformations of the v-function derived from a given bc-function. Thus, there is no objection on Sen's part to the use of functionals whose arguments are bc-functions and whose values are real-valued v-functions. However, the extra information conveyed by a v-function additional to the ordering which is thereby represented is regarded as suppressible. My notion of an SBFL does not presuppose this in advance.

The second respect in which SBFL's cover situations not covered by SWFL's concerns the possibility that a benefit comparison structure free of cardinal conflict may, nonetheless, determine a value structure which suffers not only from cardinal but even from ordinal conflict. Sen himself has explicitly acknowledged the possibility of value structures exhibiting ordinal conflict so that the categorical value ranking is at best a quasi ordering.[2] But he has restricted the ways in which such a value structure may be generated. There is nothing in Sen's theory, for example, corresponding to an SBFL defined by using the average benefit principle together with a concern structure suffering from conflict. As we have seen, however, it is precisely in cases where the concern structure is conflicted that we can begin with an SBFL generated by the average benefit principle and, by supplementing the appeal to average benefit with a hierarchy of SBFL's characterizing lexicographical maximin, display sensitivity to fairness in distributions of benefits.

In chapter 9, we considered, without saying so, several different types of SBFL's whose ordinalizations are SWFL's:

1. Let $l(i)$ be the distribution of concern which is uniquely permissible according to concern structure $L(I)$. Let $ab[l(i),bc(x,i)] = \Sigma\ l(i)bc(x,i)$. This function, for fixed $l(i)$, is an SBFL whose ordinalization is an SWFL.

2. For fixed k, both $\min(k,bc,x)$ and $\max(k,bc,x)$ are SBFL's whose ordinalizations are SWFL's.

In addition, we considered SBFL's which use the average benefit principle relative to conflicted concern structures. In general, the values of these SBFL's will suffer from ordinal conflict and, hence, we cannot ordinalize them so as to yield SWFL's.

I have already mentioned that Sen's conception of an SWFL allows for a principle deploying a lexicographical maximin principle to be an SWFL even though it is not an SBFL. And there could be a principle which begins with the use of the average benefit principle and then appeals to lexicographical maximin which is also characterized by an SWFL which is not an SBFL. In the next section, this matter is explored in a little more detail and the relation between such SWFL's and criteria of leximinb-admissibility and abl(i)leximin admissibility explained.

11.2 Lexicography

Leximin as Sen understands it proceeds by taking a bc-function and determining $\min(1,bc,x)$, which is a function of x whose values are real values, taking all elements in U which receive a specific real value, and determining $\min(2,bc,x)$ for each of them and ordering those elements of U with the same real value accordingly. If there remains a "tie", one goes to the third level and so on. The upshot is that we obtain a definite weak ordering of the elements of U for each permissible bc-function in the benefit comparison structure. If the benefit comparison structure is free of ordinal conflict, each permissible bc-function will generate the same weak ordering.

Suppose, however, that the benefit comparison structure is not free of ordinal conflict. In that case, one will obtain a set of weak orderings. One might consider as a rule for making choices an injunction to restrict choices to those options in U which come out optimal according to some weak ordering in this set. Will this set of options coincide with the leximinb-admissible options? In the case where there is no ordinal conflict in the benefit comparison structure, the answer is yes. In cases where there is ordinal conflict, the answer is, as a general rule, no. The following setup illustrates the point.

Suppose that U contains two social states x and y and I contains two individuals i and j. The benefit comparison structure is the convex hull of the following pair of benefit comparison functions:

	bc^1		bc^2	
	i	j	i	j
x	0	10	6	10
y	1	5	1	5

According to some permissible benefit comparison functions in the benefit comparison structure, the leximin SWFL ranks x on top. According to others, y is ranked on top. But x alone is leximinb-admissible. It is true that both x and y are $MINB_1$-admissible, but x is uniquely $MINB_1$-$MINB_2$-admissible.

This divergence between the verdict recommended through the use of criteria of admissibility based on Sen's leximin SWFL and the use of leximinb-admissibility disappears, of course, when the benefit comparison structure is free of ordinal conflict. These are the cases on which Sen and his associates focused in discussing leximin.

One could, in principle, consider criteria of admissibility based on SWFL's like Sen's leximin. However, when benefit comparison structures conflict, these criteria do not function well in the ways in which lexicographical principles should. The motivation for using lexicographically ordered principles is to provide a basis for rendering verdicts as to what to do when prior principles fail to do so. In the example just cited, the use of the leximin SWFL to develop a test of admissibility is no better than the test of $MINB_1$-admissibility. Leximinb-admissibility does better. We cannot always guarantee that it will do better, but it cannot do worse.

The relations just described between a test of admissibility generated by the leximin SWFL and leximinb-admissibility can be paralleled when we consider starting with the average benefit principle and then deploying lexicographical maximin. As long as the concern structure is free of cardinal conflict, we can generate an abl(i)leximin SWFL. If, in addition, the benefit comparison structure is free of cardinal conflict, the options which are optimal according to this SWFL are the abl(i)leximin-admissible options. But if the benefit comparison structure suffers from cardinal conflict, there may be options admissible according to the test using the abl(i)leximin SWFL which are not abl(i)leximin-admissible.

The contrast becomes apparent when the benefit comparison structure satisfies the assumption OLC but not CFC. As noted in chapter 9, the abl(i)leximin-admissible options coincide with the leximinb-admissible options. But if we take each permissible *bc*-function separately, determine the options which come out best relative to that function according to the abl(i)leximin SWFL, and regard as admissible all options which come out best in this way relative to some permissible *bc*-function, then for each *bc*-function, there will be at least one admissible option which is optimal relative to that *bc*-function according to the average benefit principle. Clearly the test for admissibility using the abl(i)leximin SWFL does not do very well in rendering verdicts when the average benefit principle fails us.

These considerations indicate some grounds for approaching the discussion of principles for determining the admissibility of options relative to value commitments marked by benevolence for all in a way which restricts Sen's SWFL's to those cases where the orderings which are the values of the SWFL's are not lexicographical.

11.3 Independence

SBFL's have been introduced to characterize value commitments marked by social benevolence. Although they are functional relations between benefit comparison functions and value structures, we have embraced constraints on them already which guarantee that they determine value structures from benefit comparison structures as well.

Strictly speaking, an SBFL is defined as a function from benefit comparison functions over a given domain $U \times I$ to value structures on the given U. Hence, if we shift from the given U to another set of feasible options U' or from set I of citizens to I', the original SBFL is not applicable.

But value commitments marked by social benevolence are to be understood as having scopes of applicability extending beyond a single set of feasible options. Advocates of such commitments may share a given commitment for one class of decision problems while differing concerning the applicability of the commitment to other decision problems. But only rarely will an advocate of some commitment regard his or her endorsement as restricted exclusively to one set of feasible options (i.e., to one decision problem). Thus, as a general rule, a value commitment marked by social benevolence cannot be fully characterized by an SBFL. We need to consider a family of SBFL's for all the domains of feasible options within the scope of the value commitment.

Let two hypothetical sets U and U' of feasible options have at least some options in common. Let S be the intersection of U and U'. F is an SBFL defined for benefit comparison functions over $U \times I$ and F' is an SBFL defined for benefit comparison functions over $U' \times I$. Because S is nonempty and both SBFL's are defined for all possible benefit comparison functions in their respective domains, both will be defined for benefit comparison functions bc and bc' which agree in the set $S \times I$.

One question which must be settled if we are to discuss how value commitments marked by benevolence for all determine SBFL's for different contexts of choice is when F and F' cannot characterize the same value commitment marked by social benevolence for all. This is not a problem of individuation raising issues of profound ontological importance. We are free to settle the matter in one way or another. But how we do so will contribute to our characterization of value commitments marked by benevolence for all.

For the purposes of this discussion, I shall suppose that if $F(bc) \neq F'(bc)$ when the value structures are restricted to the domain $S \times I$, the value commitments characterized by F and F' are distinct.

There may be value commitments characterizable by SBFL's but which are not individuated in accordance with this requirement. They will not be understood to be value commitments marked by social benevolence in the sense understood here.

In the special case where U' is a proper nonempty subset of U, it follows that given two benefit comparison functions bc_1 and bc_2, both of which are defined over $U \times I$ but which agree over $U' \times I = S \times I$, the value structure $F(bc_1)$ restricted to $U' \times I$ should be the same as the value structure $F(bc_2)$ restricted to $U' \times I$.

Let F' be the SBFL defined for $U' \times I$ which characterizes the same value commitment as F does for $U \times I$ and let bc' be the benefit comparison function over $U' \times I = S \times I$, which is the common restriction of bc_1 and bc_2 to $S \times I$. By the condition on the individuation of value commitments marked by social benevolence, the value structure $F(bc_1)$ restricted to $S \times I$ must equal $F(bc')$. Similarly the value structure $F(bc_2)$ restricted to $S \times I$ must also equal $F(bc')$.

Thus, the principle we have adopted to constrain the way the same value commitment determines SBFL's for different domains entails a condition of *independence* (condition I) on SBFL's, which asserts that if F characterizes a value commitment over $U \times I$ and $S \times I$ is a subset of $U \times I$, the value commitment is characterized over $S \times I$ by the restriction of F to $S \times I$. This condition corresponds to the condition of independence of irrelevant alternatives imposed by Sen on SWFL's.[3]

Condition I is a constraint on SBFL's (or in Sen's version on SWFL's). It is interesting, however, that it can be derived from a condition on

SBFL's for different overlapping sets of feasible options where the SBFL's are expressions of the same value commitment marked by social benevolence. When seen in this light, the independence condition may be understood as a corollary of procedures for individuating value commitments marked by benevolence for all.

11.4 Paretian conditions

Value commitments marked by benevolence for all are endorsed by agents concerned to promote the benefits of the clients, citizens, club members or objects of concern in I. For this reason, it is not enough to require that value structures be determined by benefit comparison structures so that the values of feasible options are determined by the benefits accruing to citizens. The dependence should, in addition, be a positive one according to which the value of an option increases with increases in the benefits accruing to members of I.

Just as Sen captures this positive dependency by means of conditions on SWFL's, we may impose corresponding constraints on SBFL's. F satisfies the *strong Pareto condition* (SP) if and only if the following two conditions are satisfied:

(i) For every x and y in U such that $bc(x,i) \geq bc(y,i)$ for all i in I, the corresponding value structure ranks x weakly better than y according to all permissible rankings.

(ii) For every y in U such that $bc(x,i) \geq bc(y,i)$ for all i in I and $bc(x,i) > bc(y,i)$ for some i in I, the corresponding value structure ranks x strictly better than y according to all permissible rankings.

If an SBFL satisfies SP, it also satisfies the following conditions: The *weak Pareto condition* (WP) is satisfied if and only if for every x and y in U such that $bc(x,i) > bc(y,i)$ for all i in I, the value structure ranks x strictly better than y according to all permissible rankings. The *Pareto indifference condition* (PI) is satisfied if and only if for every x and y in U such that $bc(x,i) = bc(y,i)$ for every i in I, the corresponding value structure ranks x equal to y according to all permissible rankings.

All of the SBFL's considered here satisfy WP, PI and clause (i) of SP, but some SBFL's violate clause (ii). Examples are those SBFL's characterizing the use of the average benefit principle with a dictator- or oligarchy-permitting concern structure (see 9.3). These are the concern structures with permissible distributions of concern assigning o weight or concern to some elements of I. All other SBFL's grounded in the average benefit principle satisfy clause (ii) of SP. SBFL's defined according to bottom-up or top-down kth-level dictatorship also violate clause (ii) of SP, as is easy to check.

We have seen that hierarchies of SBFL's often define functional relationships from benefit comparison functions to weak orderings over U which are lexicographical and, hence, not representable by value functions or sets of value functions. In particular, the leximin SWFL and a corresponding abl(i)leximin SWFL may be constructed in this manner. SP is satisfied by the leximin SWFL. And when the concern structure is free of conflict, so is the abl(i)leximin SWFL.

Keep in mind, however, that benefit comparison structures may suffer from conflict, and whether they do or do not, concern structures may do so. Although the Paretian conditions are well defined for SBFL's and for SWFL's which are not SBFL's [such as the leximin and the abl(i)leximin SWFL's], we need to consider whether we can find useful characterizations of Paretian conditions for tests of admissibility hierarchically organized as are the tests issuing in the criterion of abl(i)leximin-admissibility or of leximinb-admissibility.

When we focus on tests of admissibility associated with SBFL's as applied to conflict-free benefit comparison structures, it is obvious that those SBFL's which satisfy SP are such that no option is admissible according to the SBFL which is strictly inferior according to the requirements of clause (ii) of SP to some other feasible option, and those SBFL's which satisfy WP are such that no option is admissible according to the SBFL which is strictly inferior to some other feasible option according to WP.

We can extend these definitions to the case where benefit comparison structures suffer from conflict by saying that a test of admissibility associated with an SBFL satisfies SP (WP) if and only if no admissible option according to the SBFL is strictly inferior to some other feasible option according to SP (WP) relative to all permissible bc-functions. Such tests of admissibility guarantee that no noncontroversially Pareto-inferior option (in the sense of SP or WP as the case may be) will be admissible. It should be apparent that a test of admissibility associated with an SBFL satisfies SP (WP) if and only if the associated SBFL does.

We are now in the position to generalize to hierarchically ordered sequences of tests of admissibility such as leximinb-admissibility and abl(i)leximin-admissibility. We can say that a criterion of admissibility (whether generated from a single test or from a hierarchy of such tests) satisfies SP (WP) if and only if there is no noncontroversially Pareto-inferior option (according to any given benefit comparison structure) recognized as admissible by the criterion. Even in those cases where there is neither an SBFL nor an SWFL characterizing the criterion but only a hierarchy of SBFL's, we may make sense of these criteria satisfying SP or WP.

In 11.2, we noted that the options in U which come out optimal according to some ordering generated by the leximin SWFL from a permissible *bc*-function in a conflicted benefit comparison structure need not be leximinb-admissible, although all leximinb-admissible options are optimal according to the leximin SWFL relative to a permissible *bc*-function. Hence, leximinb-admissibility never recognizes as admissible an option which is inferior according to SP to some other feasible option in *U*. The same applies *mutatis mutandis* to the abl(i)leximin SWFL and abl(i)leximin-admissibility, provided that the concern structure is dictator and oligarchy forbidding. (To speak of an SWFL rather than an SBFL implies that the concern structure is free of conflict.) If the concern structure is conflicted and dictatorship and oligarchy forbidding, then ABL(I)-admissibility satisfies SP so that no abl(i)leximin-admissible option is inferior according to SP. Moreover, even if the conflicted concern structure is dictatorship and oligarchy permitting, as long as at least one permissible distribution of concern is neither dictatorial nor oligarchic, the appeal to leximin after resorting to ABL(I)-admissibility guarantees that no admissible option is SP-inferior to any other feasible option. This condition is satisfied unless all permissible distributions of concern in *L(I)* assign 0 concern to each element of a common nonempty subset of *I*.

11.5 Invariance

Given a set *X* of *bc*-functions, an SBFL is *X*-invariant if and only if the value structures determined by the given SBFL from all the *bc*-functions in *X* are the same.

We have already insisted that all SBFL's be CFC-invariant and noted that Arrow required that SWF's be ONC-invariant. Clearly, however, we can also entertain SBFL's which are CUC-invariant, OLC-invariant or exhibit other types of invariance. Assumptions of invariance of SBFL's ought not to be confused with the associated measurability–comparability assumptions. To assume cardinal full comparability (CFC) is to make a stronger measurability–comparability assumption than to assume cardinal unit comparability (CUC) in the sense that the set of permissible *bc*-functions under CFC is a proper subset of the set of permissible *bc*-functions under CUC. However, to assume that an SBFL satisfies CUC-invariance is stronger than to assume that it satisfies CFC-invariance in the sense that a CUC-invariant SBFL is invariant over a larger set of *bc*-functions than is a CFC-invariant SBFL so that CUC-invariance entails CFC-invariance.

If we focus attention on SBFL's which are also SWFL's, the value structure determined for a benefit comparison structure which satisfies the measurability–comparability assumption *X* is free of ordinal conflict if the SBFL is *X*-invariant or is *Y*-invariant, where *Y* is a stronger measurability–comparability assumption than *X*. Thus, an SBFL based on the average benefit principle relative to a conflict-free concern structure will not only be CFC-invariant (as every SBFL must be) but also be CUC-invariant. However, it will not be OLC-invariant, CNC-invariant or ONC-invariant. Relative to an assumption of CFC or CUC made by a benefit comparison structure, the value structure will be free not only of ordinal but of cardinal conflict as well. However, relative to an assumption of OLC, CNC or ONC, there will be ordinal conflict. This does not mean that the SBFL fails to determine a unique value structure for benefit comparison structures assuming OLC. Rather it means that the SBFL yields a value structure suffering from conflict.

Furthermore, commitment to the average benefit principle with a conflict-free concern structure does not obligate one to endorse benefit comparison structures satisfying CUC or CFC. One's value commitment may require the use of a benefit comparison structure which assumes OLC or CNC or any other measurability–comparability assumption consonant with our general requirements on benefit comparison structures. Doing so will bring conflict to the value structure which emerges, but it will not bring incoherence.

This observation is quite general. Given commitment to an SBFL satisfying X-invariance, it is unnecessary to restrict application of the SBFL to benefit comparison structures satisfying the measurability–comparability assumptions X. Applying it to benefit comparison structures which are proper subsets of those satisfying X will mean that some measurability–comparability assumptions will be irrelevant to the determination of a value structure. Applying it to benefit comparison structures which include the benefit comparison structure satisfying X will generate conflict in value structures. There is no need, however, to rule out benefit comparison structures of either kind from the range of the SBFL.[4]

11.6 Anonymity

Some SBFL's exhibit another important type of invariant property. A benefit comparison function may be transformed by permuting the members of I in the appropriate argument place in the bc-function. The result is another bc-function which is, in general, distinct from the original one. If the value of an SBFL is invariant under a permutation transformation of the bc-function, the SBFL is said to satisfy the *anonymity condition* (A) (see, e.g., Sen, 1970a: 68, 72).

All SBFL's conforming to kth-level bottom-up (or top-down) dictatorship satisfy the anonymity principle. So do all SBFL's conforming to the average benefit principle where the concern structure is symmetrical. (see 9.3). This includes the special case where the concern structure is egalitarian. To be sure, all other cases involve conflicted concern structures. Hence, when the average benefit principle is used, the only SBFL which will always take values free of cardinal conflict is the "utilitarian" one based on an egalitarian distribution of concern assigning equal concern to every element of I.

This point is of some interest, for as long as one restricts oneself to SWFL's or to SBFL's whose ordinalizations are SWFL's, one will rule out average benefit principles with conflicted concern structures and, hence, tend to think of anonymity conditions as mandating commitment to egalitarian concern structures or to some form of kth-level dictatorship such as Rawls' difference principle. Historically, something very much like this has tended to happen in the social choice literature. Once more we have testimony to the widespread but unwarranted tendency to deny or ignore cases of unresolved conflict.

The condition of anonymity as just characterized applies to SBFL's. But the idea may be extended to the criteria of admissibility obtained by appealing to a hierarchically organized sequence of tests for admissibility such as leximinb-admissibility and abl(i)leximin-admissibility. If permuting the individuals in bc-functions defined over $U \times I$ does not alter the set of admissible options according to some criterion of admissibility, the criterion satisfies anonymity. In this sense, leximinb-admissibility satisfies anonymity, and when $L(I)$ satisfies the symmetry condition, abl(i)leximin-admissibility also meets anonymity.

11.7 Benevolence for all

We are now in a position to characterize value commitments marked by benevolence for all citizens in I in terms of the SBFL's or hierarchies of SBFL's they mandate in decision problems where the feasible options belong to some set U so that the benefit comparison structure is defined over $U \times I$. Throughout this discussion, I assume that all SBFL's are CFC-invariant and satisfy the convexity condition.

We have tacitly assumed that any SBFL should be a total function defined for every bc-function possible. This corresponds to a so-called condition of unrestricted domain (U). In addition, we have introduced a condition of independence which characterizes the way in which a value commitment marked by benevolence for all determines SBFL's for different sets of feasible options where one set contains the other.

Conditions U and I by themselves fail to distinguish value commitments marked by benevolence for all from value commitments marked by malevolence for all or, indeed, from value commitments of other varieties where the value structure for U is a function of the benefit comparison structure for $U \times I$. In 11.4, however, it was suggested that WP, PI and clause (i) of SP could be invoked to distinguish value commitments marked by benevolence for all from these other value commitments characterizable with the aid of SBFL's.

To sum up, therefore, we may say that an SBFL characterizing a value commitment marked by benevolence for all should be CFC-invariant, satisfy the convexity condition and satisfy conditions U, I, WP, PI and clause (i) of SP. Furthermore, we should expect all SBFL's in a hierarchy controlled by a value commitment marked by benevolence for all to satisfy these conditions.

11.8 Potential resolutions

Some value commitments marked by benevolence for all are aimed at resolving conflicts marked by benevolence for each member of I. As understood in chapter 9, this means that the first level value structure has to be derived from the benefit comparison structure via the average benefit principle. But all such SBFL's are CUC-invariant. This means that all first-level SBFL's in a hierarchy should be CUC-invariant. Hence, $\text{MIN}B(1,bc,x)$ cannot be a first-level SBFL if the value commitment marked by benevolence for all is to provide potential resolutions of conflicts among value commitments marked by benevolence for each. Consequently, criteria of admissibility such as leximinb-admissibility are ruled out as long as the provision of such potential resolutions is a concern.

11.9 Utilitarian aggregation

It is customary to think of the anonymity condition A as a strengthening of the condition of nondictatorship. And that is true if nondictatorship is the requirement that no SBFL be such that $F(bc)$ always be equal to the benefit structure of the individual i for some fixed i. Clearly condition A rules out that alternative. However, it does not rule out bottom-up or top-bottom dictatorship. Of course, Sen and his colleagues do not think bottom-up dictatorship to be as offensive morally as dictatorship of the sort just cited (which is, in effect, the sort which Arrow sought to preclude). In any case, once we have fixed on SBFL's grounded in the average benefit principle as the first-level SBFL's in a hierarchy, condition A implies, as we have seen, that $L(I)$ should be symmetrical.

We may go even farther. If the SBFL is an SWFL so that the value structure is required to be free of ordinal conflict, condition A guarantees that the sole permissible distribution of concern in $L(I)$ be the uniform distribution assigning equal concern to all elements of I. This is, of course, the concern structure favored by utilitarianism. Taking all the results obtained thus far together, we reach the conclusion that an SBFL which is also an SWFL, which is CUC-invariant (and *a fortiori* CFC-invariant) and which satisfies U, WP, PI, clause (i) of SP, I and A is utilitarian in the sense just given.

This characterization of utilitarianism is reported by C. D'Aspremont and L. Gevers (1977: 203, theorem 3) in a study which seeks to make invariance conditions on SWFL's pivotal to a comparison of utilitarian criteria as compared to criteria based on some Rawlsian version of minimax or on a leximin ordering. Observe, however, that if we consider SBFL's which are not SWFL's, this characterization no longer captures the utilitarian principle. An SBFL satisfying CUC-invariance, convexity U, WP, PI, clause (i) of SP, I and A can have a symmetrical concern structure which is conflicted. It can, indeed, be dictatorship permitting. We may forbid both dictatorship and oligarchy by insisting that SP be observed. And, indeed, D'Aspremont and Gevers do not invoke WP, PI and clause (i) of SP, but simply appeal to SP which entails all this and more. Still, the concern structure can be symmetrical and conflicted so that we have no guarantee that the uniform distribution is the uniquely permissible one. To obtain that result, we must require that the SBFL be an SWFL so the value structure is conflict free.

This point brings out rather nicely a limitation of working with SWFL's. Analyses relying on SWFL's as the fundamental tool build in to their approaches the presupposition that the value structure to be derived will be free of conflict. Hence, the use of the average benefit principle with conflicted concern structures is ruled out in advance. The D'Aspremont–Gevers characterization of SWFL's singles out the so-called utilitarian SWFL, but once we apply the characterization to SBFL's we no longer obtain the utilitarian result.

When this point is appreciated, the issue of CUC-invariance is no longer as pivotal as it once appeared to be to the characterization of utilitarian methods of deriving value structures from benefit comparison structures. It remains, to be sure, a necessary condition for obtaining such methods, but it is far from sufficient. Nonetheless, the question of the presence or absence of conflict in the concern structure begins to seem as important as the question of CUC-invariance in assessing the status of utilitarian methods of aggregation.

11.10 Leximinb-admissibility and abl(i)leximin-admissibility

The reason CUC-invariance was pivotal for D'Aspremont and Gevers in characterizing utilitarianism is that they were contrasting a utilitarian SWFL with a leximin SWFL. The latter, like the former, satisfies U, SP, *I* and A but differs in that it is OLC-invariant. To be sure, this remains insufficient as a characterization of the leximin SWFL. The so-called leximax SWFL also satisfies these requirements. (This is the analogue of leximin obtained by appealing to top-down kth-level dictatorship.) An additional condition must be imposed (D'Aspremont and Gevers, 1977: theorem 7). Even so, this additional constraint presupposes OLC-invariance of the SWFL. Given the requirements that we are dealing with an SWFL satisfying U, SP, I and A, OLC-invariance rules out CUC-invariance. Thus, it does appear plausible to suggest that the pivotal issue in debates among advocates of the utilitarian principle and the leximin principle concerns the merits of CUC-invariance versus OLC-invariance.

Once, however, we take seriously the possibility of conflict in value structures and resort to SBFL's as the tools for analysis, we can no longer use the leximin principle, for the leximin SWFL is not an SBFL. As I have already suggested, we should, instead, consider the criterion of leximinb-admissibility which is generated by a hierarchy of tests utilizing SBFL's of the form MINB(k,bc,x). We can contrast it with the test for ABL(I)-admissibility where the concern structure recognizes only the uniform distribution to be permissible as utilitarianism requires or the test for abl(i)leximin-admissibility with the same concern structure.

But now we need to address some new issues. We have already suggested how to understand the various Paretian conditions and anonymity when discussing tests for admissibility. And it seems fairly obvious that instead of condition U we want the corresponding requirement that the test of admissibility be applicable to any well-formed benefit comparison structure. Understanding condition I and the various invariance conditions becomes more problematic.

What we do not want to require in lieu of I is the condition that the set of admissible options in subset S of U consist of all admissible options in U which are also in S and only these. This condition would be far too strong, implying in effect that properties α and β be satisfied by choice functions characterized by the standard for admissibility. This would imply that the options in U could be weakly ordered so that the admissible options in any nonempty finite subset are optimal according to the weak ordering. The upshot is that the value structures in the hierarchy with which we would begin could be invoked to determine a valuation free of ordinal conflict.

Clearly I mean to deny that this must be so. Hence, condition I cannot be extended in this manner to tests of admissibility. Instead, I suggest that we require only that the tests of admissibility be based on a hierarchy of SBFL's, all of which satisfy condition I. When this is so, I shall say the test of admissibility satisfies I as well.

Invariance conditions are even more problematic. Perhaps the best way to contrast tests of admissibility with respect to invariance is to restrict oneself to benefit comparison structures free of cardinal conflict. Here ABL(I)-admissibility is clearly CUC-invariant, leximinb-admissibility is OLC-invariant whereas abl(i)leximin-admissibility is CFC-invariant when the concern structure is not maximally conflicted but is OLC-invariant (indeed, is equivalent to leximinb-admissibility) when the concern structure is maximally conflicted. Notice that even when the concern structure is free of all conflict, abl(i)leximin-admissibility is at best CFC-invariant. To be sure, the first test is ABL(I)-admissibility, which is CUC-invariant, but the subsequent tests (amounting to leximin) are not CUC-invariant. However, when the concern structure is free of conflict, we may say that the test of abl(i)leximin admissibility is "primarily" CUC-invariant.

In chapter 9, I defended the requirement that tests of admissibility for value commitments marked by benevolence for all be "primarily" CUC-invariant. This was not because I had strong views about the feasibility or lack of feasibility of various forms of interpersonal comparisons of benefits but because I proposed to focus on value commitments marked by benevolence for all which can serve to resolve conflicts among value commitments marked by benevolence for each.

To insist on invoking a criterion of leximinb-admissibility even though it cannot serve this function seems to me to beg the question in advance against those who seek to resolve such conflicts by balancing the interests of different members of the community. To rely on ABL(I)-admissibility however, entails neglecting the question of the fairness of distributions. As I have pointed out in chapter 9, using the criterion of abl(i)leximin-admissibility skirts both Scylla and Charybdis. To be sure, to do this presupposes the possibility of conflict in benefit comparison structures and concern structures. And this requires an analytical apparatus which is somewhat more flexible than the framework of social welfare functionals.

11.11 Arrow's impossibility

Because an SWFL is a generalization of Arrow's SWF, it is possible to formulate a version of his impossibility result in terms of SWFL's as Sen (1970a: 129) has done. We suppose that SWFL's are CFC-invariant, and satisfy conditions U, WP and I. In addition, we suppose that the SWFL is nondictatorial in the sense that the value structure determined by an SWFL is not equated with the personal benefit structure of some specific individual in I no matter what the benefit comparison structure over $U \times I$ might be. Finally, we assume that the SWFL is ONC-invariant so that no matter what the benefit comparison structure might be, interpersonal comparisons of benefits are ignored.[5]

Sen's version of the Arrow result asserts that these conditions are inconsistent.

Conditions U, I, WP and CFC-invariance guarantee that conditions parallel to conditions L_1 and L_2 on potential resolutions of conflicts between value functions as specified in 5.4 are satisfied. ONC-invariance implies CUC-invariance, which in turn assures us that an analogue of L_3 can be secured. Hence, we can say that the value of an SWFL must be obtained by the average benefit principle. But no SWFL satisfying that principle is ONC-invariant unless it assigns all weight to a single individual – counter to the condition of nondictatorship.

Why is ONC-invariance assumed? Primarily because Arrow desired a way of deriving a social ranking from individual rankings (or utility indicators) without relying on interpersonal comparisons. Two demands are being made here: (a) that the value structure derived from a benefit comparison structure be free of ordinal conflict and (b) that there be no reliance on interpersonal comparisons. If we give up either requirement, we no longer need to assume ONC-invariance. Thus, if we require only CUC-invariance with the average benefit principle, say with the utilitarian uniform distribution of concern, but consider benefit comparison structures assuming ONC, we shall obtain a conflicted value structure in violation of (a). We shall not, however, be making any assumption of interpersonal comparability and so shall be satisfying (b).

Arrow, of course, always explicitly insisted that social value structures (social preferences) be free of ordinal conflict and, indeed, insisted, as so many economists do, in making this a condition of rationality. I have been arguing against this assumption throughout this book and see no reason to find it especially compelling in the context of social choice. But allowing violations of (a) is not enough to remove the sting of Arrow's impossibility result. It is one thing to allow the rationality of decision making under unresolved conflict. It is quite another to maintain that agents ought perforce to remain in a state of maximal conflict when committed to promoting the benefits of all. If we refuse to make any assumptions about interpersonal comparisons of benefits in defiance of (b), we shall remain in a permanent state of unresolved conflict.

All of this discussion has been restricted to an analysis invoking SWFL's. If we permit SBFL's, it is easy to see that we can permit nondictatorship and ONC-invariance without inconsistency. But, of course, by permitting SBFL's we will have given up Arrow's "rationality" assumption in advance. Even so, if we were to embrace an ONC-invariant SBFL (e.g., using the average benefit principle with a maximally conflicted concern structure), we could not avoid unresolved conflict as a permanent state. We must permit the possibility of resolving conflict in concern structures and, hence, in value structures, and this suggests that we can shift to SBFL's which are not ONC-invariant.

In my judgement, the discussion of Arrow's impossibility result has tended to see the endorsement or rejection of the various conditions which lead to inconsistency as a forever affair. Either we must mandate the rationality postulate forever or we must never mandate it. Nondictatorship must always be imposed or never imposed. The same is true for noncomparability, however that is construed.

My own view is far more wishy-washy. In promoting benefits for all, we often find ourselves in unresolved conflict in violation of the rationality postulate. And we may be eminently reasonable to recognize our value conflicts as unresolved. At the same time, we may hope, with Dewey, that we can somehow find considerations sufficient to resolve the conflicts, if not now then in the future. This may involve finding ways to reduce conflicts in benefit comparison structures by making stronger measurability and comparability assumptions while weakening invariance requirements on SBFL's by reducing conflict in the concern structures. We should not, in advance, postulate limits to our success or failure in reducing such conflicts. To throw such roadblocks in the path of inquiry is to frustrate the approach to moral struggle of the second kind advocated by Dewey before it can get off the ground.

12

Conflict and inquiry

Dewey once wrote:

Diversity does not of itself imply conflict, but it implies the possibility of conflict, and this possibility is realized in fact. (Dewey, 1983: 38)

According to Dewey, conflict in "habits" (which correspond roughly to what I have called "value commitments") provokes inquiries aimed at the revision of such habits to eliminate the conflict. In Dewey's view, therefore, the conditions provoking inquiry concerned with modifying values are themselves generated by the diversity of habits or value commitments endorsed by agents or members of a community. Circumstances arise, often unexpectedly, in which value commitments which heretofore have cohered well in practical applications are no longer jointly applicable. That conflict-generating situations develop is not a logical consequence of value pluralism, but it is, as Dewey says, a fact.

Coming to terms with this fact intelligently does not deny value pluralism by substituting some single standard of "intrinsic" value for it. Efforts to do so are fruitless, so Dewey would argue, and are tied to an untenable quest for certainty:

Love of certainty is a demand for guarantees in advance of action. Ignoring the fact that truth can be bought only by the adventure of experiment, dogmatism turns truth into an insurance company. Fixed ends upon one side and fixed "principles" – that is authoritative rules – on the other, are props for a feeling of safety, the refuge of the timid and the means by which the bold prey upon the timid. (Dewey, 1983: 167)

In this passage, Dewey is not expressing a skepticism about values which denies that we can be certain about values. For Dewey, both in science and in conduct, we are sure of some things and in doubt about others. To alleviate the doubt, intelligent agents devise conjectures which they seek to test and develop in order to reach a sensible conclusion as to how to reduce the domain of doubt. Dewey objects, rightly I think, to those who would deny the need to take the risks incurred in such experimentation by pretending that what is currently doubtful is after all certain.

There are many questions to be answered by someone who wishes to take Dewey's idea seriously. Precisely how one is to take the role of experimentation in investigations aimed at resolving conflicts between value commitments and the value structures they generate remains, it seems to me, an open question. Some consideration of why it seems urgent to resolve some conflicts in value whereas we can manage to live easily with others unsettled is called for. The relations among value commitments, truth-value-bearing hypotheses and probability demand scrutiny.

In this volume, I have avoided addressing these and many other important matters. My aim has been to remove one roadblock from the paths of inquiries of the sort Dewey envisaged. The fundamental premise has been that agents may make decisions without settling the question as to what they ought to do, all things considered, and still retain their credentials as rational agents. Indeed, an even stronger assumption was endorsed. On many occasions, the reasonable thing to do is to make decisions without having resolved all conflicts in values.

Such assumptions seem thrust on us if we seek to provide an account of inquiry aimed at settling controversial issues regarding what we ought to do without, on the one hand, presupposing that such issues may be settled in advance by some single standard of value or hierarchy of principles for conflict resolution or, on the other hand, insisting that such conflicts are resolved by the choices we make. Once we take seriously the idea that conflicts in values put us in a state of ignorance regarding the value commitments in competition and that relief from such ignorance may often entail investigation, we should, I believe, be prepared to reject the idea that such inquiry can always be brought to a successful conclusion before the moment of choice. To think otherwise is to give excessive credence to the miraculous.

In the previous chapters, I have sought to give a general account of decision making under unresolved conflict and to give some sense of its ubiquity – in moral deliberation narrowly defined, in cognitive decision making, in decision making under uncertainty and in efforts to promote benefits for all. It should be apparent that I have not exhausted all the possible ways in which value conflicts can arise. Nothing has been said, in particular, about conflicts between personal projects or other agent-centered value commitments and moral or other value commitments or about conflicts between liberty and welfare. Some indication has been given, however, that decision making under unresolved conflict is or ought to be a pervasive phenomenon, and an analytical framework has been proposed for use in representing conflicts of value other than those subjected to explicit examination here.

The framework for rational choice which has been proposed is more than a device for removing obstacles to a Deweyite conception of moral inquiry. To the extent that its prescriptions can and are obeyed by human and social agents, it presents a rather radical revision of as-sumptions lying at the core of most contemporary decision theory and microeconomic theorizing. As a normative account of how risks ought to be assessed by public agencies, it offers an important alternative to the orientations currently favored by public officials (Levi, 1980a: ap-pendix). It offers a general setting for comparing diverse views of how benefits are to be allocated to citizens or clients. Thus, even those who have little sympathy for my Deweyite predilections might find something of interest in the ideas which have been presented.

Even so, for me at any rate, the chief attraction of the ideas pre-sented here is their role in preparing the way for bridging the alleged gulf between science and value through a vision of problem-solving inquiry applicable to both scientific inquiry and efforts to settle unre-solved conflicts.

Notes

1. Moral struggle

1 Since I follow Dewey and Davidson on this point, I shall not seek reasons for rejecting the one-principle outlook except to observe, following R. Marcus (1980: 125), that using one fundamental principle is no guarantee against moral conflict in Davidson's minimal sense.

2 Davidson (1980: 36) suggests that there is a sort of reasoning present in moral conflict which adds up the reasons on all sides of the issue.

3 *Akrasia* so construed and violation of the total knowledge requirement are sometimes due to lapses of memory, limitations of computational capacity and the excessive costs of recovering information which can be recovered if the price is right. The remedy for this is often more extensive reliance on improved and less expensive technologies which facilitate the recovery of information and the improvement of computational capacity. Libraries and computers are examples of such technologies. Improved training in logic and mathematics may sometimes be helpful. Perhaps psychotherapies can also be of assistance. In these respects, weakness of will is a failure of rationality in much the same sense as is a failure to be certain of the deductive consequences of the propositions in whose truth one is certain, a failure to form coherent credal probability judgements or a failure to have transitive preferences. Such failures may also be attributable to failures of computational capacity and memory as well as to emotional disturbances. In all such cases, our acknowledged incapacities to live up to the prescriptions of rationality ought not to persuade us to trim our norms but to devise techniques which enhance our capacities to conform to them.

R. C. Jeffrey (1974) seeks to deploy second-, third-, and higher-order preferences to represent complex valuational attitudes including versions of weakness of will. Akrates prefers smoking to abstention but prefers that he prefer abstention rather than prefer smoking. This seems to contrast with Davidson's approach, according to which *prima facie* rankings are preference rankings relative to given "considerations" – corresponding roughly to my "value commitments". The agent's preference ranking may agree with one of these *prima facie* rankings. If the agent has proper strength of will, his ranking will agree with the *prima facie* ranking, all things considered. Second-order preferences between first-order preferences do not appear at all.

Second- and higher-order preferences may be relevant when the focus is on the revision of value commitments and the first-order preferences determined by them. Such revision is the concern of moral inquiry or moral struggle of the second kind and should not be confused with moral struggle of the first kind – i.e., weakness of will. This concern with moral struggle of the second kind is not ruled out by H. G. Frankfurt (1971). Frankfurt's second-order desires can be construed as desires for revisions of desires or wants for future preferences. Jeffrey explicitly disavows such an interpretation of his view. The second-order preferences at t are rankings of first-order preferences at t (Jeffrey, 1974: 384 and footnote 11). Jeffrey concedes that his theory of higher order preference would be trivial if the agent were constrained by rationality requirements to be certain of his first-order preferences. However, he suggests that an argument of S. Uchii (1973) to that effect is question begging; and Jeffrey (1983: 226–227) sketches a semantics for higher preference with some help from Z. Domotor. I fail to see, however, how this semantics or any other maneuver in Jeffrey's work addresses the worries raised (Levi, 1980a: 165–166) about such views.

It is, of course, undeniable that persons lack self-knowledge, but I am inclined to classify uncertainty about preferences with failures of deductive closure in the set of assumptions taken to be certainly true or failures of coherence in probability judgement as failures to live up to commitments to given ideals of rationality. Such failures are excusable because of human limitations of memory or computational capacity and emotional instabilities. Davidson sees weakness of will as a product of such failures. Jeffrey apparently intended to offer a characterization of weakness of will without failure to live up to ideals of coherence or rationality. He seems to think that uncertainty about first-order preferences is not merely something which can consistently (and truly) be said to happen but is a perfectly coherent cognitive posture for the agent in such a state of uncertainty. I disagree.

4 The agent endorsing P_i need not formulate the constraint C_i explicitly. Nor need the agent identify the scope T_i explicitly. A value commitment represents a general principle or habit of evaluation to which the agent is committed. Failures of memory or computational capacity and emotional instability may prevent the agent from living up to his, hers or its commitments and may also excuse such failure. To this extent, endorsing a value commitment resembles commitment to deductive closure of a body of assumptions taken as settled or certain (see Levi, 1980a: 9–13). The lack of feasibility referred to in clause 4 is intended to refer to factors other than those inhibiting the capacity to think clearly. Finally, the distinction between the scope of a value commitment and the constraint it imposes on evaluations of feasible options is itself context dependent and no more rigid than the corresponding distinction between the scope of a scientific law and its formula.

5 R. B. Marcus (1980: 128–129) defines a consistent set of rules as "obeyable" in all circumstances in some possible world. Marcus does not explicitly distinguish between the scope of applicability of a principle and the constraints imposed by it. But setting this point of difference to one side, her characterization of the consistency of a set of principles seems to be equivalent to my notion of the *logical* consistency of a set of value commitments.

B. Williams (1973: 205) adopts a conception of consistency of rules more or less the same as that endorsed by Marcus. He contrasts the corresponding notion of inconsistency with a conception of conflict. Conflicts arise in Williams' sense when it is "empirically impossible" for all constraints imposed by the principles to be satisfied in some specific context. I am not sure what Williams means by "empirical impossibility" over and above the fact that in some context of choice the constraints are not satisfiable. In any case, this suffices to induce a breakdown of the universal applicability of the set of principles. Williams sometimes seems to call such a breakdown "inconsistency" even though it is not logical inconsistency. The inconsistency is between the claim of universal applicability and the claim that the constraints are not jointly satisfiable in a particular case. If the agent knows this and obeys SGC, his value commitments are epistemologically inconsistent in the sense I introduce in the text. As we shall see shortly, Williams does not endorse SGC (see note 6).

6 Marcus and Williams take a different view. The existence of an inconsistency between the assumption of the universal applicability of a system of value commitments (for Marcus and Williams, moral commitments or principles) and the information that the constraints are not jointly satisfiable in the particular context of choice presenting the dilemma is not sufficient reason to modify the scopes of applicability of any of the commitments by moving to a state of suspense as to their applicability in the given dilemma-provoking predicament.

Marcus denies that the existence of such an inconsistency involves an inconsistency in the value commitments in any important sense – only an inconsistency between the assumption of universal applicability and the information that a counterinstance to that assumption exists. As I understand her, she rejects the SGC, which holds that the endorsement of value commitments (in her case, moral value commitments) presupposes the universal applicability of the several principles jointly (see Marcus, 1980: 134–135). Hence, if one who endorses such commitments finds a counterinstance to universal applicability, the agent may consistently continue to endorse these principles while recognizing that the principles are not universally applicable together.

Marcus holds that endorsement of several value commitments presupposes a readiness to undertake efforts to avoid dilemma-like predicaments wherever feasible. We try to make the world such that in the future the moral value commitments will be universally applicable. Embracing this commitment presupposes the satisfaction of a weak generalizability condition asserting that the constraints imposed by the several principles ought to be jointly satisfied except in those cases where they are incapable of being jointly satisfied.

Thus, dilemma-provoking contexts in which conditions 1–4 obtain do not, according to Marcus' view, generate struggles of the second kind. There is no inconsistency which provokes a shift to a position of suspense among value commitments. It does not become an open question as to whether any given one of the P_i's applies in the particular context. They all continue to apply at least when taken separately. They do not apply jointly. Since there is no need to move to a state of suspense, there is no need subsequently to conduct inquiries aimed at removing doubt.

I do not mean to suggest that Marcus thinks that moral dilemmas are matters for complacency. She insists that although there is no demand that the several constraints be jointly satisfiable in the particular context, they should be satisfiable individually. Moreover, there is an obligation to satisfy each constraint individually in the sense that failure to do so generates an obligation to make amends. Dilemmas are troubling, but the solution to such troubles is to avoid them insofar as the world admits. Seeking to modify the value commitments which generate the dilemma is not taken seriously.

Williams holds that recognition that a given decision problem satisfies 1–4 generates a conflict, and for him such conflict is often described as inconsistency. As stated in note 5, the inconsistency among moral principles or value commitments recognized seems to be tantamount to a breakdown of the universal applicability jointly of these principles. Rhetorically Williams affirms the existence of an inconsistency in such cases whereas Marcus denies it. But as far as I can make out, Marcus does not deny the breakdown of universal applicability, and Williams does not affirm the presence of an epistemological inconsistency in the endorsement of the value commitments.

Williams asserts that the sort of inconsistency which is present need not lead to a modification of the value commitments. In this respect, he agrees with Marcus and disagrees with me. Williams cannot, therefore, say that endorsing the several value commitments presupposes their universal applicability as SGC requires. If it did, then as soon as the agent endorsing the value commitments recognized the existence of the dilemma, there would be an inconsistency in the agent's beliefs or "assertions". Williams is quite clear that such inconsistencies should be removed (Williams, 1973: 201–205). Thus, the sense in which Williams holds that there is an inconsistency is not one which Marcus should deny.

The substantive agreement between Williams and Marcus is more profound than even this. Williams, like Marcus, holds that when 1–4 obtain, the individual principles remain in force separately if not jointly. Both agree that it is often sensible to try to avoid dilemma-like predicaments. Williams glosses this with the observation that there is often no need even to try because the contexts in which the commitments cannot be simultaneously obeyed are too rare or trivial to worry about. Williams and Marcus agree that in dilemma-like contexts, one is obliged to conform to each commitment in the sense that one should make amends wherever feasible for failure to do so.

Perhaps the chief difference between Williams and Marcus is Williams' argument that ethical realism is undermined by the fact that endorsing several moral commitments inconsistent in his sense (because not universally applicable) does not warrant modifying the commitments. It seems to me that it is the SGC that Williams is undermining. If that is an implication of ethical realism, then to that extent his argument does, indeed, undermine ethical realism. But I do not understand what the controversy over ethical realism amounts to and so avoid dealing with it. In any case, Williams and Marcus agree in rejecting SGC. If they do differ over ethical realism, it cannot be over the status of SGC.

For my part, I endorse SGC and, hence, maintain that 1–4 entail the epistemological inconsistency of value commitments in a sense which legitimately calls for their modification. The first step in revision is a shift to suspense which eliminates inconsistency but retains conflict or dilemma. Thus, I agree with Williams and Marcus that dilemmas do not involve incoherence or inconsistency in belief, but this agreement masks a rather substantial disagreement between their shared views (whatever their differences might be) and my position. I have no *a priori* demonstration that my approach is superior to theirs. I seek only to elaborate some of the ramifications of taking the approach I favor, which may then be compared with the approaches they adopt.

7 In the cases where the constraints imposed by a single value commitment cannot be implemented in a given decision problem (see Marcus, 1980: 125), consistency is achieved by restricting the scope of applicability of the offending value commitment so that it does not apply to situations of the type under consideration. Here too the agent must shift to a form of suspense, but it cannot be between erstwhile distinct value commitments and

the constraints they impose. Rival commitments must be invented for the occasion. Thus, in examples like Marcus' cases where two promises are made which by unfortunate circumstance cannot both be kept, judgement may be suspended as to which ought to be kept – perhaps according to different considerations. The rankings of the alternative options according to the two views are both recognized as permissible.

8 Even though Davidson's akratic agent might choose to join the army just as our conflicted agent does, the akratic agent fails to recognize there being any question outstanding concerning what ought to be done in a situation of that kind. The akratic agent is committed, all things considered, to some definite resolution of the conflict in favor of pacifism and conscientious objection, but he cannot bring himself to choose in conformity with his commitments. He chooses instead in conformity with patriotism. If he is wallowing in self-deception, he will consider his patriotic gesture to be right even though this judgement fails to cohere with the verdict to which he is committed, all things considered. Or if he is not fooled by his own rationalizations and recognizes his moral weakness, he may worry as to how to protect himself against similar lapses in the future. What he does not worry about is how to settle the conflict between pacificism and patriotism. All things considered, the conflict has been resolved. And according to his akratic rationalization, it is also resolved. Either way there is nothing to inquire about.

2 Dilemmas

1 Van Fraassen (1973: 15−19) does not use standards of value (my ways of evaluation) inducing weak orderings over feasible options or worlds as he does when characterizing "ought" according to the approach he regards to be "axiological". Given a set of feasible worlds, he defines the "score" of a feasible world as the set of "imperatives in force" which that world fulfills. According to van Fraassen (1973: 18) h ought to be the case if and only if there is a feasible world in which h is true whose score is not included in the score of any feasible world in which $\sim h$ is true.

The difference between van Fraassen's definition and the one I have attributed to him in the text is in formulation alone. According to van Fraassen, a subset of the set of imperatives-in-force is consistent if and only if there is a feasible world in which they are jointly fulfilled. Let us then consider a maximally consistent subset of the set of imperatives relative to the set of feasible worlds. The set of imperatives-in-force generates various such maximally consistent subsets in this sense. Each such subset picks out a subset of the set of feasible worlds which fulfill the requirements of the imperatives in that set. Any such maximally consistent subset of the imperatives-in-force may be viewed as a partial characterization of a weak ordering representing a way of evaluating feasible options. This partial characterization is sufficient to define "ought" relative to such ways of evaluation or standards of value. That is to say, it suffices to furnish a characterization of ideal worlds. Once we have this notion of "ought" relative to a way of evaluating feasible worlds as partially characterized by a maximally consistent subset of the set of imperatives-in-force, the categorical "ought" may be determined in the manner I have attributed to van Fraassen in the text. This notion is equivalent to the one explicitly proposed by van Fraassen. If h ought to be true in van Fraassen's sense, there is a feasible world in which h is true whose score is not empty. There must be at least some subset of its score which is not in the score of $\sim h$. Furthermore, there must be at least one subset of that subset which is maximally consistent. These subsets are such that h is true in every world which fulfils them, for otherwise $\sim h$ would fulfill some of them – counter to our assumptions. Hence, there is at least one maximally consistent subset of imperatives-in-force (and, hence, at least one permissible way of evaluation) relative to which h ought to be the case. Hence, h ought to be the case in the sense I attribute to van Fraassen in the text.

Conversely, if h ought to be the case according to the definition I attribute to van Fraassen in the text, there is some maximally consistent set of imperatives such that h is true in all feasible worlds fulfilling that set. Hence, these imperatives are not part of the score of $\sim h$. So h ought to be true in the sense of "ought" van Fraassen explicitly introduces.

2 The rescue of the so-called classical principles of deontic logic which is thereby achieved is effected at the cost of full recognition of their triviality – which seems to me exactly right.

3 According to Davidson, weakness of will requires the presence of a *prima facie* obligation in conflict with the *prima facie* obligation, all things considered. This is perfectly compatible with claiming, as I have done here, that in the particular context, the conflict between promise keeping and the other considerations has been resolved.

3 Values in scientific inquiry

1 In Levi (1962: 56–57), I used the expression "eliminate doubt". In Levi (1967a: ch. 4), I used "relief from agnosticism". In Levi (1967b 369–391), I used "informational utility" or "informational value".

2 I first suggested that such a trade off characterized the degree of caution exercised by an investigator in Levi (1962: 56–57). It was subsequently incorporated into the account of epistemic utility presented in Levi (1967a) and then modified in Levi (1967b).

3 Peirce himself failed to grasp the distinction until relatively late in his career. See Levi (1980b: 128–130).

4 I suggested that these desiderata be construed as determinants of informational value in Levi (1967b: footnote 34, p. 391). This suggestion was put forward as a revision of the position taken in Levi (1967a: 113–118). In that book, I thought of such informational desiderata as rivals to relief from agnosticism rather than determinants of it.

5 See Levi (1979: 419–427; 1980a: ch. 6). G. Shafer pointed out to me in correspondence that my characterization of P-admissibility in 6.3 of Levi (1980a) falters due to a mistaken claim made on p. 136 of the hardback edition. The claim is corrected in the paperback edition. However, I should say that I am not entirely satisfied with the account of this matter which emerges. As Teddy Seidenfeld keeps complaining and Patrick Maher (1984:691) has pointed out, my current view will sometimes recommend a conclusion which is not a Bayes' solution (E-admissible). I am more inclined now than I once was to regard this complaint as a just one. Its remedy cannot be considered here. However, I do not think the settling of this issue will alter the main thrust of these remarks very seriously.

6 J. Leach (1968: 99–102). P. Maher (1984: 690) asserts that it would be "irresponsible" not to take into account the practical and ethical ramifications of revisions of doctrine. My remarks about Leach should apply to Maher as well.

7 As I conceded (Levi, 1960: 356).

8 I discuss this point (Levi, 1967a) in response to oral comments made by

Rudner in reaction to my earlier criticisms of his view. I did not see Leach's paper until later, but my reaction to Rudner applies to Leach as well.

9 The conception of truth I employ is discussed in Levi (1976: 32−33; 1980a: 14−25).

4 Choice and foreknowledge

1 It is commonly held that if a deterministic characterization is to be given, it will be found at some more fundamental level of scientific theorizing (according to some suitable hierarchy). Of course, such a characterization at a more fundamental level may not be forthcoming. That appears to be the case with regard to quantum mechanics. There is no need to conclude from this that the probabilities appearing in quantum mechanics are therefore peculiarly different in a way calling for a new "single case propensity interpretation" of probability. It should also be noted that when chances relative to trials of a given kind or sample spaces relative to trials of a given kind are attributed to a system, there is a way to describe outcomes at a more "superficial" level of explanation according to which the process becomes deterministic. One can causally explain why coin a landed heads or tails up by appealing to the coin's sure-fire disposition to land heads or tails on a toss and the law or reduction sentence asserting that whenever a coin having that disposition is tossed it lands heads or tails. This is not a trivial explanation, in a sense ruling out considering it a causal explanation. Thus, relative to the description of outcomes of trials as realizing some point in the sample space, deterministic representation is always available. If one is prepared to follow D. Davidson's (1980: essay 7) approach to causality and say that the tossing of the coin on some specific occasion caused its landing heads on that occasion because the coin's landing heads or tails, which is known to be the landing heads, can be causally explained by its being tossed, not only should conditional analyses of causation be abandoned but so should probabilistic analyses be rejected. Attributions of objective probability presuppose causal generalizations in the typical cases.

2 I agree with H. G. Frankfurt (1978: 157−162) that actions may be described as such without reference to the causal factors explaining them.

3 In another version of Jones' predicament, he might have had the ability to choose to toss a coin and let the outcome determine whether Jane or Lilly were hired. Or he might have had yet another option − namely, letting his boss decide between Jane and Lilly. In both cases, one might describe the option as choosing true as strongest (relative to the agent's knowledge) that either Jane or Lilly is hired. Of course, this representation would not be helpful if both options were available and we wanted to distinguish between them. We would then need to distinguish between choosing as strongest that Jane is hired or Lilly is hired by the outcome of a toss of a coin and choosing as strongest that Jane is hired or Lilly is hired in accordance with the boss's verdict.

Even so, if we must provide for such discriminations, we can identify a set of propositions each consistent with the agent's body of knowledge K and such that K entails the truth of at least and at most one of them, so that each feasible option can be represented as choosing g as strongest relative to K, where g asserts that some member of a nonempty subset of the partition used is true. For the most part, characterizing options using so much apparatus is unnecessary. Even so, it is important to keep in mind that the stilted representations of choosings I have proposed using (namely, as choosing propositions or sentences true) should be qualified by the statement that the proposition chosen is the strongest proposition chosen true relative to the agent's knowledge and relative to some set of propositions exclusive and exhaustive relative to K, where each element is consistent with K.

4 F. Schick (1984: 10–11) agrees with Shackle that choosing is a shift from one system of propositional attitudes to another. There is one feature of Schick's view which differs markedly both from Shackle's view and from the one I favor. According to Schick's account, choosing to hire Jane is coming to want to hire her. The shift in "psychic" state is from a condition of indifference between the two options to a condition of wanting the option chosen. The choosing is that shift in attitude.

Schick seems to take the notion of wanting as a primitive propositional attitude. I have taken choosing true as a primitive. It may be that Schick's analysis of choosing in terms of coming to want and my analysis come to the same thing, involving predilections for different systems of primitives, but I doubt it.

Schick (1984:11) insists that in his sense of "want", wanting is related to preference and desire, and he goes out of his way to insist that "we don't choose what we want – we choose something and *then* we want it". I concede that under some reasonably natural understandings of "want" we do not always choose what we want. But if I have chosen something so that my implementing the choice is, from my point of view, a settled issue, there is no longer any question of my wanting it. I may enjoy the implementation or I may be disappointed. But I no longer want true what I take for granted is or will be true. It would, in short, be more accurate to say that choosing sometimes entails ceasing to want rather than coming to want.

These remarks are not intended to be decisive objections to Schick's view. In part, I am merely registering my lack of comprehension of what he means. In part, my reservations derive from the fact that I am concerned to characterize presuppositions involved when an agent is evaluating feasible options with respect to admissibility. In this context, I am supposing that the option chosen will be implemented as far as the decision maker is concerned. In contrast, Schick discusses choices and reasons for choices in an effort to provide a framework for explaining human actions. Perhaps it makes sense in such a setting to make use of a conception of choice which does not presuppose the efficacy of choice even from the decision maker's point of view (although I am not entirely convinced of this). Hence, an agent may not be certain that a chosen option will be implemented. Choosing it may then be seen as preferring it as compared with the alternatives to it which are not ruled out.

5 Schick (1984) requires that feasibility and admissibility coincide according to the agent before choice. He stipulates that the options in an "issue" must be "indifferent" for the agent before choice. Schick uses "indifferent" in the technical sense adopted by economists steeped in the ideology of revealed preference according to which "indifferent" means "equal in value or noncomparable". Although indifference in this sense is not sufficient for admissibility in my view, as far as I understand him, Schick claims that when all options are indifferent they are all admissible.

6 According to Shackle's view, the agent may assume that he will always choose an option which is admissible relative to the final information set concerning (i)–(iii) before the moment of choice. But he cannot use this alleged

"law" to predict his choice because he is never in a position to determine whether the information set concerning (i)–(iii) is the final set. This prevents first-person prediction from laws, but it does not prevent retrospective explanation; and it does not prevent someone from entertaining such principles as true lawlike claims.

I myself prefer to preserve for principles of choice a nontrivial role in determining admissibility in contexts where information concerning (i)–(iii) is taken as final. We are interested in such principles primarily for that purpose and not for the purpose of explanation.

5 Value structures

1 D. Blackwell and M. A. Girshick (1954: 116–119). Assumption L_1 is stronger than the corresponding assumption in Blackwell and Girshick. They assume, in effect, that weak preference between a pair x and y of elements of $N(U)$ is uniquely determined by comparisons induced by v_1 and v_2 without regard to comparisons with other alternatives in $N(U)$. I have assumed, in addition to this, that the potential resolution imposes a ranking on the elements of $N(U)$ representable by a real-valued function of elements of $N(U)$. This assumption rules out the possibility that the ordering of elements of $N(U)$ represented by the potential resolution is a lexicographical ordering. However, lexicography is given its due in 5.7. See also note 2.

Blackwell and Girshick formulate their conditions for individual decision making under uncertainty. The options in $N(U)$ are states of nature for them. The v-functions are payoff functions for individual options and represent options. These differences in interpretation of formalism should not mask the possibility of deploying their argument in our context where potential resolutions are being characterized.

2 The possibility ruled out by strengthening L_1 (see note 1) is reinstated. Instead of allowing lexicographical orderings to be potential resolutions, ways of evaluation assigned o weight are ruled out of consideration only to reappear in higher level value structures in the hierarchy.

6 Values revealed by choices

1 If we take relation R as primitive and define I and P according to conditions I and II, the domain of these relations is weakly ordered by R if and only if R is reflexive, transitive and complete. If R weakly orders a given domain, conditions I–VII listed in the text are satisfied. Conversely, if I–VII are satisfied, R weakly orders the given domain. For our purposes, therefore, I–VII may be taken to characterize a weak ordering.

2 Sen has offered the strongest arguments with which I am familiar for rejecting "Pareto principles" in developing theories of collective choice. See Sen (1970a: 79–81, 83–85, 87–88; 1970b: 152–157; 1976a: 217–245). For critical comment, see Levi (1982a: 239–249).

3 Satisfaction of I–V is obvious. To establish the acyclicity of R_c (condition VI), suppose that $x_i P_c x_{i+1}$, for i from 1 to $n - 1$. Then there is a subset S of the set of n options which contains x_i and x_{i+1} such that $x_i \in C(S)$, whereas there is no set S' containing these two elements such that $x_{i+1} \in C(S')$. From this it follows that the only element of $C(T)$ (where T is the set consisting of the n options) is x_1. (Remember that the choice function is defined for all finite subsets of T and such definition requires that the choice set be nonempty.) This implies the falsity of $x_n P_c x_1$.

4 This term is used to designate a kindred property for choice functions by Sen (1977: 63).

5 For a general discussion of such relations, see Sen (1971: 307−317). Much of my discussion is based on this paper, Sen (1977) and Herzberger (1973).

6 Terminology is by no means standard. I follow Sen (1977), especially pp. 63−71, where the terminology is defined and several of the results cited here are stated.

7 This result is an implication of theorem 1 and propositions 18 and 19 of Sen (1977: 175−176).

8 W. Harper (1983: 374−375) has argued that in the context of decision making under uncertainty (to be discussed in chapter 7) the analogue of my criterion of lexicographical V-admissibility leads to intransitivities in preference.

7 Uncertainty as a source of conflict

1 Let K consist of all hypotheses which constitute the agent's body of knowledge expressible in the regimented language L. The function $Q(x/y)$ is a finitely additive, real-valued and normalized probability measure in L relative to K if and only if $Q(x/y)$ satisfies the following conditions:

(i) Let E be the set of all hypotheses in L consistent with K; $Q(h/e)$ is defined for all h in L and e in E, and for all such h and e, $Q(h/e) > 0$.
(ii) If $K - h \equiv h'$ and $K \, 1 - e \equiv e'$, $Q(h/e) = Q(h'/e')$.
(iii) If $e \, 1 - \sim(h \, \& \, g)$, then $Q(h/e) + Q(g/e) = Q(h \vee g/e)$.
(iv) If $K,e \, 1 - h$, then $Q(h/e) = 1$.
(v) $Q(h \, \& \, g/e) = Q(h/g \, \& \, e)Q(g/e)$.

See Levi, (1980) 76b for further discussion.

2 The stipulation that options are to be ranked according to expected value as computed by Eq. (1) is called the method of ranking options with respect to expected utility (REU) in Levi (1980a: 95−98). Because this method of ranking does not always guarantee that one option which weakly dominates another will be ranked strictly better (the guarantee fails when seriously possible hypotheses bear credal probability 0 [Levi, 1980a: 119−121]), in 5.2−5.6 I proposed some modifications of REU which guarantee satisfaction of the requirement that when one option dominates another it is strictly preferred to it (in cases where states are probabilistically independent of options). For the purposes of this discussion, these refinements may be neglected.

3 In Levi (1980a) the VE-admissible options were called E-admissible, and the VS-admissible options were called S-admissible. The lexicographically ordered hierarchy of tests with respect to security (a version of which will be elaborated subsequently) eventuated in a set of lex-admissible options. The options surviving all the tests were called admissible rather than V-admissible. There was no reference to higher level extended value structures to be used when two or more options are admissible (i.e., V-admissible).

Another difference should be mentioned. After the test for E-admissibility and before the test for S-admissibility, a test for P-admissibility was required. This test was motivated by the recommendation that when two or more options are E-admissible, the agent ought to adopt an option which expresses suspension of judgement among them. The import of this recommendation is clearest in cognitive decision problems, where it carries its greatest importance. In noncognitive decision problems, the set of P-admissible options will normally coincide with the set of E-admissible options so that considerations of P-admissibility play a negligible role. To avoid needless complexity, therefore, I ignore P-admissibility in the subsequent discussion. There is, however, one troubling aspect of P-admissibility which, perhaps, deserves brief mention. In some special cases, the set of P-admissible options will not be a subset of the set of E-admissible options – a result in conflict with the general spirit of the use of lexicographically ordered tests of admissibility. My intellectual conscience, Teddy Seidenfeld, persists in chiding me for this and I think he is right. Fortunately the contexts in which such peculiarities arise do not seem overwhelmingly important, and there are ways of modifying the tests of P-admissibility to avoid trouble – although at the cost of some additional complexity. The pros and cons of modifying these tests would require, however, some extended consideration which would be inappropriate in a discussion where the scope of applicability for them is likely to be limited.

4 I have argued (Levi, 1978: 1–15), that the definition of conditional credal probability favored by de Finetti and Ramsey which appeals to called-off bets conflicts with de Finetti's insistence that conditional probability on conditions with probability o is well defined and that this conflict could be removed in a way which permits allowing possibilities which bear probability o while preventing options weakly dominated by others from being admissible (see also Levi, 1980a: 112–118).

5 D. V. Lindley (1980: 20–21) complains, wrongly I think, that Levi (1980a) said little about the works of strict Bayesians like de Finetti and Ramsey and then writes: "Is he [Levi] fully aware of the basic result that a man who is to act sensibly can do so only if he acts in accordance with a *unique* probability and a *unique* utility?" A reference to this "basic result" of Ramsey and de Finetti is made on p. 109 of Levi (1980a), where I explicitly point out that they formulated their arguments in a manner presupposing freedom from conflict in probabilities. I then explicitly reject this presupposition. Much of my book is devoted to elaborating the ramifications of rejecting Lindley's "basic result". Lindley seems to think that I could not reject it if I were "fully aware" of it. This response is testimony to the strong allure which the prohibition against value conflict has for many serious authors.

6 For an excellent brief discussion of recent efforts by necessitarians, see Seidenfeld (1979: 413–440).

7 See Levi (1980a, especially ch. 12), for an account of the principle of direct inference which controls how credal probability judgements are to be made relative to knowledge of statistical probabilities or chances.

8 W. Harper (1983: 367–376) appears to favor such a view.

9 Appealing to upper and lower betting quotients (or equivalently to upper and lower betting odds) was suggested by Smith (1961: 1–25). Smith did not notice that his approach could be obtained by supplementing tests for E-admissibility by tests for S-admissibility. Also, as it happens, in the simple decision problems he considers, much of the ambiguity in determining security levels is irrelevant as long as one does not appeal to degenerate security levels. In cases where there is no issue of choosing between the minimax risk approach of Wald in fixing security and the approach which favors using table 1 of our example, the idea of revealing credal states by looking at upper and lower betting quotients may be extended along lines explained in Levi (1980a: 196–208).

10 Ellsberg (1951: 658). I am taking for granted that appraisals with respect to subjective or credal probability and with respect to possibility are ap-

praisals of truth-value-bearing hypotheses. Personal or subjective or credal probabilities are not supposed to own truth values. Hence, they should not be evaluated with respect to credal probability themselves. See Levi (1980a: 183–191, 1982b: 387–417, especially 391–393). This paper comments on Gärdenfors and Sahlin (1982a: 361–386). (See also Gärdenfors and Sahlin, 1982b: 433–438 which is a reply to my paper.)

11 We may distinguish this uniquely permissible credal distribution over the hypotheses as to which color ball will be drawn from the possibly true chance hypotheses specifying chance distributions over possible outcomes of a draw. Hence, there is no conflict between the unique permissibility of this distribution of credal probability and the possible truth of several chance distributions. If the chance distributions were, as Ellsberg sometimes suggests, to be taken as subjective distributions, then his attributing possibility to them would have to be construed as attributing permissibility and his characterization would be threatened with inconsistency.

12 J. O. Berger (1980: 134–135). His reference is to Robbins (1964: 1–20).

13 I do not mean to leave the impression that I endorse an unqualified injunction against choosing dominated options. I do endorse avoiding the choice of an option which is dominated by another option in the following sense: Let there be a *finite* set of exclusive and exhaustive hypotheses (given the available knowledge) which serve as "states" such that for each state in the set, the first option is rated inferior to the second option. The first option is dominated in a finite way by the second. Although I favor avoiding the choice of options dominated in a finite way, I do not argue for avoiding options dominated in an infinite way. The cost of doing so is explained in Seidenfeld and Schervish (1983: 398–412). On p. 411, Seidenfeld and Schervish introduce an inconsistent triad and find it difficult to decide how to remove inconsistency. I am more foolhardy than they and favor giving up the first element of their triad.

14 See, in particular, D. Kahneman and A. Tversky (1979: 263–273), especially pp. 265–267, where data are reported on the Allais problem and several variations of it. Also see M. Machina (1982: 277–323) and K. R. MacCrimmon and S. Larsson (1979: 333–409).

15 Allais (1952: 78; 1953: 518). It is interesting that for Allais the requirement of a weak ordering appears to be implied by the assumption that a rational agent "pursues ends that are mutually consistent (i.e., not contradictory)". Apparently mutually consistent ends are conflict-free ends. My contention is that an agent may pursue ends which are in conflict in the sense that he is in suspense among them and still remain rational.

16 Bernoulli (1954: 23–36). See especially paragraph 5 for Bernoulli's description of an exception to the diminishing marginal utility of money.

17 A. K. Sen considers a lexicographical maximin principle formally similar to the one I am proposing in discussing questions of the distribution of goods and welfare (see, e.g., Sen, 1970a: 138, 158).

18 See the papers by Kahneman and Tversky, Machina and MacCrimmon and Larsson referenced in note 14. In addition, mention should be made of important contributions by Chew Soo Hong (1984) and E. F. McClennen (1983).

19 Of the four pairs of problems mentioned in Kahneman and Tversky (1979: 265–267) only the first three are susceptible to the treatment I have outlined above. Problems 7 and 8 cannot be treated in this manner. In problem 7, most respondents opted for 3,000 with a 90% chance over 6,000

with a 45% chance while choosing 6,000 with a 0.1% chance over 3,000 with a 0.2% chance in problem 8. Even if the utility of money is indeterminate so that both options are E-admissible in problem 7, the appeal to security will not account for the responses reported. Leximin will favor the gamble with the 6,000 payoff in both cases. I suspect experimental subjects tend to think that the difference between a 0.1% chance and a 0.2% chance so negligible that they neglect the difference (fallaciously) and treat the chances as equal. In contrast a 90% chance is regarded as signifigantly larger than a 45% chance, and it may be that the indeterminacies in the utility of money are not so great as to render both options E-admissible. Perhaps, only the gamble on 3,000 is. Similar remarks are relevant to the results on common ratio of probability problems discussed by MacCrimmon and Larsson.

20 Allais insists on the observance of stochastic dominance, or "absolute preference" as he calls it. Consider two lotteries L and M over "sure" prizes. Let $F(u)$ be the probability that L will yield a prize with utility less than or equal to u, and let $G(u)$ be the corresponding "cumulative distribution function" for M. Lottery L stochastically dominates M if $F(u) \geq G(u)$ for all u with strict inequality for at least one value of u. Machina and Chew also seek to observe it.

21 Let us suppose that V is strictly preferred to VI and VIII to VII, as these authors suppose is the case in the typical response to the Allais problem. Let $(V), $(VI), $(VII) and $(VIII) be the dollar values the agent would place on the options. Given the denial of ordinal conflict, such dollar values can be placed on the options. Let L_1 be a lottery where the agent receives V if a fair coin lands heads up and VIII if the coin lands tails up, and let L_2 be a lottery where the agent receives VI if heads and VII if tails. The dollar values on these lotteries are (L_1) and (L_2). The standard independence assumptions imply the "mixture dominance" condition (see the reference to Chew in note 18) that (L_1) lie between $(V) and $(VIII) and (L_2) between $(VI) and $(VII). Lottery L_1 is equivalent to L_2 and should be assigned the same value. This means that the independence assumption has to be given up. One can follow Chew and retain mixture dominance, but mixture dominance is clearly violated by the behavior exhibited in the Ellsberg problem. One can follow Allais, Machina and McClennen and allow violations of mixture dominance either by allowing L_1 to have a value less than both constituent lotteries or by letting L_2 have a value greater than its constituent lotteries. Let us consider the latter case. Let $(L_1) = $(L_2) = k, which is greater than both $(VI) and $(VII). Let C_1 be a new lottery in which one receives the opportunity to choose between receiving VI and receiving m if a fair coin lands heads up and choosing between receiving VII and receiving m if a fair coin lands tails up. We suppose that m is less than both $(VI) and $(VII) and, hence, less than k. If the agent faces the lottery C_1 and the coin lands heads up, he will choose VI. If the coin lands tails up, he will choose VII. Hence, the lottery is equivalent to lottery L_2, the dollar value of which is k. Let C_2 be a lottery where, if the coin lands heads up, the agent receives a choice between receiving both VI and x and receiving a cash prize y worth slightly more than $(VI) + x and, if the coin lands tails, a choice between receiving both $(VII) and x and receiving a cash prize y. In this case, the agent will choose the y regardless of the outcome of the toss so that the dollar value of C_2 is y. Finally, we can arrange matters so that k is greater y. Hence, if the agent is invited to choose between C_1

and C_2, he should choose the former. But regardless of the outcome of the toss of the coin, the dollar value of the payoff for C_2 is greater than that of C_1. Indeed, because these payoffs have dollar values in virtue of the assumption that all options and payoffs are weakly orderable with respect to value or preference, his choice of lottery C_1 over C_2 can be equated with a choice of an option which is dominated with respect to the ultimate or pure payoffs and, hence, violates stochastic dominance, which Machina and Allais both seek to avoid doing. A similar result can be obtained if we allow L_1 to be valued lower than both V and VIII. Hence, either we insist on respecting mixture dominance and give up dealing with Ellsberg and abandon stochastic dominance or, as I favor, give up the assumption that all alternatives be weakly ordered.

22 The proposals I am advocating can also rationalize the phenomena of preference reversal reported by D. M. Grether and C. R. Plott (1979: 623–638). Consider the following pair of gambles:

$$G_1 = \text{a million dollars with probability } .9.$$
$$G_2 = 5 \text{ million with probability } .8.$$

Suppose the utility function $U(\$x)$ is any function in the convex hull of $\log(x + 1)$ and $\log(0.1x + 1)$. The expected utilities of the two gambles are 12.44 and 12.34 respectively according to the first function with corresponding dollar values of \$252,000 and \$239,000. According to the second utility function, the expected utilities are 10.35 and 10.49 respectively with corresponding dollar values of \$11,000 and \$12,300.

Both options are E-admissible. Leximin favors G_2. Suppose, however, we modify the gambles slightly. We charge a small amount, say \$10, for G_2. Both gambles should remain E-admissible, but now leximin favors G_1. Observe, however, that the range of dollar values for the gambles will be negligibly altered. The smallest dollar value for G_2 will be higher than the smallest dollar value for gamble G_1. Hence, if the agent is asked for the smallest price at which he would sell G_1, the answer should be \$11,100. For G_2, it should be \$12,300.

The upshot is that in the modified version of the situation, G_1 should be chosen over G_2. Yet the lowest price at which the agent ought to sell G_2 is higher than the lowest price at which he ought sell G_1. This analysis appears to reproduce the phenomenon reported by Grether and Plott.

23 Because the security level assigned a mixture of two options is greater than the security levels of either option in the mixture, it may appear that the v-functions indexing security levels in this way lack the mixture property discussed in 5.3. And this would imply that such v-functions cannot qualify as representations of ways of evaluation which may be permissible in a value structure. No such implication obtains. The v-functions indexing security do have the mixture property according to the proposal I favor. However, mixtures of options are in general not neutral with respect to security in the sense of neutrality discussed in 5.3. Hence, the security value of a mixture is not the expected security value of its constituent pure options.

8 Conflict and social agency

1 I have advocated thinking of knowing subjects as institutions such as scientific communities as well as persons for some time – most recently and explicitly in Levi (1980a: 1–13).

2 K. O. May (1954: 1–13) argued along these lines.

3 These remarks give a rough characterization of the insight expressed by Luce and Raiffa (1958: 343–345). They point out that by reinterpreting an argument offered by Blackwell and Girshick (1954: 118) pertaining to individual decision making under uncertainty, one can derive the Arrow impossibility theorem. In 5.4 and note 1 of chapter 5, I exploit the Blackwell–Girshick view in a characterization of potential resolutions. As will emerge in chapter 9, the two adaptations can be related to one another in a useful manner. Paul Lyon and Teddy Seidenfeld drew my attention to the Luce and Raiffa discussion of Arrow's result in relation to the Blackwell–Girshick postulates for individual decision making under uncertainty independently of one another.

4 An important recent effort to develop decision theory applicable to both social and personal agents has been made by P. Lyon (1980).

9 Distributing benefits

1 A. Sen (1982: 29–32, 367–368). Sen (1985: 169–221) distinguishes functioning capabilities (these appear to be his old basic capabilities) from agent relative capabilities, which are abilities to pursue personal projects.

2 Sen calls benefit comparison structures "comparison sets" (1970a: 106, definition 7*2) or "comparability sets" (1982: 229). The list of types of interpersonal comparisons given in the text is taken from Sen (1982: 273). The formulations are tailored to the formalism I have adopted but are equivalent to Sen's.

3 A transformation of a benefit comparison function is variable unit–variable origin piecemeal positive affine if and only if it is of the form $b(i) + a(i)bc(x,i)$, where $b(i)$ is a real-valued function of elements of I and $a(i)$ is a positive real-valued function of elements of I.

4 A transformation of a bc-function is constant unit–variable origin piecemeal positive affine if and only if it is a transformation of the type given in note 5 except that $a(i)$ is a constant value for all i in I.

5 A transformation of a bc-function is variable piecemeal positive monotonic if and only if it is obtained by order-preserving transformations of each of the constituent personal benefit functions, which may be different for each element of I.

6 In 5.3, I pointed out in passing that arguments of M. Fleming and J. Harsanyi may be adapted to sustain the weighted average principle as a characterization of potential resolutions of conflicts among ways of evaluation. These arguments are alternatives to the Blackwell–Girshick arguments. In my opinion, they carry more conviction in this application than they do when applied to the defense of the average benefit principle as Harsanyi intended. The difference between the two cases concerns the legitimacy of regarding mixtures in $M(U_p)$ as neutral in the sense of 5.3. According to the doctrine of 5.3, ways of valuation must always satisfy the mixture property, but this does not imply that the value of a mixture is equal to the expected value. Only when the mixture is neutral must this be so. When one way of evaluating options in $M(U_p)$ is a resolution of a conflict among others, I take it to be plausible that if mixtures are neutral according to the ways of valuation in conflict, they should be neutral according to the potential resolution as well. This implies that the potential resolution and the conflicting ways of valuation ought all to satisfy von Neumann–Morgenstern (1944) requirements over the given domain. Taken together with the requirement that if the rival ways of evaluation agree on ranking options x and y together so should the potential resolution, this implication

suffices to secure the result that a potential resolution should satisfy the weighted average requirement. But it does not follow from this that a value commitment marked by concern for the benefit of all ought to embrace the average benefit principle as a criterion for deriving permissible ways of evaluating options from permissible bc-functions. The permissible ways of evaluating options ought, indeed, to obey the mixture property, but the mixtures in $M(U_p)$ need not be neutral. In fact, they will not be if one follows a version of a maximin or leximin rule which attends to the worst off. From this it follows that the values attributed to mixtures in $M(U_p)$ will not equal their expected values. The von Neumann–Morgenstern or Marschak axioms are not applicable to this domain for this reason. Now in those cases where lotteries carry some value or disvalue because they are lotteries of a special type, we should not expect the von Neumann–Morgenstern axioms to be satisfied. Nor should we demand that sure-thing or independence principles be observed. This is not because of some defect in these principles but because they are being applied to an inappropriate domain.

7 If I understand Sen's (1976b) position, he means to assert both that the Harsanyi argument is deficient as a defense of the average benefit principle and that utilization of the average benefit principle entails insensitivity to questions of distribution. I think his position is too strong. The Harsanyi argument is not deficient if one is seeking to deploy overall benevolence to resolve conflicts generated by efforts to promote the benefits of each member of I separately. In that case, the average benefit principle is insensitive to distributive questions and cannot be made very sensitive by invoking a secondary principle which is sensitive to distribution to break ties. But the average benefit principle can be supplemented by secondary principles to render it sensitive to distributional considerations provided that one abandons the ambition of invoking overall benevolence to resolve conflict. Thus, one of Sen's charges must be right. But at the same time, one of them must be wrong. What remains unclear is which of them is right and which wrong.

8 Sen (1970a: 138, footnote 12). Sen's tool for analysis in discussing derivations of analogues of my value structures from analogues of my benefit comparison structures is the so-called social welfare functional (SWFL), which is a functional relation between bc-functions and orderings of the elements of U. (Sen, 1970a: definition 8*2). The orderings which are values of SWFL's are not required to satisfy an Archimidean condition so that lexicographical orderings are allowed. If the benefit comparison structure is not free of ordinal conflict, one can use Sen's leximin SWFL to determine a set of lexicographical orderings of U and define a corresponding notion of admissibility – call it Sen–leximinb-admissibility. Sen-lexminb-admissibility will not always coincide with leximinb-admissibility as I have defined it.

Suppose, for example, that there are two social states in U, x and y, and two individuals i and j in I. The benefit comparison structure is the convex hull of the following pair of benefit comparison functions:

	bc_1		bc_2	
	1	2	1	2
x	0	10	6	10
y	1	5	1	5

According to some permissible comparison functions in the benefit comparison structure, the leximin SWFL in Sen's sense ranks x on top. According to others, y is ranked on top. Both are therefore Sen-leximinb-admissible. But although both x and y are $MINB_1$-admissible, only x is $MINB_1$–$MINB_2$-admissible. Hence, x alone is leximinb-admissible.

We may generalize to some degree the notion of a lexicographical ordering according to the leximin principle. Given any benefit comparison structure, the value structure determined according to bottom-up first-level dictatorship induces a categorical quasi ordering (see 6.5) over U. If x is categorically strictly preferred to y, it remains so in the lexicographical ordering. If x is categorically indifferent to y or is disconnected from y according to the first-level categorical preference but is categorically strictly preferred to y according to second-level dictatorship, it is strictly preferred to y in the lexicographical ordering. If the second level does not legislate, then x remains indifferent (or disconnected) pending consideration of third level dictatorship and so on.

This generalization can sometimes yield a weak ordering of U even when the benefit comparison structure suffers from conflict. Orderings induced by lower level dictatorship may be incomplete, but the orderings at higher levels may be complete. When this is so, we may ask whether the set of leximinb-admissible options must coincide with the options that come out optimal according to the lexicographical weak ordering. That is to say, does the lexicographical weak ordering according to the generalized leximin principle (when it exists) always satisfy what we may call the *optimality–admissibility* (OPAD) condition?

When the weak ordering is derived from a conflict-free benefit comparison structure, the answer is, as already noted, in the affirmative. But in general the answer is no. An example will serve to establish this: Suppose U contains three options x, y and z and I contains two citizens 1 and 2. Let the benefit comparison structure be the convex set of all weighted averages of the following two functions:

	bc_1		bc_2	
	1	2	1	2
x	0.26	0.00	0.26	0.25
y	0.30	0.05	0.30	0.05
z	0.25	0.25	0.25	0.00

All three options are noncomparable according to first-level dictatorship so that second-level dictatorship becomes legislative. It ranks y over x over z. Hence, y is optimal in a three-way choice according to the lexicographical ordering induced by the leximin principle. In contrast, in a three-way choice, only x and y are leximinb-admissible, y is not leximinb-admissible. The lexicographical ordering violates the OPAD condition. It should also be noticed that in a pairwise choice between x and y, y becomes uniquely admissible. Property α is violated.

Thus, optimality according to the generalization of Sen's leximin principle does not always coincide with leximinb-admissibility even in those cases where a weak lexicographical ordering according to leximin exists. In the special cases where ordinal conflict is absent from the benefit comparison structure, however, this type of optimality does coincide with leximinb-admissibility. These, of course, are substantially the cases on which Sen focused.

9 Sidgwick (1907: 416). Sidgwick's talk of an absence of cognizable differences in utility does not clearly distinguish between cases where there are differences but we do not know them and cases where value structures are subject to unresolved conflict. I suspect that he intended the former interpretation. Even so, his idea does suggest, even if he did not intend it, a role for considerations of distribution in narrowing down the set of admissible options when considerations of total welfare fail to single out a uniquely admissible option. Rawls (1971: 26, footnote 12) takes note of Sidgwick's principle for breaking ties but does not appreciate the possibilities for the use of Sidgwick's idea in accommodating questions of distribution. Both he and Sen (1979: 469–470) adopt a narrow reading of Sidgwick according to which the role for equality of distribution is restricted to the breaking of ties. But since Sidgwick himself acknowledged that the usefulness of such appeals to equity would be negligible and thought that the usefulness of the idea would emerge because one cannot always identify policies as maximizing utility, it seems to me that they have failed to take Sidgwick's suggestion as seriously as it deserves to be taken.

10 Utilitarianism and conflict

1 Rawls (1971: 161–175) is misled by the confusion involved here into arguing that an appeal to how one would choose in a state of Laplacian ignorance by maximizing expected utility yields the injunction to maximize average utility in the sense of using a variable domain. As should be apparent, I share with Rawls many reservations concerning the merits of the principle of maximizing expected utility and the principle of insufficient reason. From my perspective, deriving principles of just distribution from states of ignorance characterized by Laplacian ignorance has no more (but no less) merit than deriving principles of just distribution from maximally indeterminate credal states where invoking maximin or leximin may be warranted (see Levi, 1977: 749–754). But regardless of how matters stand concerning the merits of different "contractarian" arguments, it is simply false to assert as Rawls does that the Vickrey–Harsanyi appeal to Laplacian ignorance sustains what Rawls calls "average" utilitarianism (i.e., when a variable domain of concern is used) as opposed to what he calls "classical" utilitarianism (where a fixed domain of concern is employed). Since the domain of objects of concern is variable, when the agent is alleged to be ignorant of his position does this mean that he is ignorant also as to the domain to which he belongs – and what precisely does that mean?

2 The validity of the weak Pareto principle is, of course, an implication of the average benefit principle. These matters will be discussed at greater length in chapter 11.

3 As I read him, Robbins' denials of the testability of interpersonal comparisons of welfare ought to be construed as implying no more than what he claims when he writes that such comparison "which is never needed in the theory of equilibrium and which is never implied by the assumptions of that theory . . . necessarily falls outside the scope of any positive science" (Robbins, 1962: 139). If we delete the word "necessarily", Robbins' remarks seem right, for the positive economic science of his time (and the present so it seems) provides no useful predictive or explanatory role for interpersonal comparisons of utility. We should be more open minded than Robbins appears to have been about future developments in econom-

ics and other social sciences and, hence, should avoid the strong modal adverb "necessarily". But if his claim about the current state of social science is correct, interpersonal comparisons have no place in positive social science, just as Robbins says. I take Robbins to have this in mind when he says that interpersonal comparisons are not testable. Put this way, his remarks are correct, though misleading.

This reading of Robbins' (1962: 140) discussion is supported by his explicit acknowledgment (1962: 140) that we do make interpersonal comparisons in daily life, just as Little and Sen insist. "But the very diversity of the assumptions actually made at different times and in different places is evidence of their conventional nature" (Robbins, 1962: 140). In these passages, Robbins is not denying the testability of the assumptions, nor is he asserting that they lack cognitive content. Rather he is insisting that the specification of a conception of interpersonal comparisons of welfare is not implied by positive social scientific theory in general or economic theory in particular. Such a specification is not "interesting" from the point of view of current positive economic theory. The interest in such a specification (which may have "descriptive content") derives (as matters now stand) entirely from considerations of value.

Sen (1982: 265, footnote 1) is right to acknowledge that Robbins does not prohibit economists from making policy recommendations. He goes too far, I think, in claiming that Robbins denies descriptive meaning to such comparisons. What Robbins denies is that such descriptively meaningful comparisons are interesting for positive economic science.

11 Social choice theory

1 Aside from Sen (1970a: ch. 8*2), see Sen (1982: 228–240), P.J. Hammond (1976: 263–274), C. D'Aspremont and L. Gevers (1977: 199–209) and K. W. S. Roberts (1980: 421–439).

2 I refer to Sen's discussion of "aggregation quasi orderings" in Sen (1970a: ch. 7*; 1970c; 1982: 22).

3 Sen (1970a: 123–124, 129). Sen's version of independence of irrelevant alternatives should not be confused with the condition of robust preference of 6.3 or property α of 6.7, definition 1. The former is a condition on value structures, the latter on choice functions. Sen's condition of independence of irrelevant alternatives is a constraint on social welfare functionals.

The relation between my condition of independence and Sen's condition is much closer. SBFL's and SWFL's take benefit comparison functions as arguments. They determine different types of values. But the value structures which are the values of SBFL's and the weak orderings which are the values of SWFL's have the same intended applications – to wit, to the evaluation of options as better and worse. The differences concern the extent to which conflict is recognized, how it is to be represented and how lexicographic valuational is to be understood and represented. These differences do not undermine the essential equivalence between Sen's condition I and mine.

None of the above-mentioned requirements correspond to Arrow's (1963: 26–28) condition of independence of irrelevant alternatives. Roughly speaking, Arrow's condition is equivalent to Sen's condition on SWFL's supplemented by the condition of ONC-invariance. Alternatively stated, if we focus on SWF's (i.e., SWFL's which satisfy ONC-invariance), Arrovian independence of irrelevant alternatives does coincide with Sen's independence of irrelevant alternatives.

4 Sen (1982: 228–229) has tended to focus on situations where SWFL's exhibiting X-invariance are applied only to benefit comparison structures
making measurability–comparability assumptions X. Nonetheless, he has
always acknowledged the possibility of leaving the domain of benefit comparison structures as broad as possible. This latter approach is what he
calls "the more permissive 'intersection' approach" (Sen, 1982: 22). Chapters 7 and 7* of Sen (1970a) discuss this approach, as does chapter 9 of
1982. Chapter 8*2 of 1970a addresses the more restrictive approach and
this more restrictive approach appears to be more or less tacitly understood in much of the subsequent discussion of SWFL's and interpersonal
comparability. Because Sen has always seemed open to the possibility of
unresolved conflict generated by conflict in the benefit comparison structure, he is not committed to the error of supposing that the adoption of
an X-invariant SWFL presupposes assuming measurability–comparability
assumption X. In this respect, his position stands in advance of Arrow's
view. Arrow's SWF's are, in effect, ONC-invariant SWFL's and, because of
this, Arrow is committed to denying the relevance of measurability–comparability assumptions stronger than ONC − at least at the time he wrote
hiw 1963 book. But ONC-invariance does not entail an obligation to deny
the feasibility of making ordinal level comparisons. Nor, for that matter,
does Arrow's principle of the independence of irrelevant alternatives, which,
among other things, implies ONC-invariance redundantly. Yet Arrow de-
fends independence of irrelevant alternatives, in part, by attacking the
feasibility of making interpersonal comparisons. Even if he had succeeded,
this would not automatically decide the case for ONC-invariance one way
or the other. To be sure, if we could never make "meaningful" interpersonal comparisons of welfare or benefits, then endorsing an SWFL which
is not ONC-invariant would lead to conflicted value structures and would
do so inevitably. Since Arrow's "rationality postulate" entails that the value
of an SWF must be a value structure free of ordinal conflict, if we must
unavoidably assume ONC, then we can avoid ordinal conflict only by requiring ONC-invariance. Thus, Arrow's failure to emphasize the difference between the assumption of ONC and of ONC-invariance derives from
his insistence that value structures be free of ordinal conflict.

5 It is important to understand that the impossibility result does not require
that interpersonal comparisons of benefits not be made or that they be
nonfeasible. Rather it presupposes that they be judged irrelevant to the
valuation marked by benevolence for all.

Bibliography

Allais, M. (1952). "The Foundations of a Positive Theory of Choice Involving Risk and a Criticism of the Postulates and Axioms of the American School." Trans. in Allais and Hagen (1979), pp. 27–145.

(1953). Le comportement de l'homme rationnel devant le risque: Critique des postulats et axiomes de l'école americaine." *Econometrica* 21, pp. 503–546.

Allais, M., and Hagen, O., eds. (1979). *Expected Utility Hypotheses and the Allais Paradox*. Dordrecht, The Netherlands: Reidel.

Arrow, K. J. (1963). *Social Choice and Individual Values*, 2nd ed. New York: Wiley.

D'Aspremont, C. D., and Gevers, L. (1977). "Equity and the Informational Basis of Collective Choice." *Review of Economic Studies* 46, pp. 199–209.

Berger, J. O. (1980). *Statistical Decision Theory*. New York: Springer-Verlag.

Bergson, A. (1966). *Essays in Normative Economics*. Cambridge, MA: Harvard University Press.

Bernoulli, D. (1954). "Exposition of a New Theory of the Measurement of Risk." Transl. from Latin by L. Sommer, *Econometrica* 22, pp. 23–36.

Blackwell, D., and Girshick, M. A. (1954). *Theory of Games and Statistical Decisions*. New York: Wiley.

Bogdan R. (1976). *Local Induction*. Dordrecht, The Netherlands: Reidel.

Braithwaite, R. B., ed. (1950). *Foundations of Mathematics*. New York: Humanities Press.

Buchanan, J. M. (1964). "Social Choice, Democracy and Free Markets." *Journal of Political Economy* 62, pp. 114–123.

Chew Soo Hong (1984). *A Mixture Set Axiomatization of Weighted Utility Theory*. Unpublished working paper, University of Arizona, Department of Economics, Tucson.

Davidson, D. (1980). *Actions and Events*. New York: Oxford University Press.

de Finetti, B. (1964). "Foresight: Its Logical Laws, Its Subjective Sources." In Kyburg and Smokler (1964), pp. 95–158.

Dewey, J. (1939). *Theory of Valuation*. University of Chicago Press.

(1983). *Human Nature and Conduct*, vol.14 of *John Dewey: The Middle Works*, ed. by J. A. Boydston. Carbondale: Southern Illinois University Press.

Dewey, J., and Tufts, J.H. (1932). *Ethics*. New York: Holt.

Ellsberg, D. (1951). "Risk, Ambiguity and the Savage Axioms." *Quarterly Journal of Economics* 75, pp. 653–656.

Fleming, M. (1952). "A Cardinal Concept of Welfare." *Quarterly Journal of Economics* 66, pp. 366–384.

Frankfurt, H.G. (1971). "Freedom of the Will and the Concept of a Person." *Journal of Philosophy* 68, pp. 5–20.

(1978). "The Problem of Action." *American Philosophical Quarterly* 15, pp. 157–162.

Gärdenfors, P., and Sahlin, N.-E. (1982a). "Unreliable Probabilities, Risk Taking and Decision Making." *Synthese* 53, pp. 361–386.

Gärdenfors, P., and Sahlin, N.-E. (1982b). Reply to Levi (1982b). *Synthese* 53, pp. 433–438.

Goldman, A. (1970). *A Theory of Human Action*. Princeton, NJ: Princeton University Press.

Grether, D. M., and Plott, C.R. (1979). "Economic Theory of Choice and The Preference Reversal Phenomenon." *American Economic Review*, pp. 623–638.

Hammond, P. J. (1976). "Equity, Arrow's Conditions and Rawls' Difference Principle." *Econometrica* 44, pp. 263–274.

Harper, W. (1983). Review of Levi (1984). *Journal of Philosophy* 80, pp. 367–376.

Harsanyi, J. C. (1955). "Cardinal Welfare, Individualistic Ethics, and Interpersonal Comparisons of Utility." *Journal of Political Economy* 63, pp. 309–321.

Herzberger, H. (1973). "Ordinal Preference and Rational Choice." *Econometrica* 41, pp. 187–237.

Hïntikka, J. (1962). *Knowledge and Belief*. Ithaca, NY: Cornell University Press.

James, W. (1956). *The Will to Believe and Other Essays*, New York: Dover.

Jeffrey, R. C. (1965). *The Logic of Decision*. New York: McGraw-Hill.

(1974). "Preferences among Preferences." *Journal of Philosophy* 71, pp. 371–391.

(1977). "A Note on the Kinematics of Preference." *Erkenntnis* 11, pp. 135–141.

(1983). *The Logic of Decision*, 2nd. ed. University of Chicago Press.

Kahneman, D., and Tversky, A. (1979). "Prospect Theory: An Analysis of Decision Under Risk." *Econometrica* 47, pp. 263–273.

Kant, I. (1909). *Kant's Critique of Practical Reason and Other Works on the Theory of Ethics*, 6th ed. Trans. by T. K. Abbot, London: Longmans.

Kaufman, W., ed. (1956). *Existentialism from Dostoevsky to Sartre*. New York: Meridian.

Kripke, S. (1982). *Naming and Necessity*. Cambridge, MA: Harvard University Press.

Kuhn, T. (1970). *The Structure of Scientific Revolutions*, 2nd ed. University of Chicago Press.

Kyburg, H. E. and Smokler, H. E., eds. (1964). *Studies in Subjective Probability*. New York: Wiley.

Leach, J. (1968). "Explanation and Value Neutrality." *British Journal for the Philosophy of Science* 19, pp. 99–102.

Levi, I. (1960). "Must the Scientist Make Value Judgements?" *Journal of Philosophy* 57, pp. 345–357. Reprinted in Levi (1984). pp. 1–13.

Levi, I. (1962). "On the Seriousness of Mistakes." *Philosophy of Science* 29, pp. 47–65. Reprinted in Levi (1984), pp. 14–33.

(1967a). *Gambling with Truth*. New York: Knopf. Reprinted by MIT Press in 1973.

(1967b). "Information and Inference." *Synthese* 17, pp. 369–391. Reprinted in Levi (1984), pp. 51–69.

(1976). "Acceptance Revisited." In Bogdan (1976), pp. 1–71.

(1977). "Four Types of Ignorance." *Social Research* 44, pp. 749–754. Reprinted in Levi (1984), pp. 128–135.

(1978). "Coherence, Regularity and Conditional Probability." *Theory and Decision* 9, pp. 1–15.

(1979). "Abduction and Demands for Information." In Niiniluoto and Tuomela (1979), pp. 405–429. Reprinted in Levi (1984), pp. 87–106.

(1980a). *The Enterprise of Knowledge.* Cambridge, MA: MIT.

(1980b). "Induction as Self Correcting According to Peirce." In Mellor (1980), pp. 127–140.

(1982a). "Welfare and Liberty." In Sen and Williams (1982), pp. 239–249. Reprinted in Levi (1984), pp. 271–280.

(1982b). "Ignorance, Probability and Rational Choice." *Synthese* 53, pp. 387–417.

(1984). *Decisions and Revisions.* Cambridge University Press.

Lindley, D. V. (1980a). Review of Levi (1980a). *Nature* 288, pp. 20–21.

Little, I. M. D. (1957). *A Critique of Welfare Economics.* New York: Oxford University Press.

Luce, R. D., and Raiffa, H. (1958), *Games and Decisions.* New York: Wiley.

Lyon, P. (1980). *Preference Aggregation.* Unpublished doctoral dissertation. Washington University, St. Louis, MD.

MacCrimmon, K. R., and Larsson, S. (1979) "Utility Theory: Axioms versus Paradoxes." In Allais and Hagen (1979), pp. 333–409.

Machina, M. (1982). " 'Expected Utility' Analysis without the Independence Axiom." *Econometrica* 50, pp. 277–323.

Maher, P. (1984). Review of Levi (1980a). *Philosophy of Science* 51, pp. 690–691.

Marcus, R. B. (1980). "Moral Dilemmas and Consistency." *Journal of Philosophy* 77, pp. 121–136.

May, K. O. (1954). "Intransitivity, Utility and the Aggregation of Preference Patterns." *Econometrica* 22, pp. 1–13.

McClennen, E. F. (1983). *Sure Thing Doubts.* Paper prepared for the First International Conference on Foundations of Utility and Risk Theory.

Mellor, D. H., ed. (1980). *Science, Belief and Behaviour.* Cambridge University Press.

Mill, J. S. (1949). *A System of Logic*, 8th ed. London: Longmans.

Nagel, E. (1939). *Principles of the Theory of Probability.* University of Chicago Press.

Nagel, T. (1979). *Mortal Questions.* Cambridge University Press.

Niiniluoto, I., and Tuomela R. (1979). *Logic and Epistemology of Scientific Change.* Amsterdam: North Holland.

Plott, C. R. (1973). "Path Independence, Rationality and Social Choice." *Economica* 41, pp. 1075–1091.

Popper, K. R. (1959). *The Logic of Scientific Discovery.* New York: Basic Books.

Raiffa, H. (1961). "Risk, Ambiguity and the Savage Axioms: Comment." *Quarterly Journal of Economics* 75, p. 691.

Ramsey, F. P. (1950). "Truth and Probability." In Braithwaite (1950), pp. 156–203.

Rawls, J. (1971). *A Theory of Justice.* Cambridge, MA: Harvard University Press.

Robbins, H. (1964). "The Empirical Bayes Approach to Statistical Decision Problems." *Annals of Mathematical Statistics* 35, pp. 1–20.

Robbins, L. (1962). *The Nature and Significance of Economic Science*, 2nd ed. New York: Macmillan.

Roberts, K. W. S. (1980). "Interpersonal Comparability and Social Choice Theory." *Review of Economic Studies* 47, pp. 421–439.

Rudner, R. (1953). "The Scientist qua Scientist Makes Value Judgements." *Philosophy of Science* 20, pp. 1–6.

Sartre, J. P. (1956). "Existentialism as a Humanism." Reprinted in Kaufman (1956), pp. 287–311.

Savage, L. J. (1954). *The Foundations of Statistics.* New York: Wiley.

(1967). "Implications of Probability for Induction." *Journal of Philosophy* 64, pp. 593–607.

Schick, F. (1979). "Self Knowledge, Uncertainty and Choice." *British Journal for the Philosophy of Science* 30, pp. 235–252.

(1984). *Having Reasons.* Princeton, NJ: Princeton University Press.

Seidenfeld, T. (1979). "Why I Am Not a Objective Bayesian." *Theory and Decisions* 11, pp. 413–440.

Seidenfeld, T., and Schervish, M. (1983). "A Conflict between Finite Additivity and Avoiding Dutch Book." *Philosophy of Science* 50, pp. 398–412.

Sen, A. K. (1970a). *Collective Choice and Social Welfare.* San Francisco: Holden Day.

(1970b). "The Impossibility of a Paretian Liberal." *Journal of Political Economy* 78, pp. 152–157. Reprinted in Sen (1982), pp. 285–290.

(1970c). "Interpersonal Aggregation and Partial Comparability." *Econometrica* 38, pp. 393–409. Reprinted in Sen (1982), pp. 203–225.

(1971). "Choice Functions and Revealed Preference." *Review of Economic Studies* 38, pp. 307–317. Reprinted in Sen (1982), pp. 41–53.

(1976a). "Liberty, Unanimity and Rights." *Economica* 43, pp. 217–245. Reprinted in Sen (1982), pp. 291–326.

(1976b). "Welfare Inequalities and Rawlsian Axiomatics." *Theory and Decision* 7, pp. 243–262.

(1976c). "On Weights and Measures: Informational Constraints in Social Welfare Analysis." *Econometrica* 45, pp. 1539–1572. Reprinted in Sen (1982), pp. 226–263.

(1977). "Social Choice Theory: A Reexamination." *Econometrica*, pp. 53–89. Reprinted in Sen (1982), pp. 158–200.

(1979). "Utilitarianism and Welfarism." *Journal of Philosophy* 76, pp. 463–489.

(1982). *Choice, Welfare and Measurement.* Cambridge, MA: MIT Press.

(1985). "Well Being, Agency and Freedom: The Dewey Lectures 1984." *Journal of Philosophy* 82, pp. 169–221.

Sen, A. K., and Williams, B. (1982). *Utilitarianism and Beyond.* Cambridge University Press.

Shackle, G. L. S. (1958). *Time in Economics.* Amsterdam: North Holland.

Sidgwick, H. (1907). *The Methods of Ethics.* 7th ed. reissued by University of Chicago Press in 1962.

Smith, C. A. B. (1961). "Consistency in Statistical Inference and Decision." (with discussion). *Journal of the Royal Statistical Society* Ser. B, 26, pp. 1–25.

Uchii, S. (1973). "Higher Order Probabilities and Coherence." *Philosophy of Science* 11, pp. 373–381.

Van Fraassen, B. (1972). "The Logic of Conditional Obligation." *Journal of Philosophical Logic* 1, pp. 417–438.

(1973). "Values and the Heart's Command." *Journal of Philosophy* 70, pp. 5–19.

Von Neumann, J., and Morgenstern, O. (1944). *Theory of Games and Economic Behavior.* Princeton, NJ: Princeton University Press.

Wald, A. (1950). *Statistical Decision Functions.* New York: Wiley.

Williams, B. (1973). *Problems of the Self.* Cambridge University Press.

(1981). *Moral Luck.* Cambridge University Press.

Name index

Subject index